WEST POINT
LEGEND ON THE HUDSON

Poughkeepsie Journal

PUBLISHED BY THE
Poughkeepsie Journal

Photo on previous page: Cadets perform an artillery drill on the plain at the United States Military Academy at West Point on Sept. 24, 1903.
Image from the West Point Archives

Photo on facing page: The U.S. Military Academy at West Point as seen from the air, looking north up the Hudson River.
Photo by Spencer Ainsley

ISBN 0-9674209-1-1
Library of Congress Control Number 2003103480

Published in the United States of America by the Poughkeepsie Journal
www.poughkeepsiejournal.com

Printed by Walden Printing, Montgomery, N.Y.

WEST POINT
LEGEND ON THE HUDSON

Published by the Poughkeepsie Journal

FOREWORD

George Washington called it the "key to the continent," this bluff of granite high above the Hudson. West Point began as a strategic garrison on a bend of the river — where the British could be thwarted. But leaders — not forts or arms — make armies. So two centuries ago, a military academy was founded to help ensure the nation would remain secure and free.

Duty

The academy is both timeless and ever changing. Go there and you are drenched in history. You can see the chain — each link 100 pounds — that Washington's troops once stretched across the Hudson to deter British frigates from going north and dividing the colonies by making all of New York theirs. A bronze Gen. George S. Patton, posture fiercely erect, holds his field glasses as if he is about to check troops in the library his statue faces. You can sit on a stone bench with the words "loyalty" and "courage" carved into its sides. Everything at West Point wears that venerable gray wool coat of tradition. Yet you can see a new world in the diverse faces of the cadets who represent every state and many nations.

Honor

The academy's graduates have helped define our history — Robert E. Lee, Ulysses S. Grant, Douglas MacArthur, Dwight D. Eisenhower, H. Norman Schwarzkopf. One day a graduate who is a woman will reach that acclaim. It is a place of the famous, on occasion the infamous, and the soldier-statesmen who have led not just in war but in peace.

Country

In 1962, Gen. MacArthur won West Point's coveted Sylvanus Thayer Award and told cadets that the academy's motto, "Duty, Honor, Country," teaches you "to face the stress and spur of difficulty and challenge; to learn to stand up in the storm but to have compassion on those who fall; to master yourself before you seek to master others; to have a heart that is clean, a goal that is high." The academy's cadets, despite regimented lives, are still taught to question and analyze. And they're expected to embrace the highest moral standards. The minds trained at West Point are secondary to the character molded there. West Point is a fortress, a school and a legend — as intrinsic to America's heritage as the stone beneath its walls. Here is its story.

Photo: Spencer Ainsley

ACKNOWLEDGEMENTS

Dozens of people, noted below, contributed to this book. It is based on a special Poughkeepsie Journal project, commemorating the 200th anniversary of the U.S. Military Academy at West Point in 2002. The Poughkeepsie Journal, which covers the mid-Hudson Valley in New York, was assisted by The Journal News, which covers the lower Hudson Valley, Gannett News Service, based in McLean, Va., and Army Times in Springfield, Va.

POUGHKEEPSIE JOURNAL
Richard K. Wager, publisher
Margaretta A. Downey, executive editor
Dean DiMarzo, art director and book designer
Spencer Ainsley, photo/graphics director
Laurie Hlavaty, book copy editor
Mark H. Bickel, West Point project coordinating editor
Carol Trapani, senior writer
Richard L. Kleban, managing editor

Writers: Nik Bonopartis, Michelle Carroll, Nicole Edwards, Anthony Farmer, Mike Ferraro, John Ferro, Kim Gaffney, Elizabeth Lynch, Sean T. McMann, Rasheed Oluwa, Lee Park, Dan Pietrafesa, Jeremy Pond, Rebecca Rothbaum, Dan Shapley
Editors: Jim Konrad, Julie Doll, Kathy Norton, Kathleen Dijamco, Ron Bittner
Photographers: Darryl Bautista, Karl Rabe, Kathy McLaughlin, Lee Ferris
Graphic artists: Larry Seil, Sten Miller
Correspondents: Greg Marano, Nancy Haggerty
Production: Mary Kay Hummel, Glen Chapman, Jerry Grape
Indexing: Jacqueline Bono DiMarzo
Contributors: Rose Ann Simpson, Bonnie Soto

THE JOURNAL NEWS
Henry Freeman, editor &VP/news
CynDee Royle, senior managing editor
Tony Davenport, managing editor

Writers: Nancy Cacioppo, Greg Clary, Laura Incalcaterra, Steve Lieberman, Richard Liebson, Cara Matthews, Christopher Mele, Kari Neering, Khurram Saeed, James Walsh

GANNETT NEWS SERVICE
Caesar Andrews, editor
Fran Mears, managing editor/news
Ronald E. Cohen, former national editor

Writers: John Hanchette, John Machacek, John Omicinski

ARMY TIMES
Tobias Naegele, editor in chief
Robert Hodierne, senior managing editor

Writer: Jane McHugh

USMA, West Point
The Poughkeepsie Journal thanks the following individuals for their help:

Lt. Gen. William J. Lennox Jr., superintendent, U.S. Military Academy at West Point; Lt. Col. James Whaley, USMA Public Affairs Office; Theresa Brinkerhoff, public affairs specialist; Andrea Hamburger, USMA Public Affairs Office; Dr. Stephen B. Grove, West Point historian; Victoria Best, director of corporate relations, USMA Association of Graduates; Suzanne Christoff, USMA Archives; Alicia Mauldin, USMA Archives; Michael Moss, director, West Point Museum; David Reel, curator of art, West Point Museum; Michael McAfee, curator of history, West Point Museum; Lt. Col. John J. Cook, West Point chaplain; Lt. Col. Casey Neff, special assistant to the commandant for systems and planning, West Point; USMA Sports Information Office.

CONTENTS

AMERICA'S ACADEMY
THE PLACE WHERE OFFICERS ARE MADE WITH HONOR

Cadets prepare to fire during an artillery drill on the Plain in September 1903.

'The purpose has never changed and that is to provide leaders of character.'

Retired Lt. Gen. Dave Palmer, West Point superintendent from 1986 to 1991

'The Long Gray Line has never failed us.'

Gen. Douglas MacArthur, in his farewell speech at West Point in 1962

The Corps of Cadets at the U.S. Military Academy marches in formation across the Plain, an expansive field where cadets drill.

AMERICA'S ACADEMY

Grueling training shapes leaders

The core mission of the U.S. Military Academy is to train cadets to become officers in the U.S. Army. And the academy doesn't make it easy. The Army doesn't want just leaders from the West Point Corps of Cadets. The Army wants leaders of character, individuals who can live up to the academy's famous motto: Duty, Honor, Country.

So, from the day cadets arrive they are immersed in an environment that can seem as hard as the granite cliffs enfolding the 16,000-acre campus and military post. Students at most other colleges don't have to march to lunch or go through something called beast barracks — cadet basic training.

"In a regular military situation, you might have one formation a day; our first summer we had 13 (a day)," said Poughkeepsie resident Anthony Leo, USMA Class of 1963. "But all that was done with a flavor to be able to operate under stress."

Most cadets make it through graduation, since the academy is far from cavalier about whom it selects from the pool of 2,500 qualified candidates each year.

Understanding the academy's strategy helps some cadets succeed.

"It's a big mind game. You keep telling yourself, 'I can do this,' " said cadet Meghan Wilmore shortly before graduating in 2001.

Officers of character

There has been tinkering with the wording of the academy's mission over the years. That the academy will produce officers of character has always been implicit; the current mission statement declares it.

"The purpose has never changed and that is to provide leaders of character," said retired Lt. Gen. Dave Palmer, who was West Point superintendent from 1986

UNITED STATES MILITARY ACADEMY
WEST POINT

COUNTRY · WEST POINT · HONOR · DUTY · MDCCCII · U.S.M.A.

Above left, The academy's official seal displays its motto.

Left, Cadets from the USMA Class of 1883.

Class photo: USMA Archives
Montage: Dean DiMarzo

Words to live by since 1898

"Duty, Honor, Country" has been the motto of the U.S. Military Academy since 1898.

But little information exists about the reason for the selection or why a committee was established in 1896 to consider a "Device for the Military Academy."

The committee, at a meeting in January 1898, when it selected the academy's crest and motto, stated the selection of a "satisfactory motto includes some of the foregoing, such as significance, propriety, intelligibility and suitability, as well as dignity, conciseness, and to a certain extent sonorousness and tradition."

The "U.S. Military Academy Staff Records" contain only this mention involving the reasoning behind the selection of the motto's words:

"After much thought and inviting the opinion of many others, the Committee is satisfied that the sentiment expressed by the words: 'Duty, Honor, Country' more clearly and concisely express the genius of the institution than that embodied in any other motto or quotation which has suggested itself or has been suggested by others. It has met the approval of those to whom it has been submitted."

The board decided on Feb. 4, 1898, that the motto's words should be arranged as "Duty, Honor, Country."

On Aug. 14, 1898, the board resolved to recommend to the Secretary of War the design for a seal and arms and the motto be adopted.

The board on Dec. 15, 1898, "Resolved that the sum of one dollar and five cents be allotted from the Contingent Fund of the Military Academy appropriations for the current fiscal year, to be expended under the direction of the Academic Board for the payment of the fee for copyrighting the Arms, Motto and Seal of the Military Academy and Descriptive Text of same."

— *Stephen Grove, U.S. Military Academy historian*

Spencer Ainsley

Lt. Gen. William J. Lennox Jr., West Point superintendent, holds the coin minted in 2002 to commemorate the academy's bicentennial.

to 1991. "There are leaders who are evil — Hitler, dictators — who ruin their countries. But leaders of character who are loyal, who can be trusted, who have integrity, that's all important, particularly in your military leaders."

The academy's mission was never formally articulated until the 1920s, academy historian Stephen Grove said. "From the earliest days of the military academy, graduates were assuming leadership positions in the Army.

"What they are going to be doing in the Army has changed."

The Army's needs determine what happens at West Point, the source of 25 percent of today's Army officers.

There is not a single experience, course, instructor, monument or tradition at West Point that turns a cadet into a leader with character. The honor code and honor system by themselves don't do it; the military training alone doesn't, nor do athletics, handsome uniforms, military discipline or the eternal emphasis on "the Corps."

The academy is designed so virtually everything and everyone a cadet touches, hears, sees or talks to stretches, challenges, strengthens or enhances the character she or he already possesses.

And when the program backfires, the academy strives to change.

Even at its high point, the Civil War, West Point had its critics: those who charged it was an elitist haven and a hotbed of sectionalism. Football and academic cheating scandals erupted in the 1950s and the mid-1970s amid cadet perceptions the honor system was being used to enforce regulations.

Hazing eventually was stopped

Palmer established the Cadets Leadership Program to change the culture which, in the guise of discipline, tolerated unduly harsh treatment of lowerclassmen by upperclassmen, behavior that grew from silly pranks and hazing of plebes — freshmen — in the academy's early years.

Congress banned hazing in 1901, but it persisted. Douglas MacArthur, who graduated in 1903 and was superintendent from 1919 to 1922, was subject to awful hazing himself, wrote Thomas J. Fleming in "West Point: The Men and Times of the United States Military Academy." As superintendent, MacArthur initiated reforms — including the creation of the Cadet Honor Committee.

"We said at West Point all four years ought to be a developmental program, not just the first year," Palmer said. "The idea is to instill discipline, but not to be demeaning either."

After World War II, when asked by Superintendent Maxwell Taylor

'You're drilling in the mud'

A West Point cadet's rigorous academic and military training begins on the first day and doesn't end for years.

Although the academy's military training has become more intense and sophisticated over the years, much about applying the nuts-and-bolts practical part of being a soldier comes after graduation, through experience and at post-graduate schools.

West Point prepares cadets well, said Capt. Sakima A.G. Brown, a Poughkeepsie native who graduated in 1998.

"You do most of your soldiering as a second lieutenant," she said. As a first lieutenant, she gained staff experience and managed a $2.9 million budget as part of her duties at Ft. Bragg, N.C. Brown was promoted to captain in 2001. After officers' school, she returns to soldiering, commanding a company.

Once exclusively an engineering school, the academy today offers 21 optional majors. All cadets must take a core of 31 courses that includes foreign language, physics, chemistry and engineering.

"After you get past the first year, the academics are the most challenging," said Brown, who majored in psychology with a minor in systems engineering.

It's difficult to draw many similarities between West Point and other four-year colleges.

"You're forced to take things you're not good in, there are no summers off, you're drilling in the mud," academy historian Stephen Grove said. "Other kids have beer parties. You can't do that here."

Brown said her West Point experience was one of the most challenging times of her life.

"I would not change it for anything," she said.

Spencer Ainsley

Cadet Betty Simbert, of the Class of 2002, practices defensive hand-to-hand combat skills. Physical training is part of the core curriculum at West Point.

what West Point lacked, Dwight Eisenhower suggested the academy address the psychology of the citizen soldier and broaden curriculum to include leadership training.

West Point is not immune to the rest of the world, and long-held prejudices found succor there, too.

Prejudice was a reality

Henry O. Flipper, Class of 1877, the first black graduate, spent four years largely silenced by cadets, Grove said. Benjamin Oliver Davis Jr., Class of 1936, whose father was the Army's first black general, was treated to silence his first year. He graduated 35th in a class of 276 and joined the Air Corps and then the Air Force. In 1965 he attained the rank of lieutenant general, the first African American to do so.

Former academy military historian Jim Johnson, Class of 1969, who spent 15 years teaching at West Point, said he saw none of the behavior Flipper endured.

Another sea change occurred in 1976, when women were admitted to the academy. They faced hostility at first.

"I feel it is my duty to the alumni and the entire Army to run out as many females as possible," wrote one cadet, according to Theodore J. Crackel in "The Illustrated History of West Point."

In 1989, Kristin Baker became the first woman to be named first captain of the Corps of Cadets, West Point's highest cadet honor.

The issue with women was the "macho" connection to leadership, Johnson said. "That if you cannot physically lead, then you can't be a leader."

But the enactment of Title IX — federal legislation that banned sex discrimination in schools, whether in academics or athletics — resulted in equality for women in fitness and sports programs.

"And there is no intellectual issue," Johnson said. "Combat is still an issue. The great debate might be, are we prepared to draft young women?"

And while the academy has evolved, the mission is the same: producing leaders of character in the U.S. Army and beyond.

Character is difficult to describe, said former superintendent Palmer. "But you know when you see it or you see its absence."

UNITED STATES MILITARY ACADEMY AT
WEST POINT

Guide to the buildings

1 Amphitheater — Band concerts held here during summer.

2 Bartlett Hall — Chemistry and physics classrooms and labs.

3 Bradley Barracks — Cadet barracks — or dormitories — are similar to those at a civilian college. There are generally two or three cadets to a room. Cadets live with other members of their class within their cadet company. (A company consists of about 110 cadets of all four classes). Each cadet's desk is equipped with a private telephone line and a fiber optic telephone connection for Internet access.

4 Cadet Chapel — The largest church organ in the world is here.

5 Catholic Chapel — This was built in 1899 and expanded in 1959.

6 Commandant's Quarters — Home of commandant, who is in charge of the military and physical training programs.

7 Dean's Quarters — Home of the dean of the academic board.

8 Eisenhower Barracks

9 Eisenhower Hall — 193,000-square-foot venue, has been home for performing arts for more than 25 years.

10 Fort Putnam — One of many forts at West Point during the American Revolution; no charge to visit, open for limited hours from May to September.

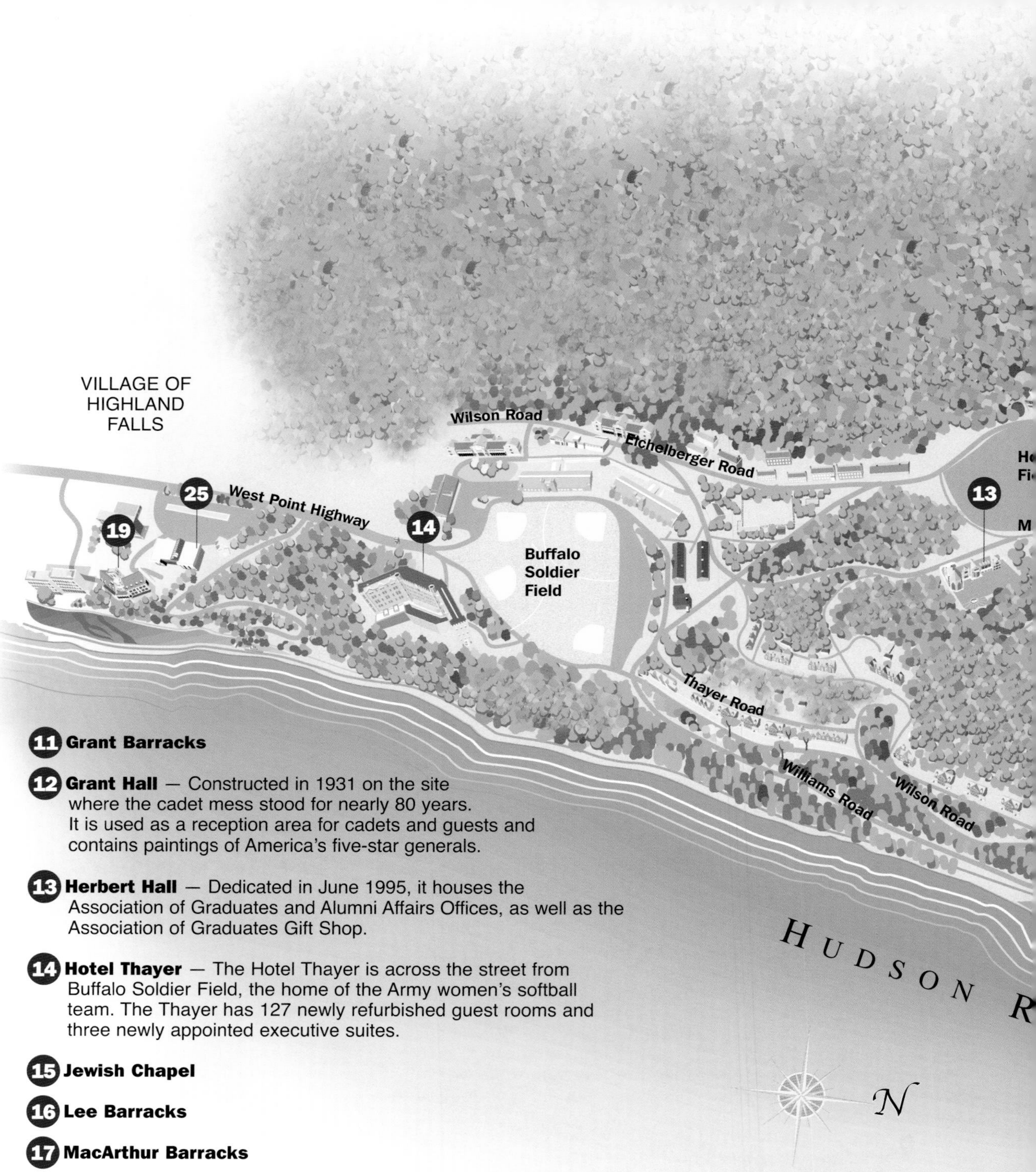

VILLAGE OF
HIGHLAND
FALLS

Wilson Road

Eichelberger Road

West Point Highway

Buffalo
Soldier
Field

Thayer Road

Williams Road

Wilson Road

11 Grant Barracks

12 Grant Hall — Constructed in 1931 on the site where the cadet mess stood for nearly 80 years. It is used as a reception area for cadets and guests and contains paintings of America's five-star generals.

13 Herbert Hall — Dedicated in June 1995, it houses the Association of Graduates and Alumni Affairs Offices, as well as the Association of Graduates Gift Shop.

14 Hotel Thayer — The Hotel Thayer is across the street from Buffalo Soldier Field, the home of the Army women's softball team. The Thayer has 127 newly refurbished guest rooms and three newly appointed executive suites.

15 Jewish Chapel

16 Lee Barracks

17 MacArthur Barracks

HUDSON R

N

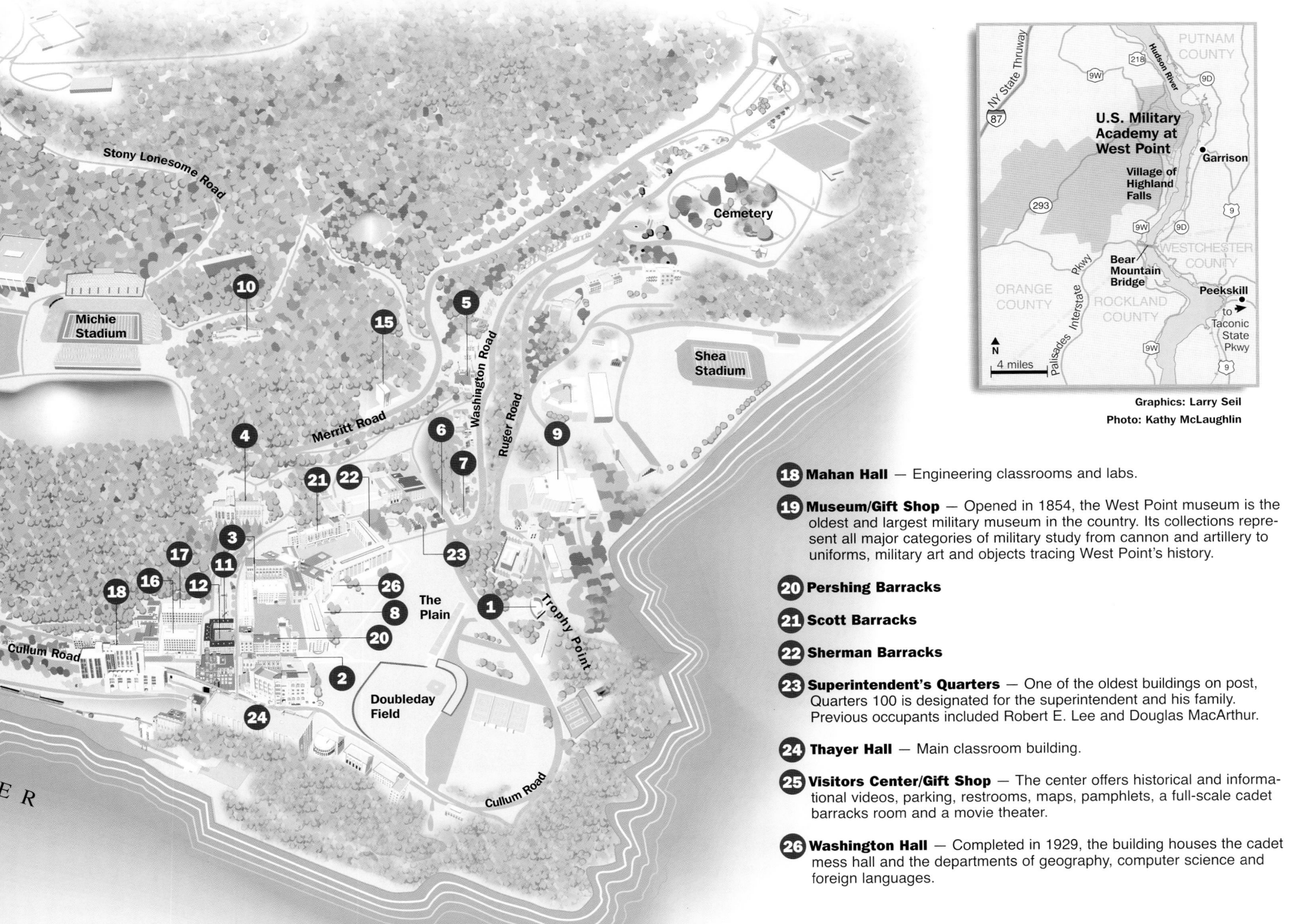

U.S. Military Academy at West Point

Village of Highland Falls

Garrison

Bear Mountain Bridge

Peekskill

to Taconic State Pkwy

PUTNAM COUNTY

WESTCHESTER COUNTY

ORANGE COUNTY

ROCKLAND COUNTY

Hudson River

NY State Thruway

Palisades Interstate Pkwy

N

4 miles

Graphics: Larry Seil
Photo: Kathy McLaughlin

18 **Mahan Hall** — Engineering classrooms and labs.

19 **Museum/Gift Shop** — Opened in 1854, the West Point museum is the oldest and largest military museum in the country. Its collections represent all major categories of military study from cannon and artillery to uniforms, military art and objects tracing West Point's history.

20 **Pershing Barracks**

21 **Scott Barracks**

22 **Sherman Barracks**

23 **Superintendent's Quarters** — One of the oldest buildings on post, Quarters 100 is designated for the superintendent and his family. Previous occupants included Robert E. Lee and Douglas MacArthur.

24 **Thayer Hall** — Main classroom building.

25 **Visitors Center/Gift Shop** — The center offers historical and informational videos, parking, restrooms, maps, pamphlets, a full-scale cadet barracks room and a movie theater.

26 **Washington Hall** — Completed in 1929, the building houses the cadet mess hall and the departments of geography, computer science and foreign languages.

Above, One of the U.S. Military Academy's two U-H1 helicopters used for training missions and official transportation purposes.

The helicopters are housed and maintained at Stewart International Airport and are flown by crew members of the 2nd Aviation Detachment, New Windsor, N.Y.

Right, The statue of Gen. Douglas MacArthur, Class of 1903, as seen in front of Washington Hall. MacArthur was academy superintendent from 1919 until 1922.

Statues and memorials

A **Air Cadet Memorial** — Erected in 1945 by the USMA classes of 1943, 1944 and 1945 as a memorial to all air cadets who died while undergoing flight training. The artist for the statue is Walter Hancock, who also sculpted the MacArthur statue.

B **The American Soldier Monument** — In 1980, a statue of three American World War II soldiers was presented to the academy and the Corps of Cadets by the classes of 1935 and 1936, and became the first statue at West Point to honor our nation's enlisted personnel. The nine-foot bronze sculpture was sculpted by Felix de Weldon, who also did the Iwo Jima Statue at Arlington National Cemetery.

C **Battle Monument** — Perhaps the most prominent and majestic monument at the academy, Battle Monument was dedicated in 1897 "in memory of the officers and men of the American Army who fell in battle," specifically the Regular Army casualties of the Union during the Civil War. The shaft is reportedly the largest polished granite shaft in the Western Hemisphere. Approximately 2,230 names are inscribed on the monument.

D **Eisenhower Monument** — The nine-foot bronze statue was sculpted by Robert L. Dean Jr. and erected in May 1983 on a pedestal of red granite. Dwight D. Eisenhower was a 1915 graduate of the USMA and served as president of the United States from 1953-1961.

E **Kosciuszko Monument/ Fort Clinton** — Thaddeus Kosciuszko, a Polish artillery officer, provided vital assistance to the Americans, leading to their victory at the Battle of Saratoga. In 1778, he came to West Point and spent two years designing and overseeing the construction of the elaborate fortifications. The base pedestal of the monument was erected in 1828 by the Corps of Cadets (Robert E. Lee was on the design committee); the statue was added in 1913.

F **MacArthur Monument** — Forty years after he served as superintendent, Douglas MacArthur returned to West Point in 1962 to receive the Thayer Award. At that time, he delivered his famous "Duty,

Honor, Country" speech. The statue was sculpted by Walter Hancock and was dedicated in 1969 by Gen. MacArthur's wife, Jean.

G **Memorial to the Army Athlete** — Dedicated in 1987 by Earl Blaik, the memorial stands outside the Holleder Sports Center.

H **Patton Monument** — Designed by James Fraser, the Patton Monument was "erected by his friends, officers and men of the units he commanded." It was unveiled by Mrs. Patton and subsequently dedicated in 1950. Gen. George Patton served as commander of the 7th Army in North Africa and Sicily in 1943 and of the 3rd Army, European Theater, from 1944-45.

I **Sedgwick Monument** — The memorial to Maj. Gen. John Sedgwick from the members of his last command, the 6th Army Corps, was dedicated in 1868. Legend holds that if a cadet is deficient in academics, the cadet should go to the monument at midnight the night before the term-end examination, in full dress, under arms, and spin the rowels on the monument's spurs. With luck, the cadet will pass the test.

J **Southeast Asia Memorial** — Its bronze plaque, inset in a granite boulder, dedicates the site to classmates of West Point's classes of 1960 through 1969 and other service members who fell in battle in Vietnam and other conflicts in the region.

K **Thayer Monument** — Known as the "Father of the Military Academy," Sylvanus Thayer strengthened the caliber of the faculty and quality of the academic instruction, brought discipline to the military environment and recognized the importance of instilling honor and integrity in cadets. Erected in 1883, the monument was sculpted by Carl Conrad.

L **Washington Monument** — The statue was sculpted by Henry Kirke Brown and unveiled in 1916. Washington recognized the critical importance of the military position at West Point. He spent much time in the area, especially near the end of the Revolutionary War, and he was among the foremost advocates of the establishment of a military academy.

Source: United States Military Academy at West Point

Michie
Stadium

Shea
Stadium

Merritt Road

Washington Road

Ruger Road

Trophy Point

The
Plain

Cullum Road

Doubleday
Field

Cullum Road

H U D S O N   R I V E R

N

Larry Seil

'Half of all graduates have been produced in the last 30 years. '

Stephen Grove, West Point historian

Spencer Ainsley

This aerial photograph of the U.S. Military Academy at West Point, which was established in March 1802, looks west toward the heart of the campus.

THE PLACE

Academy infused with tradition

War with Europe loomed in late 1793 when President George Washington told his Cabinet that U.S. harbors must be fortified.

Flustered, Secretary of State Thomas Jefferson interrupted him. Leave it to the states, he urged. The anti-Federalist Virginian wanted no standing army acting as a shadow government. War Secretary Henry Knox jumped in, saying Washington's order was moot, anyway, because "no one in America knows how to build a fort."

Knox was painfully right.

Without the help of French and German engineers and artillery officers trained at L'Ecole Militaire and Berlin Academy, the unskilled American revolutionaries would almost certainly have lost to the professional British army.

Washington and Knox, as well as Alexander Hamilton, badly wanted the new country to have a military school. But it was a divisive political issue.

Yet something — it remains unclear exactly what — changed Jefferson's mind when he became president. In March 1802, he signed a bill siting a federal engineering school and a military academy at West Point.

And so the Army's "Long Gray Line" began its march more than 200 years ago with the graduation of two cadets, Joseph Swift and Simon Levy. By 1804, however, there were doubts it could continue when officers refused to attend classes or parades. It took defeats during the War of 1812 with Great Britain and a poor showing by the Army to persuade Congress to put some serious money into West Point.

Despite ups and downs, West Point continues to turn out officers trained to be the most elite of the Army's elite, directors of the largest single organization in the United States.

No school in America claims more distinguished alumni.

From the moment you pass through the gray granite gates — donated by the Class of June 1943, which lost more cadets to war than any other — you are in the midst of deadly serious business.

'Assertion of timelessness'

Historian Geoffrey Perret aptly describes West Point as "an assertion of timelessness less friable than the marble of the Parthenon and turning a more obdurate face to eternity than the striated sandstone face of the Sphinx."

Compared with its long history, however, West Point's graduates are surprisingly few: Only about 58,000 in 200 years.

"Half of all graduates have been produced in the last 30 years," West Point historian Stephen Grove notes. That's a reminder of eras when the Army shrank to 27,000 (1897). It stood at only 189,000 on the 1939 doorstep to World War II.

A $214 million annual U.S. Military Academy budget gives West Pointers a great deal. For that, the Army expects five years of service plus exceptional leadership.

On paper, it seems the West Pointer's influence at the top may be in decline.

Promotion is less automatic than it once was: None of the last four Army officers who chaired the Joint Chiefs of Staff — Gens. John Vessey Jr., Colin Powell, John Shalikashvili and Henry Shelton — was a West Pointer.

Indeed, West Point hasn't produced a JCS chairman since 1974.

Above, Cadets use surveying equipment on Nov. 4, 1903, as part of their training.
U.S. Military Academy Archives

Left, West Point cadets load a 12-inch mortar on Oct. 6, 1903.
U.S Military Academy Archives

'From your ranks come the great captains who hold the nation's destiny in their hands the moment the war tocsin sounds.'

Gen. Douglas MacArthur
former USMA superintendent and noted World War II and Korean War general, during his 1962 farewell speech

Yet no other school in America has such a palpable weight of tradition.

Cadets see constant reminders of the Army's high expectations of them: Custer's ghost lurks in the cemetery, and around every corner, statues of legends like Omar Bradley, Dwight Eisenhower, George S. Patton and Douglas MacArthur await.

When heading for a game at Michie Stadium, the Black Knights of the Hudson slap a plaque quoting World War II Joint Chiefs of Staff Chairman Gen. George Marshall (a Virginia Military Institute graduate) as saying: "I need an officer for a secret and dangerous mission. I want a West Point football player."

Cynics need not apply.

"You are the leaven, which binds together the entire fabric of our national system of defense," former superintendent Gen. Douglas MacArthur told the cadets in his still-stirring 1962 farewell. "From your ranks come the great captains who hold the nation's destiny in their hands the moment the war tocsin sounds.

"The Long Gray Line has never failed us.

"Were you to do so, a million ghosts in olive drab, in brown khaki, in blue and gray, would rise from their white crosses, thundering those magic words — duty, honor, country."

For many in the Army, it is a powerful magnet that never lets go.

On his deathbed, five-star general and former president Dwight Eisenhower dwelt not on his eight-year presidency or his wartime exploits, but on his West Point days.

"All he wanted to talk about was West Point," Gen. Mark Clark said. "West Point was all, ever."

Top, New cadets at West Point attend one of their first classes with one of their first lessons being to field strip a rifle in June 1999.

Kathy McLaughlin

Bottom, Cadets at the U.S. Military Academy work as tank crews as they maneuver across a desert landscape during an intensive "War Games" class.

Spencer Ainsley

Soldiers appreciate comforts of the Point

West Point sure beats Korea as a place to be stationed, according to two enlisted soldiers who have lived in both places.

Because the living conditions are rough and the place is a huge culture shock to the mind and body, Korea is classified as a hardship tour. To go from there to refined, renowned West Point was a real treat for Sgt. Christopher Bamberg and Spec. Sean-Paul VanGorp.

In Korea, Bamberg, who is single, shared a room in an old barracks with two other soldiers. At West Point, he lives in a building that looks more like an apartment complex than a barracks and has a bedroom area, living room area, bathroom and closets.

"I've heard lots of people here say they're the nicest barracks they've ever seen," he said. Bamberg is a military police officer in charge of the post's bicycle patrol. When not working, he likes to play softball with the MP team and venture off-post with friends.

"There's plenty of stuff to do around here. Newburgh has movies and places to eat, and Poughkeepsie has them, too. New Paltz is a college town about 45 miles away and has a lot of clubs and activities for people my age," he said.

VanGorp, who is married with two young girls, is more of a homebody. His Army job is crane operator, but he's been detailed to administrative work where he coordinates ceremonies, funerals and the like.

In Korea, he was posted at the demilitarized zone, the grim frontier between the North and South patrolled by armed soldiers. It was lonely because he had to leave his wife.

"I was there during the monsoon season in '99 and it was terrible," he said.

West Point has its quirky weather — the average yearly snowfall is 50 inches — but life is good at the post, VanGorp said. Whatever soldiers and their families need is within easy reach.

"I use everything from the shopette to the PX to the commissary. I like living here. I'm from a small town in Iowa. It's great to live in a place that's this historic," he said. "I'm grateful to have come here."

A lamp on a building in the Main Quad at West Point.

From schools to groceries, you name it, it's available

West Point isn't your average military installation. After all, what other post is visited by 3 million tourists a year?

But West Point resembles other installations in that it offers its 4,000 active-duty soldiers and their family members, most of whom live on post, the same Department of Defense amenities and services as other garrisons.

No resident has to travel far to get hospital treatment (at Keller Army Community Hospital), buy groceries and toilet articles (at the post exchange and commissary), play tennis (Lichtenberg Tennis Center), send their children to school (West Point Elementary School and West Point Middle School), watch the home team play football (Michie Stadium), listen to live music (the U.S. Military Academy Band) or be laid to rest (West Point Cemetery).

And residents can work out in a new, state-of-the-art health club, the $40 million Kimsey Athletic Center, named after its benefactor, Jim Kimsey (Class of 1962), co-founder of America Online.

West Point has all these amenities plus 4,000 cadets who, like Kimsey, will lead the world in years to come. And that gives it a different atmosphere from other posts, said Col. Joe Adamczyk (Class of 1972), head tactical officer of the brigade of cadets.

"It's got a more academic feel to it, whereas when you step onto other posts, there's a frenzy of activity of soldiers coming and going and getting ready to deploy or just coming back from a deploy-

ment," Adamczyk said.

"It's viewed as a very good family post. But it's remote as far as large department stores, malls, restaurants and things like that go. You have to travel over the mountain and through the valley to get to these kind of places."

Amid beauty, garrison active 225 years

West Point is one of the Army's more scenic installations, not to mention one of the most historic. Indeed, it is the Army's oldest garrison, having been continually manned since 1778.

And, like nearby New York City, West Point never sleeps.

It's open for business day and night. Except for a couple of times.

"In January 1996, 500 cadets didn't make it back from Christmas break due to heavy snow," said Tony Marchesani, executive assistant to the garrison commander. "Also that year, we had a major ice storm that wiped out all the electrical power for six to eight hours. But we only lost class that time for one day."

The snow was cleared by engineers from the 1st Battalion, 1st Infantry Regiment, the unit that takes care of the post by providing security, construction, engineering and administrative services.

Besides its military component, West Point has 3,000 civilian employees. Among the most important are the food service workers whose job is to feed the entire Corps of Cadets at the same time.

"The cadets have breakfast and lunch as a group. Lunch is 24 minutes. The food service workers put the food on warming carts and bring it to tables of 10 where it's served family-style by being passed around," Marchesani said. Which goes to show the real point of the Point.

"Everything here centers around the cadets," he said.

Spencer Ainsley photos

Above, Like everything else at West Point, meal time is organized and efficient as thousands of cadets are served at once.

Right, A juice container touts West Point's legendary rivalry with the Naval Academy.

Long Gray Line has a hearty appetite

At West Point, it takes efficiency, discipline and coordination to get the job done.

And more than 300 mess hall workers do it every day.

"This is the biggest dining facility in the U.S. Army," said Lt. Col. Derek Smith, officer in charge of the cadet mess hall. Each day, 96 cooks prepare up to 12,000 meals. If they're making spaghetti, this means 550 pounds of it. When serving lamb, they have to make 1,800 pounds.

The staff consists of 200 contract workers to serve meals and clean up, and 148 full-time

government workers to cook, including several graduates of the Culinary Institute of America in Hyde Park.

The first shift starts at 3:30 a.m., when workers begin the massive job of breakfast for 4,000 cadets. After the meal, they clean up and prepare for the next daily challenge: lunch.

And for each meal, they have six minutes to serve 4,000 cadets. Each waiter is assigned to 10 tables, and each table has 10 cadets.

"They've been doing this a long time," Smith said. "They have this down to an art."

There are tricks to make everything go smoothly. Condiments are already on the table. Anything that can be prepared ahead of time is ready. When noon rolls around, the only thing left to worry about is the hot entrees.

While the staff is preparing in the kitchen, 4,000 hungry cadets assemble outside with their companies. They fall into formation all around the building's six wings, regardless of the weather, awaiting the order to enter the building to eat.

"It's a really efficient way of moving 4,000 people into one place," said David Rokhlin, a cadet from Oceanside, Nassau County,

N.Y.

Once seated, cadets scramble to be ready for the entree. If hamburgers are coming, the cadets grab the buns first, so no time is wasted when they are served.

One cadet is responsible for announcing the day's soup. Another makes sure the condiment dispensers are arranged in height order. Others divvy up plates and milk containers. At the head of the table, a commandant ensures everyone follows procedure.

Meal time is limited

They are dismissed in stages, with upperclassmen allowed to leave first. Between assembling, entering the mess hall, waiting for permission to begin, and leaving in time for their next class, some cadets say they have only 15 minutes of eating time.

For Jennifer Pampuch, a third class cadet sergeant from Evansville, Ind., this is a pace she's used to.

"This is the way I've always eaten," she said, "because I've always been busy. It's a lot like high school." She usually doesn't eat optional dinner in the mess hall, however. "If the food's good, the line is going to be out the door," she said.

Breakfast and lunch during the week are mandatory. Dinner is mandatory only on Thursdays. For the picky eaters, there are alternatives when the main course isn't something that appeals to them.

"There's always peanut butter and jelly on the table," said Theresa Brinkerhoff, public affairs specialist.

Rokhlin said when he was admitted to West Point, his family thought he would have trouble with military food.

"My family considers me a conservative eater," he said, but added he has no complaints about the meals. "I was pleasantly surprised."

'They've been doing this a long time. They have this down to an art.'

Lt. Col. Derek Smith, officer in charge of the cadet mess hall, speaking about how quickly students are fed

Spencer Ainsley

Four thousand West Point cadets eat a hasty lunch at the cadet mess in Washington Hall.

Dedication, service honored at cemetery

Above, a football-shaped stone marks the grave of West Point football coaching legend Earl "Red" Blaik. **Right,** An ornate monument for Major General Daniel Butterfield, a Civil War era officer, but not an academy graduate.

Above, a buffalo head on the gravestone of George Armstrong Custer.

The U.S. Military Academy at West Point is a place for the young, but it's obsessed with the past.

Fit, confident and blessed with the near-invincibility of youth, men and women with their lives stretched out in front of them spend four years there. Nearly everything they experience — from the names of the buildings they study, eat and sleep in to the monuments they see and the drills they practice — is meant to connect them with the spirits of those they followed.

Along Washington Road, and overlooking the eternal Hudson River, is the West Point cemetery. Here, the gravestones speak volumes, granite reminders that death awaits every living thing, that in life there are no guarantees and that soldiering is, indeed, a dangerous occupation.

Maj. John A. Hottell III, USMA Class of 1964, is buried here. Hottell, who was awarded two Silver Stars for service in Vietnam, was killed with his division commander in a helicopter crash in 1970. He was 27.

Second Lt. Spencer Dodge, USMA Class of 1994, is buried here. He died in 1995 while attending Ranger School the winter after graduation. In violation of regulations, the students were sent out in chest-deep water in a Florida swamp. Dodge was among those who became hypothermic. Cadet Curt Sansoueie also died.

Paul Bunker, USMA Class of 1903, is buried here. A commander in the Philippines in 1941, Bunker survived the fall of Corregidor. He died in a Japanese prison camp in 1943.

Place for those who fought

More than 7,000 individuals are buried in the West Point cemetery, officially named a military cemetery in 1817. This is the final resting place for 16 Medal of Honor winners. Buried here are men who fought in America's battles, beginning with the American Revolution. Here, too, is "Captain Molly," Margaret Corbin, who fought at Fort Washington in New York City in 1776, after her hus-

band was killed by her side.

Generally, according to academy regulations, eligibility for burial at the West Point cemetery is reserved for academy graduates, their spouses, widows and widowers and their minor children, and active-duty military personnel assigned to the academy at the time of their death.

Visitors can begin a walking tour of the cemetery at the Old Cadet Chapel, moved to its site in 1910 from near where the library is today. The chapel opened in 1837.

"It was going to be taken down, and the old grads said, 'Don't you dare,' " academy historian Stephen Grove said.

Inside, a plaque denotes the seat reserved for Gen. Winfield Scott, a hero of the War of 1812 and the Mexican War. He served as general-in-chief of the army for 20 years. Though not an academy graduate, he loved the Point and spent many of his later years there and died there. His gravesite is in the West Point cemetery.

Tour begins at chapel

Commemoratives inside the chapel honor generals of the Revolutionary War, the first graduates, officers of the Seminole War and Spanish-American War, and others. One plaque has no name. It is for Benedict Arnold, the American officer turned traitor who would have handed West Point to the British during the American Revolution. The plaque says only "Major General, born 1740."

Of the gravestones, a few are ornate, strange and fanciful — such as the pyramid-shaped vault guarded by two sphinxes that is the final resting place for Egbert Viele, USMA Class of 1847, chief engineer of Prospect Park in Brooklyn.

There is George Armstrong Custer's monument, complete with buffalo head, and the wedding cake-like monument of Daniel Butterfield of Cold Spring, who is generally credited with helping create the funeral music of "Taps."

Sightings of ghosts just add to the lore

Several days before Halloween 1972, two cadets woke in the middle of the night to see the shimmering figure of a U.S. cavalryman, uniformed and mustached, walking through the doors and walls of their room in the 47th Division barracks.

It was the first of several such "ghost sightings" at the United States Military Academy at West Point that fall. One of the wackier chapters of the legendary institution's history, it drew the attention of local, national and international press. The New York Times and Time, Newsweek and Life magazines were some of the news organizations that reported the story.

"This is one everybody is interested in," except the academy, said Stephen Grove, West Point historian.

Grove said the room was closed off shortly after the sightings and has since been "demolished" in the course of renovations.

"Are we going to spend the time and resources to investigate this kind of thing? No," Grove said.

Ghost tale a popular topic

In 1972, however, the story of the apparition was the talk of the campus. According to an Information Office "Ghost Story Update," dated December 1972, the first sighting occurred during the "early morning hours of 22 October 1972." Eight other sightings were reported, according to the update, and a total of four cadets said they saw the apparition.

The ghost story even became fodder for the longstanding rivalry between the Army and Navy. Newspaper reports in November 1972 quote a Naval Academy midshipman who said the ghost was a hoax, a prank before the upcoming Army-Navy football game.

West Point did not embrace this explanation, according to reports published at the time.

Left, The Old Cadet Chapel sits at the entrance to the West Point cemetery, where more than 7,000 men and women are buried.

THE MISSION

For more information about the cemetery at West Point and an online tour, log on to *www.dean.usma.edu/history/wp%20cemetery/index.htm*

Spencer Ainsley photos

Above, The grave of Brig. Gen. Joseph B. Kiddoo.

Below, A soccer medal adorns the grave of Roy W. Mase.

Man's battle was for respect

Above, The back of the Hotel Thayer overlooks the Hudson River.

> **'**I've felt like I've done what I was put here at the Thayer Hotel to do as far as helping my own.**'**
>
> **Collin Dixon,**
> Hotel Thayer employee

Right, Collin Dixon, 72, has worked at the Hotel Thayer for decades.

He walks erect, offers a firm handshake, and is "yes, ma'am" polite.

After a more-than-70-year affiliation, Collin Dixon carries himself as a man of West Point is expected to — even though he never wore the uniform and war for him was defined as a battle for respect and opportunity.

Dixon, born at West Point in 1929, can talk about first-hand encounters with famed World War II generals and their families, with POWs, Hollywood celebrities and the athletes and coaches who added to academy history.

But it was with a promise made at age 12 that this son of a World War I veteran and grandson and grandnephew of Buffalo Soldiers — who rode with Teddy Roosevelt's Rough Riders during the Spanish-American War — secured a little piece of that history for himself.

"I won't let you down," Dixon told then-Hotel Thayer Manager James Boyce when hired to be the first black to work in public areas of the academy-owned hotel.

Now, more than 60 years later, it's clear Dixon, named Hotel Thayer employee of the year in 2002, kept his word.

Employee is much loved

"Everybody in this hotel loves him," said Jim Brady, hotel concierge and security chief. "Collin is the best of the best. Personally, it's a distinct honor to work with him."

Twice in recent years, Dixon, now a security officer, has had to evacuate the hotel, room by room, during fires.

But seemingly as important as the duties he performs is the historical record he keeps in his head.

Dixon's family moved to Highland Falls, nestled next to West Point, when he was 4 or 5. Before that, he lived on post. His grandfather and granduncle had been assigned there in 1907 to teach required horsemanship.

By 12, he was ready to get a full-time, after-school job to aid his mother, father and 10 siblings.

The high school principal sent him to Boyce, a man Dixon came to admire very much.

Dixon recalled what Boyce told him: "Collin, we've never had any of your kind here before. If you do well, then we'll hire more of your kind."

Today, the words might offend. But Dixon was well aware of the climate and understood Boyce's bluntness. Born with undeveloped fingers on his left hand and undeveloped toes on his left foot, he had come to realize his real handicap was his color.

Initially hired at Thayer to operate the elevator, Dixon's real assignment was to open doors for other blacks.

Most guests lived at the hotel full time. They included retired officers, the families of current cadets and the wives of men assigned overseas. Many did not embrace Dixon's presence.

"I went through pure hell," he said. "I learned to turn the other cheek — to endure. I wanted to quit (after just a few weeks). It was really rough. I'd hear remarks and see people pointing," said Dixon, who noted some female guests ordered him not to speak to their children.

So Dixon quietly did his job. He would drive the elevator, fill the hotel lobby's mammoth fireplace with wood, serve ice water to the generals' wives, and through the years, handle assignments as a bell-boy, baker's assistant and housekeeper.

Some guests of high pedigree were kind.

"They were very nice, not uppity," he said. "They treated me like I was somebody and back in those days I needed to get all of that I could get."

A favorite was Mamie Eisenhower, wife of general and later president Dwight Eisenhower. He also found a friendly face in beloved West Point instructor Marty Maher, upon whose life the movie "The Long Gray Line" was based. Dixon noted Maher also taught swimming, though he didn't swim and refused to get in the water.

During World War II, Dixon earned $45 a month in salary, but took home $200 to $300 a week by doing favors for guests and cadets. One time, after much cajoling, he accepted $20 from an officer to sneak the wedding gift of a calf up to a fourth-floor room. After the incessantly bleating animal was discovered and ordered removed, the officer demanded his $20 back.

"I said: 'I'm keeping it. I may get fired today,'" Dixon recalled with a laugh. Dixon, now 73 and a widower with two grown children, never was fired.

He has come and gone at the hotel, always on his own terms. He worked at the hotel full time until taking a base job in 1948. After leaving there in 1953, he worked off and on part time at the hotel over the years while holding down pharmaceutical and bookstore jobs. Finally, he returned "home" for full-time work 11 years ago.

"I love it. I don't know what I'll do when I can't do this anymore," Dixon said.

Times are different now

Much has changed in the years Dixon has spent at the Thayer and at West Point.

"That has big meaning to me," he said. "I've seen it grow from one or two (black cadets) to 20 and hundreds now, and females."

The change mirrors changes in society, he said, and, to some extent, he knows he helped foster that.

"I've felt like I've done what I was put here at the Thayer Hotel to do as far as helping my own," he said. "I'm proud of my heritage and what I've accomplished. It was not easy, but I'm glad I've endured. If I've done nothing outstanding, at least I've accomplished something and reaped the awards of being loved and appreciated."

Cadets begin service with community, kids

Selfless service is one of the seven core Army values cadets at the U.S. Military Academy at West Point are taught to revere.

It ranks with loyalty, duty, respect, honor, integrity and courage. But over the past few decades, community service has taken on a larger role, moving from the realms of individual choice to collective responsibility endorsed by the academy.

Each year, hundreds of cadets give their time and energy to community groups, mainly in local Orange County, N.Y. Cadets serve as mentors to children, volunteer at the Special Olympics, help organize the Boy Scouts annual jamboree, build homes for the homeless side by side with Habitat for Humanity volunteers and visit veterans who are ill.

"There are really a number of reasons behind it," said Capt. Chris Engen, tactical officer for Company D-3 and the person who guides the 130 cadets in his company in their community service work. "It fosters social responsibility. It provides an opportunity for cadets to give something back to the local community. Cadets are here essentially on a full scholarship and can show their appreciation through service."

Joining volunteer programs

Each of West Point's 32 companies has a tactical officer — a major or captain — who is responsible for mentoring their cadets, including getting them involved in volunteer programs.

The system is fairly new. When Engen graduated from West Point in 1991, he said individual cadets quietly went about serving the community. Now, there's more emphasis on giving back as a unit.

Much of cadets' free time is limited to the weekend since they are busy meeting the many academic, military and physical demands required of them.

Nancy Kosloski, executive director of the Big Brothers/Big Sisters of Orange County, has been working with West Point cadets since 1978. Because of their time constraints, they spend a day with a child once a month.

Over the years, the cadets and their Little Brothers and Sisters have visited the Bronx Zoo and Liberty Science Museum in Jersey City and spent time on the slopes snow-tubing.

Kosloski said the cadets make particularly good "Bigs," as the mentors are known, because they come from all over the country, aren't that much older than the children they are working with and are wonderful role models. They exemplify academic excellence, physical health and discipline.

For the cadets, "it gives them an opportunity to loosen up and be a kid themselves," she said. "And it gives the children unconditional love and something to look forward to."

Spencer Ainsley
Cadets at the USMA

'They are phenomenal young men and women. They're young enough where they'll still rough and tumble with the kids, but they also make the child feel like they are special in that person's life.'

Nancy Kosloski
executive director
Big Brothers/Big Sisters
of Orange County on
cadets relating to children

HISTORY AT EVERY TURN

State seals are painted on the ceiling beams in a reception area in Grant Hall.

Right, The Washington Monument, unveiled in 1916, is pictured under a glowing spotlight attached to the roof of Washington Hall. The monument honoring the visionary commander in chief and president was moved in 1971 from the northern side of the Plain to its current location.

Left, A majestic eagle over the entrance to Thayer Hall at the military academy.

> **'The Cadet Chapel continues to be a place where our cadets are both nurtured and challenged in their faith.'**
>
> **Lt. Col. John J. Cook,** chaplain of Cadet Chapel

Spencer Ainsley photos

The organ inside the U.S. Military Academy's Cadet Chapel is the largest church organ in the world. The organ was installed in 1911. This series of organ pipes, perpendicular to the window, is located at the rear of the church to provide sound from all directions.

ON THE WEB

Visit the Web site of the U.S. Military Academy library: *http://usmalibrary.usma.edu*

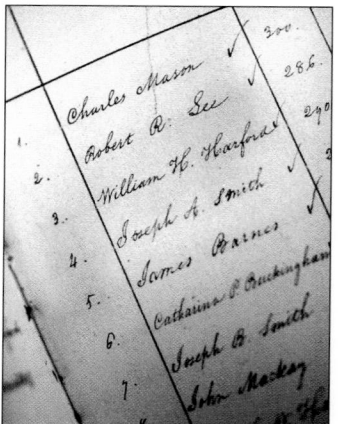

Spencer Ainsley

Robert E. Lee's graduation rank, second, is shown in the register for the Class of 1829. The listing reads Robert R. Lee because of a scrivener's error.

'I think it's very inspiring looking at material about people you've learned about all your life.'

Suzanne Christoff
associate director
Special Collections
and Archives
USMA Library

Library preserves memories, histories

"During the time of war, my life is the rightful property of my country."

So wrote 1st Lt. Philip Barbour in his final journal entry. The date was Sept. 20, 1846, the night before he died fighting for the United States in the Mexican War.

Today, his journal rests on a shelf in the Special Collections room at West Point, surrounded by writings of other American soldiers. Hundreds of thousands of memorabilia include letters to family members, antique brown-and-white photographs of soldiers and note cards Ulysses S. Grant used to communicate during the final days of his life.

"We have items ranging from a sheet of paper to volumes of collected works," academy Librarian Joseph Barth said.

Historical documents fall under one of two categories at the West Point library — Archives and Special Collections.

Left, The academy fencing team was the 1904 intercollegiate champion.

the paper, touching the pages only to turn them — carefully.

To protect them from wear and tear, the curators stress — very reluctantly — these collections are not available to the public. Most users are cadets, faculty members, graduate students from other schools and occasional filmmakers.

"The reason we're here is to support the curriculum of military students," Barth said.

This doesn't mean these resources are completely inaccessible to non-cadets. At the library's Web site, the public can get a peek at a small sampling of the

Archived materials include anything from West Point and date from 1802, when the academy was founded.

Personal papers kept

Special Collections can include personal papers of graduates, annotated books — such as George S. Patton's collection, in which he made notations in the margin when doing his reading — photographs and books about West Point. The oldest item in Special Collections is a book from the 15th century, entitled "De Re Militari" by Flavius Vegetius Ranatus. The book on medieval military history was published by Benedictus Bononiensis in 1496.

Preservation of these collections is not easy. According to Suzanne Christoff, the library's associate director of Special Collections and Archives, the temperature in the rooms where these items are stored is regulated near 70 degrees, with a relative humidity of 45 percent.

When she is reviewing any of the material, her fingers glide above

materials stored at the West Point archives.

Cadets studying American history have priority for gaining access to the original documents, including Barbour's journal.

"The collection comes to life when there's a particular point of interest," Christoff said, adding cadets wanted to see Barbour's handwritten journal after reading a published version.

"I continue to learn new things," Christoff said of her 16 years at her post. "I think it's very inspiring looking at material about people you've learned about all your life."

Such material includes demerit listings kept by the academy. These records document how Gen. Abner Doubleday, Class of 1842 — whose name has been associated with the beginnings of baseball in Cooperstown — was often late for meals. Doubleday served in the Mexican War, and in the Civil War he reportedly fired the first Union shot from Fort Sumter.

Gen. Robert E. Lee, on the other hand, who led the Confederate Army, had a perfect record at West Point.

A late 19th-century image of a horse show held at the U.S. Military Academy at West Point.

Movies, TV give a peek into academy

The film "We Were Soldiers," released in 2002 and starring Mel Gibson, isn't the first time the U.S. Military Academy at West Point was featured on television or in the movies.

Since the early 1900s, films like John Ford's 1955 drama "The Long Gray Line" and the 1979 CBS television movie "Women at West Point" focused on the historic academy by the Hudson River.

In "We Were Soldiers," the West Point Cadet Glee Club sang "The Mansions of the Lord," a hymn dedicated to fallen soldiers.

The various portrayals of the academy not only recognize the academic aspect but also let the world in on other obstacles of military life; cadets facing war, love and death.

During the academy's bicentennial year, the Eisenhower Hall Theatre at West Point offered a film series that included "Francis Goes to West Point" (1952), "Flirtation Walk" (1934) and "The West Point Story" (1950) with James Cagney and Doris Day.

"They're more comedic than anything," said Kathleen Colley, marketing director of the Eisenhower Hall Theatre at West Point, about movies like "Francis Goes to West Point," a film about a talking mule whose owner is training at the academy. "None of these films are really historic, but they do show kind of an insight of cadet life at West Point."

Fascinated with military life

Film and television crews have centered story lines and movies around military life, or the academy itself, for years. Records at the U.S. Military Academy's Cadet Library list a 16mm motion picture "Daly of West Point Winning Hurdle Race" copyrighted Dec. 9, 1902, as one of the earliest films in the archives.

Aside from films, West Point has been featured on television networks like CBS and NBC. CBS' "60 Minutes" and NBC News both aired programming with West Point cadet and faculty interviews con-

Left, The USMA Cadet Glee Club warms up with help from director Connie Chase, front right, in the basement of the Cadet Chapel at West Point. The club was preparing to record the hymn "The Mansions of the Lord" for the movie "We Were Soldiers," starring Mel Gibson.

Karl Rabe

cerning current world affairs and the threat of terrorism after Sept. 11, 2001.

West Point football players Felix A. "Doc" Blanchard and Glenn Davis starred in the 1947 movie "Spirit of West Point."

Warner Brothers released "Flirtation Walk." Flirtation Walk actually refers to a historic landmark below Trophy Point where cadets are allowed to take their dates.

Shot on location

Scenes were shot on the celebrated campus for Paramount's "Beyond Glory" (1948) starring Alan Ladd and Donna Reed, while one of the most celebrated films, "The Long Gray Line," was based on the true story of West Point athletic trainer Marty Maher, played by Tyrone Power.

Films also addressed issues like homosexuality in NBC's 1986 military mystery "Dress Gray," starring Alec Baldwin.

Women enrolled at the academy in 1976. Film director Alan Sacks, who produced the television series "Welcome Back Kotter," explored the historic event in 1979 by directing the CBS television movie "The Plebe Year of Jennifer Scott."

Mike Piepel of Iowa has been collecting movie posters for 25 years, one of which includes "The Long Gray Line."

"The films we were able to look for all over the United States, they are hard to come by," Piepel said.

In 1981, the academy was also featured in Bob Hope's 78th birthday special on NBC. Hope has been noted for entertaining United States military troops since World War II.

EARLY HISTORY
OLDEST ARMY POST SAVES A NEW COUNTRY

This engraving by George Catlin shows a view north from the military academy as it looked in 1828 during Sylvanus Thayer's superintendency.

West Point Museum Collections, U.S. Military Academy

'It's almost hallowed ground for Americans.'

Stephen Grove, U.S. Military Academy historian, about West Point

Fort Putnam, a key defensive post in the Revolutionary War, was restored in the 1970s and offers a majestic view of West Point and the river.

Fort helped shape nation

Gasp your way up and down West Point's rigorous hills, and you can't help but imagine the men who sunk a country's military roots here. Why did they settle in these unforgiving granite mountains?

You get the answer when a glorious glimpse of the Hudson River comes into view.

Those cliffs and boulders lead to the narrow stretch of water that was the difference between the birth of a nation and the death of hope for one.

At this rugged spot in the Hudson Highlands, the Continental Army dug in more than 200 years ago. Those soldiers knew that if they stayed in control of the river, there was a chance of defeating the British.

From their victory and from this spot grew the world's greatest army and the finest tradition in military academies. Its stamp is on every era of American history.

West Point graduates designed railroads, bridges and dams demanded by a burgeoning nation. Others went to the White House. A few walked in space.

Some horrifically faced their classmates and friends in a civil war. Generals, presidents, inventors, engineers and astronauts — they all drilled on the same land where the first American soldiers stood down the mightiest military power of its time.

Right, A cadet sabre rests against the back of a chair in the cadet mess at Washington Hall.

Spencer Ainsley

Englishman Henry Hudson sailed the Half Moon, above, during his 1609 exploration of the river that would bear his name. The Hudson River was pivotal in the creation of West Point, first as an Army post and later as a military academy.

'Let us defend the North River and hold West Point, and the end of our campaign will be glorious.'

Baron Frederick von Steuben,
Continental Army's drillmaster and inspector general who was born in Prussia

'For some reason, they completely overlooked the commanding position of West Point.'

Sidney Forman, author, 'West Point: A History of the United States Military Academy'

Spencer Ainsley

Above, Constitution Island sits across the Hudson River from West Point. Also known as Martalear's Rock, the island was fortified before West Point.

IN THE BEGINNING

Future forged at the Point

Imagine New Yorkers Christopher Tappan and James Clinton overcoming the rock cliffs, precipitous drops, thick woods and dense underbrush of the wild and rugged Hudson Highlands in 1775.

There was no fortress or academy at West Point when the Continental Congress handed responsibility for the Hudson River's defense to the New York Assembly more than 200 years ago.

But in 1778, three years after Tappan and Clinton surveyed the Highlands to determine from where the Americans would have the best chance of guarding and defending the Hudson River, the first troops drilled at West Point. The Army has been there ever since. West Point is America's oldest Army post and the nation's first military academy.

"It's almost hallowed ground for Americans," said Stephen Grove, historian at the U.S. Military Academy at West Point.

Today — more than 200 years after Thomas Jefferson signed the document that created America's first military academy in 1802 — West Point is as solidly embedded in America's history as the billion-year-old Hudson Highland granite from which it is carved.

Rising from the canyon-like banks of the river it was built to protect, West Point still works at building officers of character for the United States Army. West Point has survived the conflicting whims of critics and advocates, of war and peace, of interference and indifference.

Counted across the eons of time, the academy's history is but a moment. But in the story of the United States, West Point and its graduates figure prominently.

From the first graduates in 1802: Joseph Gardner Swift, who helped develop New York's fortifications, and Simon Levy, who performed administrative duties for the Corps of Engineers during his brief military career; to the mid-20th century graduates who would one day strap themselves into rockets; to the thousands who summoned the pluck to endure the rigid discipline; to the people of color and the women who had the grit to plow through prejudice, West Point graduates have shaped the America that is today.

"It was grueling," City of Poughkeepsie resident Anthony Leo, Class of 1963, said of his time at the academy. "You come out without too many people being able to put much over on you."

Guarding the Hudson Valley

West Point's strategic location in the Highlands midway up the Hudson River led to its selection for fortification.

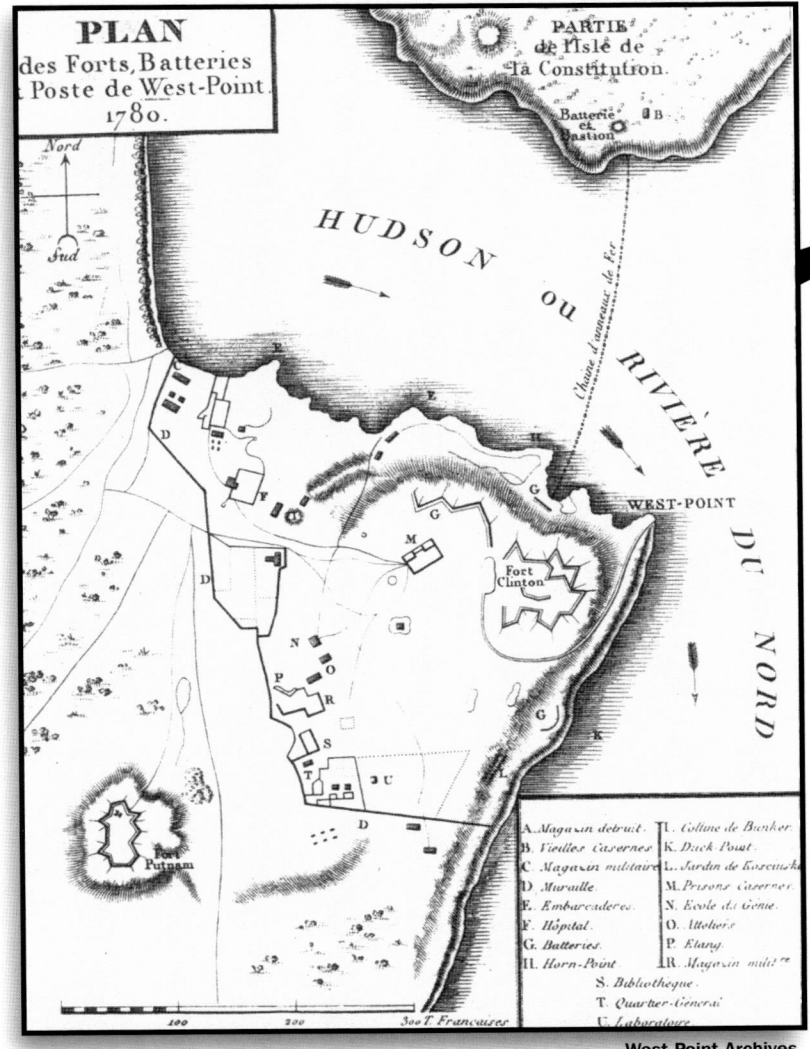

West Point Archives

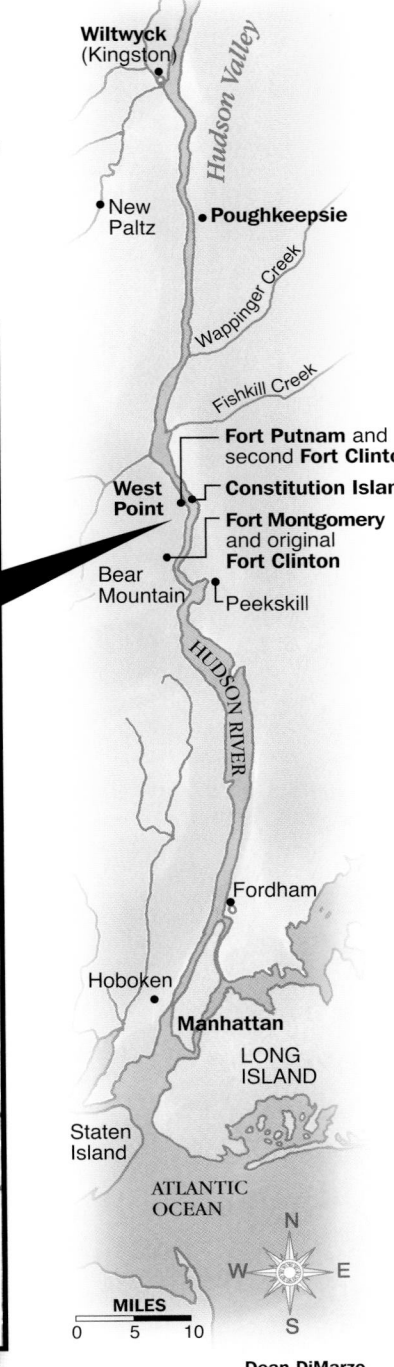

Dean DiMarzo

Kathy McLaughlin

Above, Cadets parade past a statue of George Washington prior to graduation day ceremonies in 1995.

> ‘ In 1778, the first troops arrived on the Plain at West Point and every graduate has drilled on that same field. ’

Stephen Grove
West Point historian

Gerald Richardson of Beekman, Class of 1956, was a private first class on his way to Korea when the Army asked if anybody wanted to go to West Point. "I didn't have the foggiest notion of what West Point was, but it sure sounded better than Korea," Richardson said.

"I went back to the barracks and everybody said you don't want to go there, it's tough." Richardson spent 21 years in the service, including in Vietnam in 1967 and 1968.

Key to the continent

But before West Point was an academy, it was an Army post built and manned to defend the vital Hudson River. If the British had made the river theirs, the American Revolution quite likely would have sputtered to failure. West Point was the key to the continent, George Washington wrote to Alexander Hamilton in 1783.

Baron Frederick von Steuben, who transformed patriot farm boys into a disciplined force worthy of the term "army," wrote from West Point in 1779 that there was one British objective that would determine America's future: West Point.

"Let us defend the North River and hold West Point, and the end of our campaign will be glorious," Steuben wrote.

A study of a map shows that if the British succeeded in controlling the Hudson, they could isolate New England — the fount of revolutionary zeal — from the rest of the colonies. Lines of transportation and communication critical to the Americans would be severed. The access the Hudson gave the Americans to the interior and western regions would be forfeited and American exposure to attacks by Indians would be greater. The British also would have an unobstructed path from British Canada to British-held New York City.

Tappan and Clinton knew the untamed Highlands and its perils. The Dutch Tappan was a native and trustee of Kingston, north of West Point. Clinton, of English forebears, was a soldier and surveyor and a native of Little Britain, just west of Newburgh.

Forts built in 1778

West Point and Martalear's Rock (also known as Constitution Island) were chosen because there the river bends sharply and both currents and winds make sailing treacherous. In "The River and the Rock: The History of Fortress West Point, 1775-1783," Dave Palmer, a former West Point superintendent, wrote that the Hudson River

sloop was developed specifically to cope with the river's tricksters: the winds and tides confronting boats as they attempted to sail through the Hudson Highlands.

Time would pass and failures would accrue, however, before the Americans realized the need to fortify West Point itself. That would not happen until 1778, when the Army had established itself there and began work on various forts, including Fort Putnam and Fort Arnold (renamed Fort Clinton after Benedict Arnold's treason), and the chain stretching from Constitution Island to West Point.

"For some reason, they completely overlooked the commanding position of West Point," wrote Sidney Forman in "West Point: A History of the United States Military Academy."

Constitution Island was fortified in 1775. By the fall of 1776, two forts, Montgomery and Clinton, had been built about six miles south of West Point, near Bear Mountain. A chain was stretched across the river there.

In 1777, the situation looked bleak for the Americans in the Highlands. The British took both forts on Oct. 5 and 6. On Oct. 8, they broke the chain at Bear Mountain and captured Constitution Island — only a day after the Americans defeated the British at the Battle of Saratoga. It was the Battle of Saratoga that handed the Highlands back to the Americans. When Sir Henry Clinton — on his way up the Hudson to relieve British Gen. John Burgoyne — learned of Burgoyne's defeat at Saratoga, he returned to New York City. But before he did, he destroyed the two Hudson Highland forts. Kingston, then the state capital, was burned on Oct. 16.

With Sir Henry Clinton back in New York City, and with a victory at Saratoga, the Americans looked to the ruined forts Clinton and Montgomery. George Washington decided West Point must be strengthened. Gen. Israel Putnam, headquartered in Peekskill, assembled troops and on Jan. 27, 1778, American soldiers trudged through snow and crossed the Hudson River ice to reach West Point.

"In 1778, the first troops arrived on the Plain at West Point and every graduate has drilled on that same field," Grove said.

Ever since, West Point has belonged to Americans.

"I feel that West Point is part of my American heritage," City of Poughkeepsie resident Richard Purdy said. "I feel that it belongs to me."

Saratoga 1777

It was the summer of 1777, and British forces were moving toward Albany from three directions, including from captured New York City. The vital Hudson River was at risk, and the Americans desperately needed a victory.

Gen. Benedict Arnold, front, is wounded at Saratoga

● **June 17** – British Gen. John Burgoyne leaves St. Johns, Canada, with a force of 9,000, including British, German and Canadian troops, and American Indians.

● **July 6** – Burgoyne takes Fort Ticonderoga on Lake Champlain.

● **Aug. 6** – British Col. Barry St. Leger, coming through the Mohawk Valley, defeats American forces at the battle of Oriskany but retreats when he hears of a larger American force on its way.

● **Aug. 16** – Troops sent to Bennington by Burgoyne are defeated by New England militiamen.

● **Sept. 19** – British defeat the patriots at Saratoga at great cost. The British hold their position and wait for Sir Henry Clinton.

● **Oct. 7** – Burgoyne sends soldiers south again only to be defeated by American troops led by Gen. Horatio Gates and Gen. Benedict Arnold.

● **Oct. 8** – Burgoyne begins a retreat to the north.

● **Oct. 16** – Sir Henry Clinton, delayed near West Point, sends a ship to Kingston, New York's capital at the time. Under Maj. Gen. John Vaughan, the British burn the city.

● **Oct. 17** – Surrounded and outnumbered, Burgoyne surrenders at Saratoga. The Americans take 6,000 prisoners and a large supply of arms.

'During the Revolution there was no fighting at West Point — the garrison did its fighting elsewhere. The enemy might be kept away, but not death. Excavations ... not infrequently uncover the remains of Revolutionary soldiers. Their homes are unknown, and no monument marks the resting place of these soldiers who kept their vigil in these Highlands and who first raised the American flag over West Point, the oldest U.S. military post over which it has continuously flown.'

Capt. Horace M. Reeve
17th Infantry, U.S. Army,
General Staff, USMA 1892
'The Centennial of the
United States Military
Academy at West Point,
New York'
Government Printing Office,
1904

Painting from the West Point Museum Collections, U.S. Military Academy

Graphic: Dean DiMarzo

THE PLAYERS

From hero to traitor

Call him vain. Call him greedy. Call him traitor. But first, call Benedict Arnold hero.

The officer in the Continental Army who plotted to sell the fortifications at West Point to the British was a patriot before he became a turncoat.

Magnificent and victorious at the Battle of Saratoga in October 1777, the turning point for the Americans in the Revolution, Arnold rode into the thick of fighting. Exposed constantly to British fire, he was wounded. His horse was killed. Had Arnold been killed, there's little doubt he would have been revered, not reviled. Instead, "the story of Arnold's treason, with all its blackness, is one of the most thrilling in all history and the Hudson River country was its background," Nelson Greene wrote in "The Valley of the Hudson: River of Destiny."

Arnold began plotting treachery around 1778, about the time he was put in command of Philadelphia and subsequently married his second wife, Margaret "Peggy" Shippen, daughter of wealthy Philadelphia loyalists.

As commander in Philadelphia, Arnold persuaded Gen. George Washington to put him in command at West Point. By 1779 it was considered to be the strongest military post in America. And Arnold had proved his bravery and military brilliance by then: Ticonderoga, Quebec, Lake Champlain and Saratoga were all behind him.

Arnold's West Point scheme failed in September 1780 when Arnold's British contact, Maj. John Andre, was caught out of uniform behind enemy lines carrying in his stocking the design for West Point's defenses in Arnold's handwriting. Andre was hanged as a spy a few days later. There was much sympathy for Andre, even in the American army. Many believed Andre was doing his duty as a British officer and that Arnold needlessly put Andre in harm's way.

"Washington would have saved him if the rules of war had not prevented his action," Greene wrote. Andre, out of uniform, was judged a spy, and spies were executed.

Arnold learned of Andre's capture at his headquarters near West Point, the Robinson House, where Gen. George Washington, the Marquis de Lafayette, a French aristocrat and major general in the Continental Army, and Maj. Gen. Henry Knox had arrived two days early to meet with him. It was to have been the day Arnold surrendered West Point. Arnold, learning of their arrival, had bolted 30 minutes earlier — leaving behind his new baby and his wife, who fainted. Arnold escaped to the British ship Vulture near Croton Point.

An influential wife's pressure

In "The River and the Rock: The History of Fortress West Point, 1775-1783," Dave Palmer, a former academy superintendent, wrote that Peggy Arnold at one point received Washington in her room. The commander in chief found her "propped on pillows in a diaphanous gown," her baby at her breast, her dishevelled hair around her shoulders.

"She was into it up to her ears," Clare Brandt, author of "The Man in the Mirror: A Life of Benedict Arnold," said of Peggy Shippen Arnold's role in her husband's defection. "She pulled herself out of it with remarkable hysterics with Washington and Lafayette."

Arnold's betrayal was a "betrayal of the heart" for Washington, said Jim Johnson, former military historian at the academy.

Frustration, pride and vanity pushed Arnold to treachery, historians speculate.

Arnold didn't get the promotions he believed he deserved despite his valiant conduct and his sustaining wounds at Fort Ticonderoga and Saratoga, said Stephen Grove, historian at West Point.

"Arnold's grievances, and there were many — officers going broke, Congress really not supporting the war," Brandt said. "But every single officer shared these grievances with Arnold, and he was the only one who turned his coat."

Arnold's foolish blunders doomed traitorous plan

Benedict Arnold, the officer who displayed military genius and personal courage on the battlefield fighting for the patriot cause, was a flop when it came to treason.

"He just blew this," said Rhinebeck resident Clare Brandt, author of "The Man in the Mirror: A Life of Benedict Arnold."

Arnold's plan to sell the West Point fortifications to the British was foiled in 1780 when his British contact, Maj. John Andre, was caught. Andre was out of uniform and had the fortification designs, in Arnold's handwriting, hidden in his stocking.

Andre was hanged as a spy, but Arnold escaped. He participated in a couple of battles against the Americans, but then went to England and Canada.

Arnold was never highly regarded in England either.

"Nobody loves a failed traitor. If he managed to turn over West Point, the British would have loved him, but he didn't. It was his own damn fault that he didn't," Brandt said, ticking off a list of what went awry. One of Arnold's biggest blunders, Brandt said, was his insistence that Andre carry the plans for the fortifications of West Point in Arnold's handwriting.

"That was remarkably stupid," Brandt said. "Andre could have memorized these. My guess is that Arnold wanted to be sure there was a paper trail and he would be able to say, 'Look what I tried to do for you.'"

No one should be sorry for Arnold, she said, even though he pulled the Americans' fat out of the fire several times and risked his life for the patriot cause until he decided to switch sides for money.

His treachery likely began about 1778 or 1779, when he was placed in command of Philadelphia and married, at age 35, Margaret "Peggy" Shippen, 18-year-old daughter of wealthy Philadelphians described by some historians as loyalists but called public fence-sitters and closet Tories by Brandt. Peggy's father, a lawyer, became chief justice of Pennsylvania after the war.

A native of Norwich, Conn., Arnold's status had been reduced by his father's bankruptcy, which forced Arnold in early adolescence to leave school and become an apothecary apprentice.

'An amazing leader'

Arnold spent much of his life seeking assurance, Brandt said. As the War for Independence began, Arnold, by this time a druggist and bookseller in New Haven, Conn., embraced the patriots' cause.

"He was an amazing soldier and an amazing leader of men," Brandt said.

"He was brilliant tactically, and he was even more brilliant on the battlefield. He would never ask his men to do anything he wouldn't do first. ... His men loved him for it," she said.

But Arnold personally knew the men who would have been attacked when he handed West Point to the British, Brandt said.

"Some of them had been on the march to Quebec with him. He was condemning them to either being killed or being wounded or captured. ... That tells me a lot about Arnold. He had no connection to other people, no regard for other people he knew, people he should have been counting as friends."

Arnold died in England in 1801, at the age of 60, leaving his wife, Peggy, debt-ridden. She remained his constant defender until her death in 1804.

EXECUTION SONG

An excerpt from:
"Major Andre's Arrest And Execution"

Andre found that his contrivance would soon be brought to light,

He called for pen and paper, and begged for time to write

A line to Gen'ral Arnold, to let him know his fate,

And pray'd for his assistance, but alas it was too late.

When Gen'ral Arnold read the news, it put him in a fright,

He escaped on board the Vulture, and New York he reached that night,

There went among the Brittish troups, a fighting for the King,

And left poor Major Andre there on the gallows to swing.

H.De Marsan, 1860,
New York City

Far left, An image of Benedict Arnold.

Left, For his collaboration with Benedict Arnold, Maj. John Andre was convicted of spying. He was hanged at the American encampment at Tappan in Orange County, N.Y., on Oct. 2, 1780.

West Point Museum Collections, U.S. Military Academy

Above, a set of pistols belonging to Gen. George Washington.

Right: A portrait by John G. Chapman depicts George Washington as a member of the Virginia Militia at the age of about 40.

BY THE NUMBERS

Threepence

The duty paid by Americans to the British for each gallon of imported molasses, as spelled out by the Sugar Act of 1764.

43

George Washington's age when he became commander in chief of the Continental Army at the start of the Revolutionary War.

340

British tea chests destroyed by patriots at the Boston Tea Party in 1773.

Over 3,000 miles

Distance British troops had to sail from Europe to battle Americans in the Revolution.

6 to 12 weeks

Time it took for British commands to travel from London to commanders in the field.

Washington saw Hudson's strategic value

West Point was a fortress before it was a military academy because commander-in-chief George Washington and others recognized its strategic importance to the defense of the Hudson River.

Washington also recognized the need for a military academy.

"I cannot conclude without repeating the necessity of the proposed Institution, unless we intend to let the Science (of war) become extinct, and to depend entirely upon the Foreigners for their friendly aid." This was Washington in 1783, supporting Maj. Gen. Henry Knox — who would become secretary of war — on the need for military academies, historian Stephen E. Ambrose wrote in "Duty, Honor, Country."

Academy proponents, realizing America needed a defense policy, wanted to create a military academy that would turn out officers who came from all classes of society, not just the elite. These officers would command a citizen army, or militia, while the Regular Army would have no role in the academy, Ambrose wrote. The idea of a large standing army was anathema to those Americans, who saw it both as a support and a breeding ground for aristocracies.

Congress wasted little effort after the Revolutionary War supporting an army. When the war formally ended with the signing of the Treaty of Paris in 1783, and the British had departed New York, the United States Army numbered around 80 men, most stationed at West Point.

A summer stay at West Point

West Point was Washington's headquarters in 1779 and he knew the area well.

Although Washington was spoiling for battle in the summer of 1779, in many other ways his stay at West Point was idyllic. New York City residents, including thousands of British troops, were in the grips of a fever, former U.S. Military Academy Superintendent Dave Palmer wrote in "The River and the Rock: The History of Fortress West Point, 1775-1783."

Jefferson established academy

One man who initially opposed the formation of a national military academy ended up figuring prominently in its creation.

President Thomas Jefferson signed legislation that created the United States Military Academy at West Point in 1802.

Jefferson, as secretary of state, had voiced his opposition at a Cabinet meeting with President Washington and Secretary of War Henry Knox in 1793. Jefferson argued that no power given by the Constitution would authorize the creation of a national academy, historian Stephen E. Ambrose wrote in "Duty, Honor, Country."

That opinion was to change, molded by the practical needs of the young nation, democratic ideals and fresh thinking about the purpose of higher education.

"Historians suspect he (Jefferson) saw a practical benefit to the nation for the enhancement of education, and perhaps even as an opportunity to bring about social diversity in the ranks of the military," said Stephen Grove, historian at the academy, speculating about why Jefferson changed his mind about establishing a military academy. The nation would need well-trained officers who came from many walks of life, not just the privileged class, to lead its militia and standing army.

In "West Point: A History of the United States Military Academy," author Sidney Forman noted that when Jefferson took office, he was dealing with foreign and domestic issues that would underscore the nation's need for an army: pirates in the Mediterranean, the potential restoration of French authority in Louisiana, border disputes, and the aftermath of Shays' Rebellion, a farmers' uprising in Massachusetts in 1786 and 1787 against inequitable taxes and laws.

Education reform was taking root, too: There was a growing conviction that higher education should produce not just philosophers, religious leaders and scholars, but the country's future public servants, scientists, builders and entrepreneurs, Ambrose wrote.

The rise of democracy, capitalism and science had a profound effect.

Several sites and plans for a military school were proposed. In 1794, the grade of cadet was created, and a military school was established at West Point, continuing until destroyed by fire in 1796. In 1795, the Corps of Artillerists and Engineers assembled at West Point. Maj. Jonathan Williams, Benjamin Franklin's grand-nephew, was ordered to assume the superintendency of the military school at West Point in 1801, but a formal military academy was not yet established.

The president was authorized by Congress on March 16, 1802, to organize a corps of engineers which "shall be stationed at West Point ... and shall constitute a military academy."

Right, a mural at the Poughkeepsie Journal depicts Thomas Jefferson.

Spencer Ainsley

Above, The 2002 USMA Bicentennial Commemorative Coin was minted to honor the 200th anniversary of the founding of the academy. The coin depicts a cadet color guard in parade exercise with the Academy's Washington Hall and Cadet Chapel in the background on one side and the U.S. Military Academy's bicentennial logo on the other.

Headquartered at the Moore house, Washington played ball with his aides and entertained at dinner by the river's edge. He flirted, went to several Masonic meetings at the Beverly Robinson house across the river and tried to stop the soldiers' swimming naked on hot afternoons, Palmer wrote.

Washington was at West Point in 1780 on the day he learned one of his most competent officers, Benedict Arnold, planned to turn it over to the British.

In 1781, when Washington marched 5,000 men south to what would become the Battle of Yorktown, the war's final battle, he left 4,000 men at West Point. In 1782, a victorious Washington returned to the Hudson Highlands to await a formal peace and keep an eye on New York City, still in British hands. The last cantonment of the American army was in New Windsor; Washington was headquartered two miles away in Newburgh. There, he spurned the suggestion from Col. Lewis Nicola, stationed at Fishkill with the invalid troops, that he become king.

"Washington replied the same day," said Tom Hughes, historic site manager. "Nicola was a political thinker. He built his case about how monarchies are tried and true and that there hadn't been a successful democracy or republic for centuries."

Washington replied: "Banish these thoughts from your mind. You cannot have found a person to whom your schemes are more disagreeable."

$11,000 seals the deal for West Point land

America's oldest continuously occupied military post, West Point, first was home to Native Americans. The arrival of Europeans changed all that and the property, over the years, became part of land grants.

The West Point property eventually came under the ownership of John Moore in 1747. Moore, a wealthy New York resident, built a large, three-storied house on the land across from Constitution Island. The house, one of several built in the Highlands, was used as a retreat and a summer home by the Moore family even through the early years of the Revolutionary War. By then it had been inherited by John Moore's son, Stephen, of North Carolina. Locals called it "Moore's Folly," likely because of its size and elegance amid the Hudson Highlands.

Stephen Moore by 1779 had petitioned Congress for payment for damages to the property and compensation for the material that had been used to build barracks and fortifications.

Congress paid Moore something — including rent — but nothing near the amount the Quartermaster General estimated the damages to be: $292,000 in Continental scrip, a sum that was later reduced.

Henry Knox, secretary of war, issued a report on the property's military value in response to Congress' notion to buy the West Point property.

"In case of an invasion of any of the middle or eastern states by a marine power the possession of Hudson's River would be an object of the highest importance as well to the invader of the United States," his report said.

Stephen and Griselda Moore signed the deed transferring West Point to the U.S. government on Sept. 10, 1790. The government bought it for $11,085.

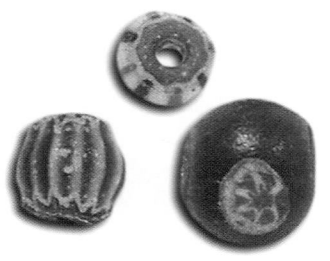

George Van Sickle

Native American artifacts from the Grapes site in Ulster County, dating from the 17th century.

HISTORIC TIMES
Events at West Point and around the nation

1625
Dutch settlers begin building New Amsterdam – now New York City. The British take it over in 1664 and rename it after the Duke of York.

1752
Ben Franklin uses a kite during a lightning storm to prove lightning is a form of electricity.

1763
British pass Stamp Act taxing printed material, including newspapers and legal documents.

1773
Boston Tea Party.

Americans battle the British for their independence.

1775-1783

| 1750 | 1755 | 1760 | 1765 | 1770 | 1775 |

FRENCH - INDIAN WARS
1689-1763

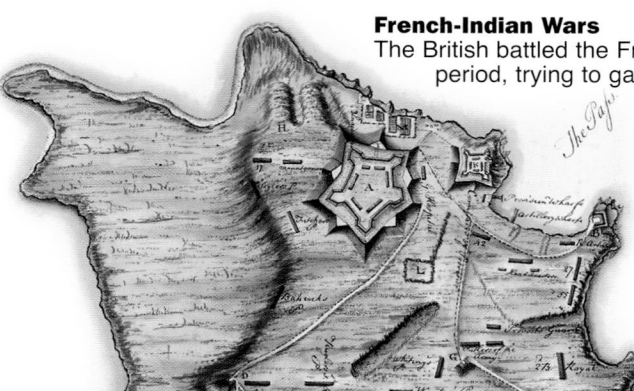

French-Indian Wars
The British battled the French in four wars during this period, trying to gain control of eastern North America. The British won in 1763, taking control of North America from the Atlantic Ocean to the Mississippi River.

Left, a map of the British fort at Crown Point on Lake Champlain during the war.

Archiving Early America

1770
American civilians are killed by British troops at the Boston Massacre.

Left, an engraving by Paul Revere shows a sensationalized version of the Boston Massacre.

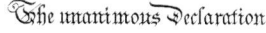

1776 — The Declaration of Independence, drafted by Thomas Jefferson, is adopted by Congress on July 4.

Baron Frederick von Steuben was a master trainer

Cadet regulations at the U.S. Military Academy are still called "the Blue Book," named for the regulations set down by Prussian-born Baron Frederick von Steuben for the U.S. Army early in the 19th century. Steuben is credited with shaping the ill-trained Continental troops into an army.

In 1783, Steuben, the Continental army's drillmaster and inspector general, used the Gulian Verplanck house, now Mount Gulian, in Fishkill, as his headquarters.

Arriving in America in December 1777, Steuben had risen to the rank of captain in the Prussian army during the Seven Years War (1756-63) and for a time was attached to the general staff of Frederick the Great. In a letter of introduction to Washington, Benjamin Franklin described Steuben as a lieutenant general, not his true rank. Washington was impressed and so was Congress, which sent Steuben to train the troops at Valley Forge, Pa., during the terrible winter of 1777-78.

At Valley Forge, Steuben found appalling conditions and an undisciplined bunch of men not used to taking orders. Steuben became the drill sergeant, barking and shouting orders. He formed a model drill company that was copied throughout the ranks, improved sanitary conditions and wrote "Regulations for the Order and Discipline

of the Troops." It served as the country's military guide until 1812.

In 1778, Steuben was named inspector general of the army and given a field command.

In the summer of 1779, when Washington established his headquarters at West Point, Steuben treated the troops he found there much the same as he did the men at Valley Forge, according to former USMA Superintendent Dave Palmer's "The River and the Rock: The History of Fortress West Point, 1775-1783."

'Matchless profanity'

The men at Valley Forge found Steuben funny. "Steuben's matchless profanity was a constant source of mirth to the clumsy men he was struggling to convert into soldiers," Palmer wrote.

By the time Steuben arrived at West Point, his English had improved "and his repertoire of American oaths was proportionately larger," Palmer wrote.

Steuben participated in the battle at Yorktown and lived in New York City after the war. Despite grants of money from Congress and 16,000 acres of land from New York state, his extravagant living put him in debt. Congress, in 1790, voted him a life pension of $2,500. He died in 1794 near Remsen in upstate New York.

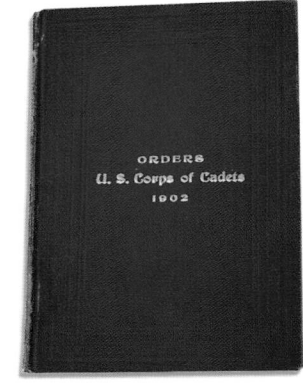

U.S. Military Academy Archive

Above, The "blue book" governs the command and administration of the Corps of Cadets and includes the honor and disciplinary system. This book is from 1902.

There are about 10,000 military casualties in the Revolutionary War.

1785-1790
New York City is the capital of the United States.

1789-1797
George Washington is first U.S. president.

1794
First artillery and engineering training at West Point school.

1797
Sojourner Truth, a slave who became an abolitionist, is born in Ulster County, New York.

REVOLUTIONARY WAR

1780   **1785**   **1790**   **1795**   **1800**

1780
Maj. John Andre, Benedict Arnold's British contact, is caught and Arnold's plan to hand West Point to the British is exposed.

West Point Museum Collections
The capture of Maj. John Andre is portrayed in this copy of an oil on canvas originally painted by Asher B. Durand.

1788
New York's Constitutional Convention is held in Poughkeepsie.

New York ratifies the Constitution and becomes the 11th state on July 26.

1790
New York population reaches 340,120.

1796
Physician Edward Jenner introduces vaccine in England for the deadly smallpox.

1801
Thomas Jefferson becomes president.

Images: Library of Congress and West Point Museum Collections, U.S. Military Academy

Brilliant engineer from Poland designed fortress

Thaddeus Kosciuszko
**West Point Museum Collections,
United States Military Academy**

'To the scientific skill and sedulous application of Kosciuszko, the public was mainly indebted for the construction of the military defences at West Point.'

Roswell Park
in 'A Sketch of the History and Topography of West Point and the U.S. Military Academy'

Spencer Ainsley

A statue at West Point pays homage to Thaddeus Kosciuszko, a Polish artillery officer who played a vital role in the Battle of Saratoga and who helped design and build the defenses at West Point.

A son of a noble Polish family and educated at Warsaw's military academy, Thaddeus Kosciuszko arrived in America in 1776, just in time to join the patriot cause.

This was a man who would advocate for his native Poland all his adult life, whose views would be forward-thinking enough to allow him to free his slaves. Thomas Jefferson called him "as pure a son of liberty as I have ever known."

Kosciuszko is credited with designing the defenses that would turn West Point into a fortress.

It was another man, however, who began them, a French engineer, Lt. Col. de la Radiere. Radiere "traces in the snow the first fortification at West Point," said West Point graduate James Johnson, who taught for 15 years at the academy and is writing a book about the Hudson Highlands during the Revolution.

"Everybody knows about Kosciuszko, but he's standing on Radiere's fort," Johnson said, referring to the Kosciuszko monument on the academy grounds.

Kosciuszko was given the rank of engineer colonel after he helped plan the defenses of the Continental Congress in Philadelphia. In 1777 he was at Fort Ticonderoga, where his warning — that the fort would be lost if the British succeeded in fortifying the steep Mount Defiance overlooking the fort — was ignored. The Americans abandoned Ticonderoga when the British did, indeed, fortify the mountain. To slow the British pursuit, Kosciuszko felled trees and flooded fields, giving the Americans time to prepare for the Battle of Saratoga, the clash that would be the turning point in the war and the Americans' first major victory. At Saratoga in 1777, Kosciuszko fortified Bemis Heights overlooking the Hudson River.

A fruitful time

Kosciuszko spent the next two years directing and guiding the building of defenses at West Point. He arrived at West Point in 1778.

"To the scientific skill and sedulous application of Kosciuszko, the public was mainly indebted for the construction of the military defences at West Point," Roswell Park wrote in 1840 in "A Sketch of the History and Topography of West Point and the U.S. Military Academy."

He utilized the chain that stretched across the river from West Point to Constitution Island, to block the British from sailing up the river.

In 1780 at West Point, Kosciuszko was named chief of the engineering corps and made a brigadier general when the war ended.

He returned to Poland in 1784. Warsaw fell in 1794 after a two-month siege by Russians and Prussians. Kosciuszko, who led Warsaw's defenses in the siege, was imprisoned. He was freed in 1796 and returned to the United States in 1797. His friendship with Jefferson flowered.

Before departing again for Europe in 1798, Kosciuszko arranged to free some of his slaves and to educate them. He lived in France, and then in Switzerland, where he died in 1817.

FIRST IMPRESSIONS

West Point Museum Collections, U.S. Military Academy

THE VIEW FROM 1823

'The Point and Country adjoining it far exceeds the most Sanguine expectations I had formed of it. I had anticipated entering a wilderness where there was nothing to gratify the optical sense but a few old Buildings used as habitation for the Cadets, but instead of that I find 7 or 8 large brick buildings occupied by professors and officers. Two very large Stone Buildings 2 Story High, one used as the Hotel and mess-hall for the Cadets, the other as a Library, Chapel and Examination Hall & two very large Stone buildings one 3 and the other 4 Story High, used as barracks for the Cadets ... '

Abner Riviere Hetzel
USMA 1827, to his father, John Hetzel, June 28, 1823, from 'Cadet Life Before the Mexican War,' USMA Printing Office, 1945

THE FIRST DAYS

An officer's description
from 'The Centennial of the United States Military Academy at West Point, New York, 1802-1902,' Washington, Government Printing Office, 1904

'Coming on to a small plain surrounded by high mountains, we found it covered with a growth of yellow pines 10 or 15 feet high; no house or improvement on it; the snow waist high. We fell to lopping down the tops of the shrub pines and treading down the snow, spread our blankets, and lodged in that condition the first and second nights. ... In two or three weeks we had erected our huts. '

A view from West Point today looking north up the Hudson River. Constitution Island is at the right.

IN WARTIME
DEFENDING AMERICA, ITS FREEDOM, ITS TERRITORY

An oil painting by Ken Riley depicts the "Surrender at Appomattox," one of the key battles of the Civil War.

'Abandon your animosities, and make your sons Americans.'

THE 1800s

ROLL CALL

16 died from West Point

16 of the 89 USMA graduates serving died in the War of 1812.

Thayer making a name

1808 USMA graduate Sylvanus Thayer, later called the "Father of the Military Academy," first served in this war, as colonel for the Army Corps of Engineers.

Battling the British again

WAR OF 1812

The War of 1812 put America back into battle with England, primarily over oppressive British maritime practices rising from the Napoleonic Wars. The United States declared war on Britain on June 18, 1812. Despite early U.S. naval victories, Britain maintained a blockade of eastern U.S. ports. The Americans were able to gain control of the Great Lakes, but the British burned the Capitol, White House and other buildings in August 1814. On Dec. 24, 1814, both sides signed the Treaty of Ghent, which essentially restored territories captured by each side. The United States won the Battle of New Orleans before news of the treaty reached home, leading it to later proclaim the war a victory.

Library of Congress

An engraving of the Battle of New Orleans, one of the battles in the War of 1812.

1802
The USMA at West Point is established by an Act of Congress on March 16.

WAR OF 1812
1812-1815

1825
363-mile Erie Canal connects Great Lakes to Hudson River.

1837
Samuel Morse builds first working telegraph.

1843
Congress provides for one cadet from each congressional district.

Mexican War
Dispute over Texas sparks war with Mexico.

MEXICAN WAR
1846-48

| 1800 | 1805 | 1810 | 1815 | 1820 | 1825 | 1830 | 1835 | 1840 | 1845 | 1850 |

1812
The size of the Corps of Cadets at West Point is set at 250. Entrance requirements and qualifications are also established.

USMA band is established.

Left, Altazimuth telescope, from 1838.

1817
Sylvanus Thayer, a graduate of the Class of 1808, takes command of the academy.

Right, a portrait of Thayer by Robert Weir.

West Point Museum Collections

1836
The Old Cadet Chapel at West Point opens. It is moved to its present location in the cemetery, shown at right, when a new chapel is built in 1910.

Spencer Ainsley

1846-48
Military successes in the Mexican War establish national confidence in West Point training.

Southwest takes shape

MEXICAN WAR — 1846-1848

The war began with a Mexican attack on American troops along the southern Texas border in April 1846. Fighting ended when U.S. Gen. Winfield Scott occupied Mexico City on Sept. 14, 1847.

In addition to recognizing the U.S. annexation of Texas, Mexico ceded nearly all of what is now California, Utah, Nevada, Colorado, Arizona and New Mexico.

Right, "General Scott's entrance into Mexico City" by C. Nebel.

West Point Museum Collections, U.S. Military Academy

1859
Abolitionist John Brown is hanged for his raid on the U.S. Arsenal at Harpers Ferry, Virginia. Brown lost control of the arsenal to Marines led by Col. Robert E. Lee.

1865
President Abraham Lincoln is assassinated.

ULYSSES S. GRANT PRESIDENT 1869-1877

1879
Thomas Edison invents first viable light bulb.

1890
First Army-Navy football game.

1899
Black, gold and gray uniforms are adopted for use in all USMA games.

1855	1860	1865	1870	1875	1880	1885	1890	1895	1900

CIVIL WAR
1861-65

Civil War
Graduates of West Point figure prominently in the war, contributing hundreds of generals to both sides, including Robert E. Lee and Ulysses S. Grant.

Right, a detail from "Gettysburg — The First Day," a painting by James Walker.

West Point Museum Collections

1877
Henry Flipper becomes the first African American to graduate from West Point.

SPANISH- AMERICAN WAR – 1898

Spanish-American War
Teddy Roosevelt, left, leads his Rough Riders to a bloody but decisive battle against Spain at San Juan Heights in Cuba.

1898
West Point motto "Duty, Honor, Country" is selected.

Coat of arms and academy seal are adopted.

West Point Museum Collections, U.S. Military Academy

THE CIVIL WAR

Academy brother against brother

ROLL CALL

Generals for North and South

There were 294 Union generals and 150 Confederate generals who had graduated from West Point. In 55 of the Civil War's 60 major battles, West Point graduates commanded on both sides of the conflict. In the remaining battles, a West Point graduate commanded one of the sides.

From West Point to history books

In addition to Ulysses S. Grant and Robert E. Lee, the top USMA generals included Thomas "Stonewall" Jackson and William Tecumseh Sherman. Jefferson Davis, president of the Confederate States of America, was also a West Point graduate.

He served only days

Gen. Pierre Beauregard served as West Point superintendent for only five days in 1861, before being relieved for Confederate sympathies.

CIVIL WAR 1861-65

After Abraham Lincoln was elected president, the South Carolina Legislature voted to secede from the United States. Its secession was followed by Mississippi, Florida, Alabama, Georgia, Louisiana and Texas. Virginia, Arkansas, Tennessee and North Carolina threatened to secede as well. These 11 states eventually formed the Confederate States of America.

The first shots of the war were fired at Fort Sumter, S.C., on April 12, 1861, by rebel troops under the command of Gen. Pierre G.T. Beauregard, USMA Class of 1838.

In the war, West Point graduates Gen. Robert E. Lee, in charge of the Confederate Army, and Gen. Ulysses S. Grant, in charge of the Union, led opposing forces. Lee surrendered his army to Grant at Appomattox Court House in Virginia on April 9, 1865.

Many West Point graduates figured prominently in the war between the states.

Top, A Civil War era sword from Dutchess County, N.Y.

Left, The charge of the 22nd Negro Regiment at the Battle of Petersburg, Va., in an 1892 oil painting by Andre Castaigne.

West Point Museum Collections
U.S. Military Academy

❝The war with Mexico gave the Academy its laurel wreath, the Civil War a lasting crown.❞

Maj. Gen. Thomas H. Ruger, U.S. Army (USMA 1854) and Civil War veteran

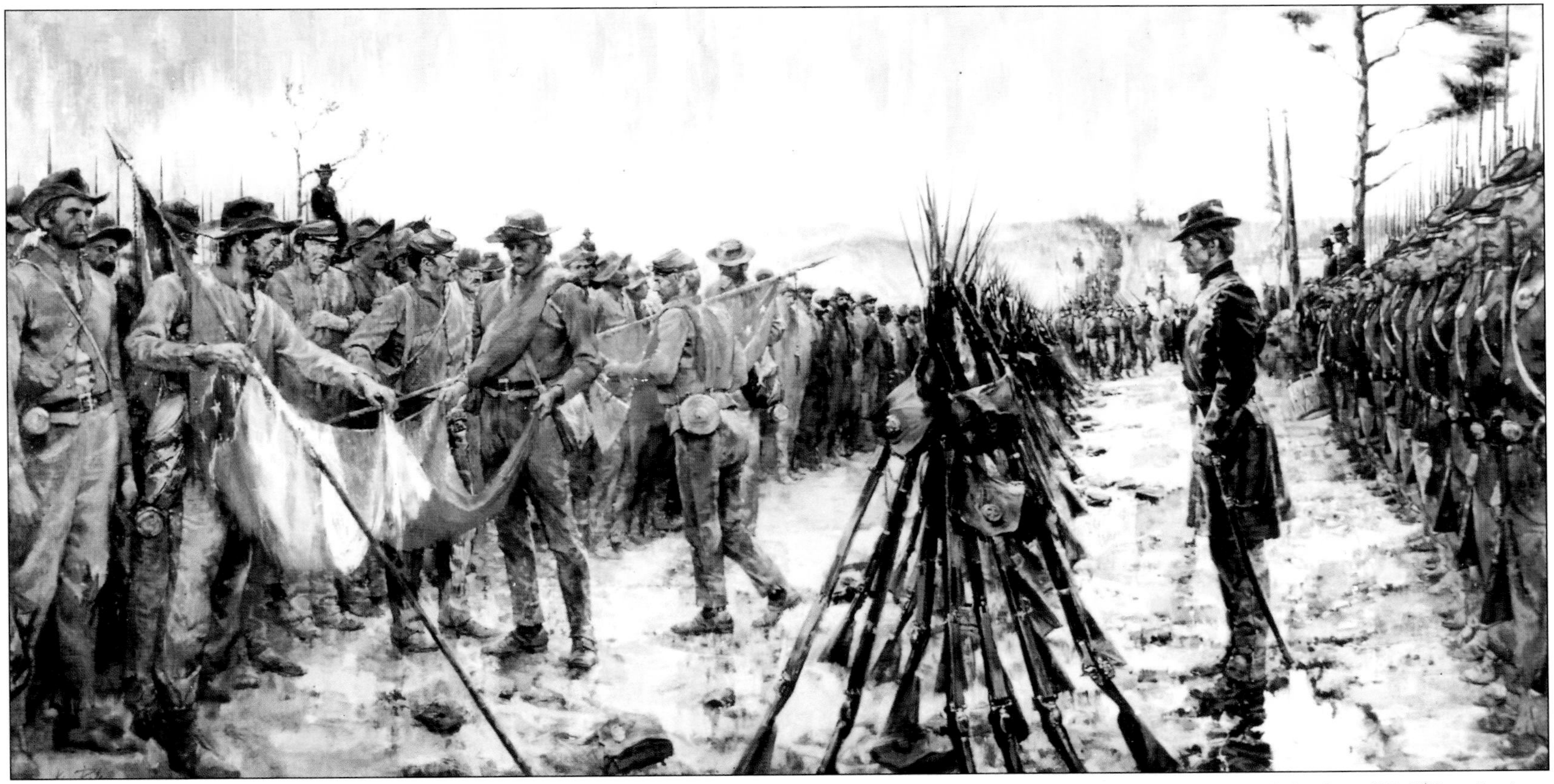

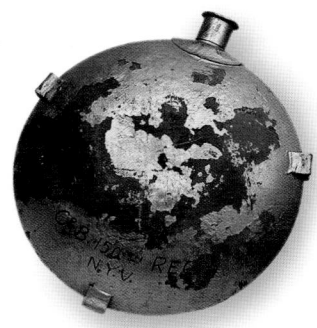

West Point Museum Collections, U.S. Military Academy

Ken Riley, in an oil on canvas, depicts "Surrender at Appomattox." West Point graduates had an immense impact on the Civil War.

Point links comrades and enemies

Confronting college classmates in later years on a routine life-and-death basis is not the normal course of events. Yet, 140 years ago, an astonishing number of West Point graduates found themselves in combat with old comrades on each side in the bloody Civil War.

In the first six decades of the 19th century, the U.S. Military Academy produced about 450 generals — and several hundred other line officers — who fought for the Union and the Confederacy in the conflict that tore a nation in half.

Fifty-five of the 60 most significant battles were commanded on both sides by West Pointers. The U.S. Military Academy was the wellhead of command for the Civil War. West Point, in many respects, helped shape a very different nation.

Most famous, of course, are the two commanders who effectively ended the war at Appomattox — Robert E. Lee for the South and Ulysses S. Grant for the North. In terms of West Point, they couldn't have been more different. Lee, who graduated second in 1829, incredibly had no demerits during his four years. He was so concerned with protocol his colleagues later nicknamed him "Granny." By the end of the war, his soldiers affectionately called him "Uncle Robert."

A different path for Lee

Lee compiled such a sterling record before the Civil War — Mexican War hero, superintendent at West Point — he was offered command of the Union forces by President Abraham Lincoln, but he could not bear to fight against his home state of Virginia.

Grant graduated 21st out of 39 in the Class of 1843, and by all

Civil War canteen

ROLL CALL

Allegiance to the South

There were 278 cadets at the academy the day Lincoln was elected president; 86 were from the southern states and 65 were discharged, dismissed or resigned because their loyalties were with the southern states.

Hundreds of thousands died

3 million fought and 600,000 died in the Civil War.

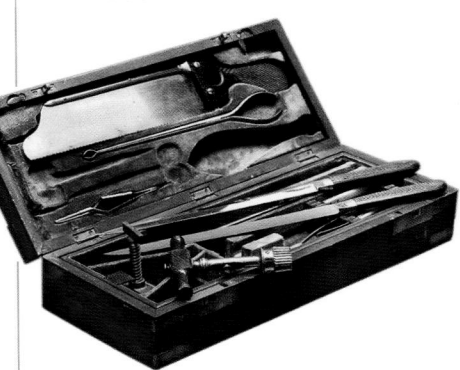

This kit, from a West Point graduate and member of the U.S. Sanitary Commission, contains medical tools used during the Civil War era.

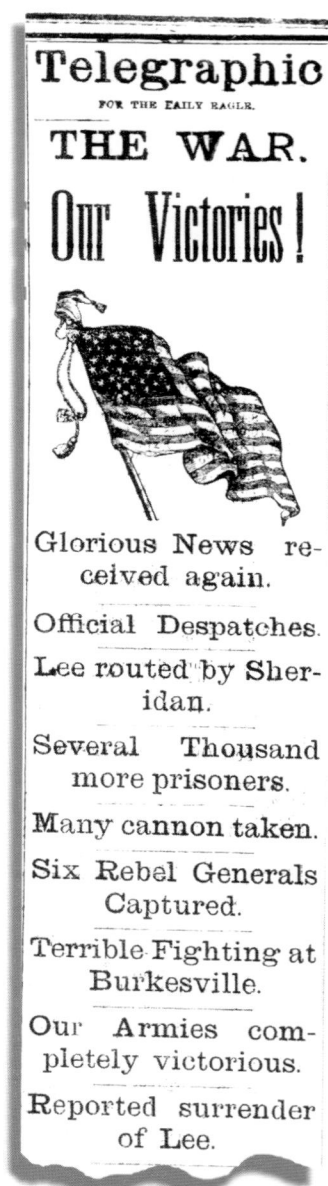
Above, Headlines from the April 8, 1865 edition of the Poughkeepsie Daily Eagle, a forerunner of the Poughkeepsie Journal.

accounts felt uncomfortable there. Fond of the bottle, Grant nonetheless performed well in the Mexican War but was clerking in an Illinois leather goods store by the time Civil War hostilities broke out and he rejoined the Army. Grant knew how to grind the Confederacy down. Lee was 54 when the war broke out; Grant, only 39.

The common experience of West Point produced considerable irony and overlapping experience among its generals.

Maj. Robert Anderson — A month away from appointment as a general, he commanded the small garrison of Union troops at Fort Sumter off Charleston, S.C., when the war began there. Anderson (Class of 1825) was highly regarded as an artillery instructor, and was fired upon at Sumter by Gen. Pierre G.T. Beauregard (Class of 1838), who less than three months earlier had been removed from his post as West Point superintendent after serving only a week, probably due to his southern leanings.

Some compiled better records during the war than they did at the academy.

Lewis A. Armistead — The southern general at Gettysburg in those "highwater mark of the Confederacy" paintings — who's urging his troops on during Pickett's Charge with his hat spiked at the top of his sword — was expelled from West Point 23 years before the war when he shattered a plate over fellow cadet Jubal Early's head. Armistead was felled a few seconds after the moment in the paintings. Early (Class of 1837) fought well for the South in early major battles, including Antietam, Chancellorsville and Gettysburg, but lost his command after several failures in the latter part of the war.

Some famous military men never made it to the hallowed halls above the Hudson.

Arthur MacArthur — A bright Wisconsin lad desired admission in

Left, "Civil War Drummer Boys Playing Cards" by Julian Scott, 1891. The painting had special meaning for the artist who had once been a drummer boy himself.

West Point Museum Collections, U.S. Military Academy

1861 but failed to gain appointment to the overflowing academy. Anxious to fight, he joined the 24th Wisconsin and a year later found himself a teen-aged colonel. Arthur MacArthur fought in 14 major battles, and at Missionary Ridge near Chattanooga, led such a valiant and successful charge he won the Medal of Honor — the same decoration his famous West Point son Douglas MacArthur (Class of 1903) would garner eight decades later.

A few of the other West Point graduates who stood out include:

George Pickett (Class of 1846) — Dead last in a class of 59 cadets, Pickett was outshone by classmates George B. McClellan and Thomas "Stonewall" Jackson but performed well in the Mexican War and during the Civil War Battle of Fredericksburg. His name sticks on a precise and foolish maneuver on the third day at Gettysburg, Pickett's Charge, when Lee ordered his division to assault the federal center on higher, well-protected ground. The three brigades were blown away. After the war, Pickett sold insurance in Richmond.

James Longstreet (Class of 1842) — Another top performer in the preceding Mexican War, Longstreet showed such great leadership during the early part of the Civil War, he was soon given command of a corps and became heavily relied upon by Lee. A master of tactical defense and position strategy, Longstreet was liked by southern soldiers because he never marched them directly into fire. He disagreed strongly with Lee's decision to do so at Gettysburg. After the war, he criticized Lee in a book, turned Republican and was appointed by Grant ambassador to Turkey.

LEADING NORTH & SOUTH

One of the 75 Medals of Honor awarded to West Point graduates

JEFFERSON DAVIS

Title: USMA Class of 1828; U.S. House of Representatives 1845-46; U.S. Senate 1847-51, 1857-61; secretary of war 1853-57; president, Confederate States of America, 1861-1865.

Born: June 3, 1808, Christian County, Ky.

Died: Dec. 6, 1889, New Orleans, La.

Contributions: Davis is credited with winning the Battle of Buena Vista in 1847 during the Mexican War. He served in the U.S. Senate, where he chaired the military affairs committee; in 1853 President Franklin Pierce named him secretary of war. After Mississippi seceded in 1861, he resigned from the Senate and was chosen president of the Confederacy. Upon Gen. Robert E. Lee's surrender, he fled Richmond and hoped to continue the fight until he could secure better terms from the North. He was indicted for treason, although he was never tried, as he was released due to poor health in 1867.

'If the secession of So. Ca. should be followed by an attempt to coerce her back into the Union, that act of usurpation, folly and wickedness would enlist every true Southern man for her defence.'

Jefferson Davis
in a personal letter
written Nov. 10, 1860

WILLIAM TECUMSEH SHERMAN

Title: USMA Class of 1840; Union commander of the military division of the Mississippi during the Civil War; U.S. Army chief of staff, 1869-1883.

Born: Feb. 8, 1820, Lancaster, Ohio.

Died: Feb. 14, 1891, New York City.

Contributions: Unlike many of his fellow West Point graduates, Sherman saw little action during the Mexican War, when he was stationed in California. Later, in the Civil War, with Ulysses S. Grant he captured Vicksburg, Miss., in 1863, opening the Mississippi to northern traffic once more. He captured the southern industrial center and railway hub of Atlanta in 1864. Then, in keeping with his mission to split the Confederacy, Sherman led 62,000 federal troops on the march to the sea, from Atlanta to Savannah, destroying anything in a 60-mile swath that could be useful to the enemy.

Facts: Sherman was named after the Shawnee chief, Tecumseh. Sherman resigned from the Army in 1853 to join a bank in San Francisco. The Panic of 1857 ended his banking career. At the brink of the Civil War he was superintendent of a new military school in Louisiana, a post he resigned when Louisiana seceded. That school became Louisiana State University.

Quote: While he was at West Point, in a letter to Ellen Ewing, his adoptive father's daughter who would become his wife, Sherman wrote: "... Indeed the nearer we come to that dreadful epoch, graduation day, the higher opinion I conceive of the duties and life of an officer on the United States Army and the more confirmed in the wish of spending my life in the service of my country."

MEDAL OF HONOR

Medal recognizes an elite group

More than 3,400 Medals of Honor have been awarded since the program was created in 1861 to recognize extraordinary valor during war. More than 1,500 were awarded for actions during the Civil War alone. Seventy-five graduates of the U.S. Military Academy have been among the recipients of the nation's highest military honor.

‘(I feel) sad and depressed at the downfall of a foe who had fought so long and valiantly, and had suffered so much for a cause, though that cause was, I believe, one of the worst for which a people ever fought.’

Ulysses S. Grant
writing of how he felt about the Civil War

ULYSSES S. GRANT

Title: USMA Class of 1843; general in chief, armies of the United States; president of the United States, 1869-77.

Born: April 27, 1822, Point Pleasant, Ohio; he was born Hiram Ulysses; it was converted in error by the congressman appointing him to West Point. He was registered as Ulysses Simpson Grant and he had to retain the name.

Died: July 23, 1885, Mount McGregor, Saratoga County, N.Y.

Contributions: During the Civil War, he made a name for himself conducting offensive campaigns, making the Union Army's superior numbers count. Relentless, he drew criticism for his tactics that resulted in high numbers of casualties and earned him the nickname "The Butcher." But the surrender terms Grant offered Confederate Gen. Robert E. Lee at Appomattox Court House in Virginia were not punitive. Though his second term as president was tainted by financial scandal, Grant backed amnesty for Confederate leaders and civil rights for former slaves and supported the ratification of the Fifteenth Amendment, which abolished race as a voting qualification.

Fact: He was cited for bravery in the Mexican War. He began smoking and drinking while stationed at Fort Humboldt, Calif. There, he became lonely, bored and disenchanted with the Army. After being reprimanded, Grant resigned from the service in 1854. He then rejoined his family near St. Louis and tried to become a businessman in attempts to earn enough money to support his family. Additional failed ventures as a civilian led him to join the leather goods store owned by his father and managed by his brothers in Galena, Ill. The Civil War brought him back into the Army.

Quote: In his memoirs, Grant wrote that his 10 furlough weeks from West Point "were shorter than one week at West Point." He also wrote of the Civil War that he felt "sad and depressed at the downfall of a foe who had fought so long and valiantly, and had suffered so much for a cause, though that cause was, I believe, one of the worst for which a people ever fought."

ROBERT E. LEE

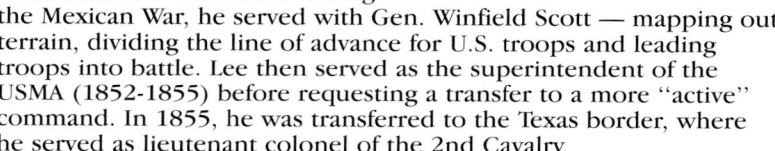

Title: USMA Class of 1829; assistant to chief engineer of the Army 1834-37; USMA superintendent 1852-55; lieutenant colonel of 2nd Cavalry 1855-57; commander of Virginia forces in Civil War 1861-65; president of Washington College 1865-70.

Born: Jan. 19, 1807, Stratford, Va.

Died: Oct. 12, 1870, Lexington, Va.

Contributions: After West Point graduation, Lee worked on several engineering projects. He helped build the St. Louis waterfront and worked on coastal forts in Brunswick and Savannah. During the Mexican War, he served with Gen. Winfield Scott — mapping out terrain, dividing the line of advance for U.S. troops and leading troops into battle. Lee then served as the superintendent of the USMA (1852-1855) before requesting a transfer to a more "active" command. In 1855, he was transferred to the Texas border, where he served as lieutenant colonel of the 2nd Cavalry.

In 1859, Lee commanded the force that put down an insurrection by radical abolitionist John Brown at Harper's Ferry. Before the formal start of the Civil War at Fort Sumter, Lee was offered command of the Union forces but said he could not fight against his home state of Virginia. He was named commander of the Virginia forces in April 1861. His last great victory of the war at the Battle of Chancellorsville was followed by his final invasion of the North, which ended at Gettysburg in July 1863. He surrendered on April 9, 1865, at Appomattox Court House in Virginia. Lee then devoted his life to setting an example for ex-Confederates. He served as president of Washington College from 1865 until his death in 1870. The school was later renamed Washington and Lee University.

Fact: Lee graduated second in his class and never received a single demerit as a cadet at the academy.

Quote: To those who did not want him to give up the fight in the Civil War: "Abandon your animosities, and make your sons Americans."

GEORGE G. MEADE

Title: USMA Class of 1835; commander, Army of the Potomac, 1863-1865.

Born: Dec. 31, 1815, Cadiz, Spain.

Died: Nov. 6, 1872, Philadelphia.

Contributions: Meade fought at Fredericksburg, Antietam and Chancellorsville. As commander of the Army of the Potomac, a position he was named to just three days earlier, he defeated Confederate Gen. Robert E. Lee at the Battle of Gettysburg. The victory turned the tide of the war, but Meade was criticized by some for allowing Lee's army to escape.

Fact: Ulysses S. Grant was named general in chief of the army in 1864, effectively making Meade a subordinate. After the Civil War, Meade served in the South during Reconstruction.

Quote: Meade rode to visit Lee the day after Lee's surrender at Appomattox. "Good morning, General," Meade said to Lee. "What are you doing with all that gray in your beard?" Lee asked. "You have to answer for most of it," Meade replied.

THOMAS J. 'STONEWALL' JACKSON

Title: USMA Class of 1846; notable service in the Mexican War; professor of engineering, Virginia Military Institute; lieutenant general, Confederate States of America.

Born: Born Jan. 21, 1824, Clarksburg, Va. (now West Virginia).

Died: May 10, 1863, near Guiney's Station, Va., as a result of wounds from friendly fire after the Battle of Chancellorsville.

Contributions: Acquired his nickname after the Battle of Bull Run (First Manassas). When Jackson and his troops maintained their positions against Yankee troops, Gen. Barnard Bee shouted, "There is Jackson standing like a stone wall." Historians disagree about whether Bee was praising or deriding Jackson for failing to come to his aid; Bee died in the battle. During his successful Shenandoah Valley campaigns, Jackson outmaneuvered four Union commanders, whose troops outnumbered Jackson's four to one.

Fact: When the Civil War began, he called it "the sum of all evils," but sided with the South; his sister denounced him and supported the Union.

'If I were an Indian, I would greatly prefer to cast my lot among those of my people who adhere to the free open plains rather than submit to the confined limits of the reservation, there to be the recipient of the blessed benefits of civilization with its vices thrown in without stint or measure.'

Lt. Col. George Armstrong Custer

GEORGE ARMSTRONG CUSTER

Title: USMA Class of June 1861.

Born: Dec. 5, 1839, New Rumley, Ohio.

Died: June 25, 1876, Little Bighorn River, Montana Territory.

Contributions: During the Civil War, he distinguished himself in numerous battles and his pursuit of Confederate commander Robert E. Lee contributed to Lee's surrender at Appomattox.

Fact: Custer graduated at the bottom of his USMA class; although he had been a fierce defender of the South at the academy, he fought for the North. His prowess as a cavalryman propelled him from lieutenant to the rank of brigadier general at the age of 23. Custer had been relieved of command of the 7th Cavalry as it was about to depart on its mission to pacify the Sioux, but Custer wrote President Grant an impassioned letter "appealing to you as a soldier to spare me the humiliation of seeing my regiment march to meet the enemy and I to not share its dangers." Custer and all of his men were killed at the Little Bighorn — "Custer's Last Stand." It was Custer's error of dividing his troops into four sections without knowing the size of the opposing force that cost him his life and the lives of his men.

ROLL CALL

Long journey for Custer

Lt. Col. George A. Custer was originally buried at the site of the Battle of Little Bighorn (1876). In 1877 his remains were shipped east and temporarily held at Poughkeepsie Rural Cemetery before being transported by steamboat to their final resting place in West Point cemetery.

Memorials at battle site

The site of the Battle of Little Bighorn is a national monument, run by the National Park Service. Work is under way to erect an Indian Memorial.

West Pointers fought and died

72 USMA graduates were killed and 68 were wounded in battles with Indians.

West Point Museum Collections, U.S. Military Academy

Territory gained at natives' expense

INDIAN WARS — 1866-1890

The Indian wars, which began with the colonial settlers, stretched into the 19th century, as white settlers battled Indians for land. The fighting essentially ended in 1890 when the U.S. cavalry nearly obliterated Big Foot's band of Sioux at Wounded Knee, South Dakota.

After the War of 1812, the U.S. government moved eastern tribes west of the Mississippi River to clear the way for white settlements. Most moves did not require force, with the notable exceptions of Florida's Seminole Wars, and the Black Hawk War in Illinois and present-day Wisconsin. Several intense battles took place with the Sioux and the Cheyenne of the northern Plains from 1876-1881, including Custer's Last Stand at the Battle of Little Bighorn in Montana. More than 200 men of the 7th U.S. Cavalry under West Point graduate Lt. Col. George A. Custer perished on June 25, 1876.

West Point Museum Collections, U.S.M.A.

Casualties

USMA graduates were line officers, regimental commanders and staff officers; 16 were killed and another 22 died in the subsequent Philippines insurrection.

Rough Rider to president

Theodore Roosevelt — who led the Rough Riders — became the youngest U.S. president, at 43, when President William McKinley was assassinated in 1901.

Freeing Cuba from Spain

SPANISH-AMERICAN WAR 1898

The war originated in Cuba's struggle for independence from Spain and was fueled by anti-Spain sentiment after the mysterious explosion of the USS Maine in Havana Harbor on Feb. 15, 1898. Congress declared Cuba's right to independence and demanded Spain withdraw its forces. The war lasted less than eight months and ended with the Treaty of Paris, on Dec. 10, 1898, in which Spain renounced its claims to Cuba and ceded Puerto Rico, Guam and the Philippines to the United States.

Right, The wreck of the USS Maine.

Library of Congress

Below left, Painting of Cpl. C. Thompson, 15th Infantry, in 1918.
West Point Museum Collections, U.S. Military Academy

Courtesy of Kathy McLaughlin
World War I era sheet music

U.S. Military Academy Archives

Cadets drill at the "Water Battery" at the USMA's north dock, 1916.

U.S. joins European allies in 'Great War'

WORLD WAR I – 1914-1918

The "Great War" started in Europe on July 28, 1914, when Austria-Hungary declared war on Serbia, accusing it of provoking the assassination of Archduke Franz Ferdinand, heir to the throne of the Austro-Hungarian Empire. On Aug. 4, 1914, President Woodrow Wilson declared a policy of U.S. neutrality.

On Feb. 24, 1917, the Zimmerman Telegram was passed to the United States by Britain, detailing an alleged German proposal of an alliance with Mexico against the United States.

The U.S. declared war on Germany on April 6, 1917, and for the first time, Americans fought a war in continental Europe — with allies France, Great Britain, Russia and Italy. The defeat of the Central Powers of Germany, Austria-Hungary and Turkey ended the war — on Nov. 11, 1918, at 11 a.m.

BY THE NUMBERS

West Point's strong showing

When the war broke out, there were 4,900 officers of the Regular Army who had at least one year of commissioned service; about half were West Point graduates. Thousands of emergency officers were commissioned to lead the 4 million-man army needed. West Point graduates were 1.5 percent of the total. But 74 percent of the generals were USMA graduates.

Death by battle and sickness

More than 116,000 people in the U.S. armed forces died during the war, many by disease that hit military camps.

Graduates served

About 2,500 West Point graduates served during World War I; more than 100 died in it.

JOHN J. PERSHING

West Point Museum Collections, U.S. Military Academy

John. J. Pershing

Title: USMA Class of 1886; commander in chief of the Allied Expeditionary Force in World War I; general of the armies, 1919.
Born: Sept. 13, 1860, Laclede, Mo.
Died: July 15, 1948, Washington, D.C.
Contributions: Pershing organized the largest American army ever, more than 2 million men.

Determined that American troops would fight under their own command, he resisted Allied generals' efforts to use his men as replacements for their fallen troops.

Pershing's "fire and movement" strategy contributed to breaking the bloody monotony of trench warfare that had taken millions of lives.

Fact: His nickname, "Black Jack," came from his service with a black regiment early in his career and later it referred to his discipline and stern manner.

Pershing victories

Gen. John J. Pershing, a West Point graduate, was appointed commander-in-chief of the American Expeditionary Force. He led the successful assault of the St. Mihiel Salient in September 1918 and helped defeat German forces in the Meuse-Argonne offensive.

Post-war career

After his success in World War I, Pershing served as Army chief of staff from 1921 until 1924.

Quote: A plebe wrote in his diary about Pershing, who was named cadet captain in his first class year: "We have an awful mean captain. He turned me out yesterday right in the middle of washing my face, made me bundle on my jacket and hat and go out and pick up two or three matches and minute pieces of paper in front of my tent."

1901
Act of Congress forbids hazing.

1903
Wright brothers fly first plane at Kitty Hawk, N.C.

1920
Prohibition begins; women get the right to vote.

1900 **1905** **1910** **1915** **1920** **1925**

WORLD WAR I
1914-1918

1902
USMA Centennial, President Theodore Roosevelt is guest of honor.

1905
Boxing and wrestling added to USMA curriculum.

Right
Various uniforms worn by cadets at the USMA in 1914.

1917-1918
Ex-cadets serve as 34 of the 38 corps and division commanders in the First World War.

America allied with France, Britain, Russia and Italy when it joined the war in 1917.

1924 Michie Stadium completed at USMA.

DOUGLAS MACARTHUR

Title: USMA Class of 1903; USMA superintendent 1919-22; Army chief of staff, 1930-35; supreme commander of the Pacific, 1941-45; supreme commander, U.N. forces, Korea, 1950-51.

Born: Jan. 26, 1880, Little Rock, Ark.

Died: April 5, 1964, Washington, D.C.

Contributions: A veteran of World War I, by 1930 he was a general and selected as army chief of staff. MacArthur retired in 1937, but was recalled to active duty in July 1941.

As supreme Pacific commander, his island-hopping strategy utilizing Army, Marine, Navy and air forces ultimately undermined Japanese supremacy in the Pacific. He was in charge of the surrender ceremony in Tokyo Bay on Sept. 2, 1945, and as Allied commander of the Japanese occupation demobilized Japan's military and instituted significant reforms.

In Korea, MacArthur's strategy returned troops to the offensive. The landing of his U.N. forces at Inchon behind North Korean lines is regarded as brilliant. But when his troops moved deeply into North Korea, he was unprepared for the Chinese attack that followed and the Americans retreated down the Korean peninsula.

In April 1951, when MacArthur's disagreements with President Harry Truman about continuing the war with China became public, Truman fired him. His farewell speech in Congress — "Old soldiers never die, they just fade away" — has become part of the fabric of American history.

Fact: MacArthur graduated West Point at the top of his class and was hazed unmercifully while there. As superintendent, he ushered in a series of reforms, from the attempt to eliminate hazing and "Beast Barracks" — on the principle that bullying soldiers is no way to lead them — to ending the academy's isolation from the rest of society, to modest curriculum reform and codification of the cadet honor system.

West Point Museum Collections, U.S. Military Academy

Douglas MacArthur

> 'How long are we going on preparing for the War of 1812?'
>
> **Douglas MacArthur,** speaking about the logic of breaking tradition at the academy

---

1927
Charles Lindbergh, left, flies solo across Atlantic Ocean.

1929
The stock market crashes.

1933-1942
Academy acquires additional territory for tactical military training.

1939
USMA Doubleday Field named in honor of Maj. Gen. Abner Doubleday, right, USMA Class of 1842, often called the father of baseball.

1946
Maj. Gen. Maxwell D. Taylor revises and modernizes USMA curriculum.

Images are from the West Point Museum Collections, USMA, West Point Archives, The FDR Library and Museum, and the Library of Congress

1930   **1935**   **1940**   **1945**   **1950**

WORLD WAR II
1939-1945

1933-1945
Franklin D. Roosevelt of Hyde Park, at left seated, serves as president for four terms.

1941-45
Academy graduates, including Gens. Eisenhower, MacArthur, Bradley and Patton, lead Allies to victory in World War II.

1942
USMA classes divided into two groups: Air and Ground Cadets.

1943
Three-year course of instruction temporarily adopted at USMA due to World War II.

1944-46
Glory days of Army football under Coach Earl H. "Red" Blaik. The Army team includes Heisman Trophy winners "Doc" Blanchard, right, and Glenn Davis, left.

Above, This poster was published by the Office of War Information in 1943.

Right, This painting by William L. Prescott shows troops during the D-Day invasion.

BY THE NUMBERS

59
Number of generals from the USMA Class of 1915

5 million
U.S. troops in World War I

116,000
U.S. troops died in World War I

16 million
U.S. troops in World War II.

405,000
U.S. troops died in WWII

17 million
Number of civilians who died worldwide during World War II.

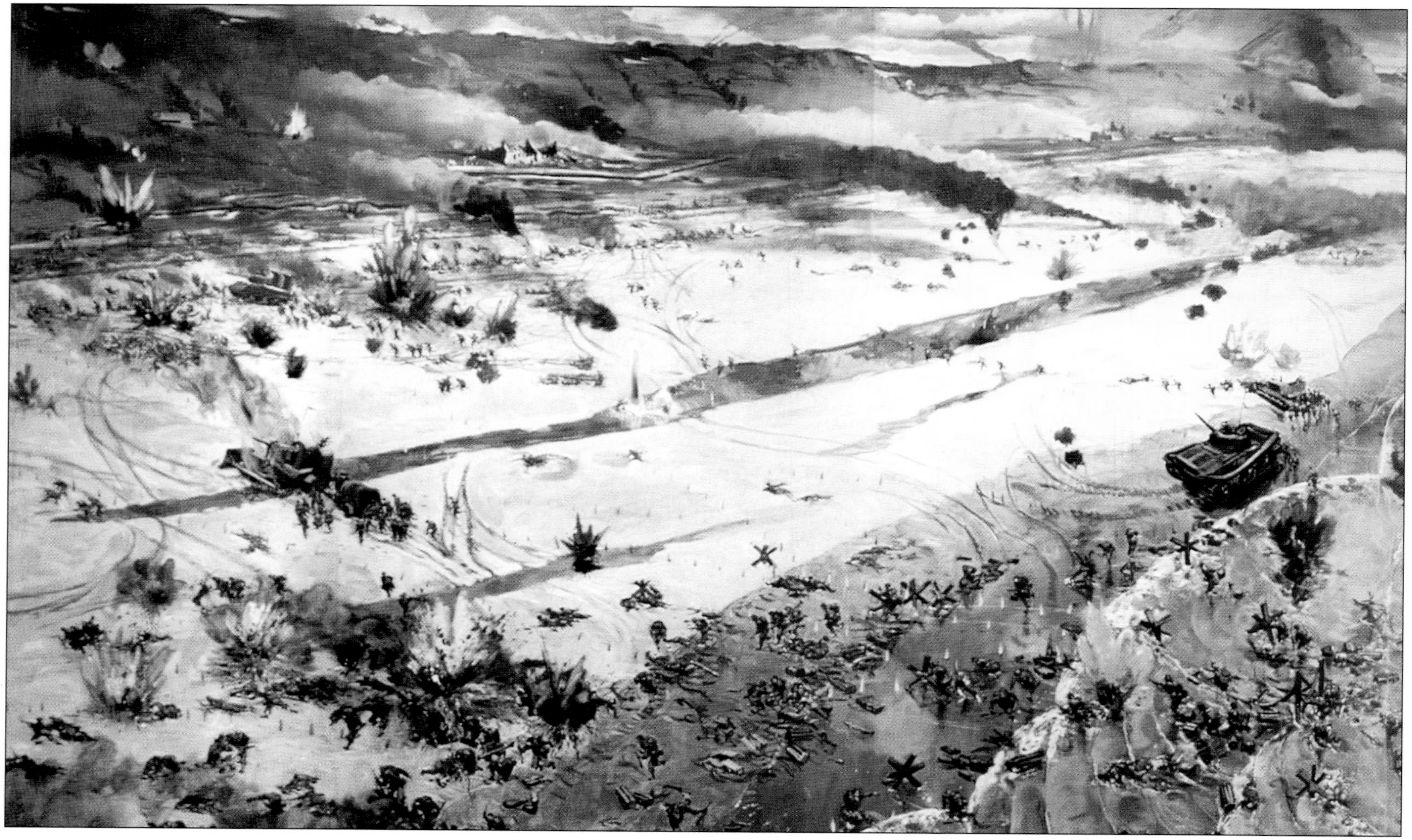

War spans the globe in Allies vs. Axis

WORLD WAR II — 1939-1945

France and Great Britain declared war on Germany — in the grips of dictator Adolf Hitler — on Sept. 3, 1939. On the morning of Dec. 7, 1941, Japanese forces attacked the U.S. naval base at Pearl Harbor. The next day, the United States declared war on Japan. Germany and Italy responded by declaring war on the United States four days later.

The war teamed up the Axis powers, including Germany, Italy and Japan, against the Allied powers, including Great Britain, the United States and the Soviet Union.

On June 6, 1944, known as D-Day, the United States and its allies invaded Normandy. Less than three months later, the Allied troops liberated Paris, more than four years after it had surrendered to Germany. The forces pushed the German troops past their border on Christmas Eve 1944.

On the Pacific front, American forces liberated the Philippines on Jan. 12, 1945, and took Okinawa six months later. On Aug. 6, the United States dropped its first atomic bomb on Hiroshima, Japan. Two days later, the second atomic bomb was dropped, on Nagasaki. Japan formally surrendered on Sept. 2 aboard the USS Missouri in Tokyo Bay, ending the war.

DWIGHT D. EISENHOWER

Title: USMA Class of 1915; Supreme Commander Allied Forces Europe, 1943-45; Army Chief of Staff, 1945-48; president of the United States, 1953-61.

Born: Oct. 14, 1890, Denison, Texas.

Died: March 28, 1969, Washington, D.C.

Contributions: No academic star shone on Ike, as Eisenhower was called, at West Point. He was in the middle of his class and also piled on the demerits. But the man who would bear the responsibility for the awesome D-Day invasion on the beaches of France that ultimately led to the end of WWII excelled after West Point. He graduated first in a class of 275 from the army's command and general staff school at Fort Leavenworth, Kan., and then graduated from the Army War College in Carlisle, Pa. He served with Gen. Douglas MacArthur in the Philippines, and by March 1941 was a full colonel. Promotions came quickly, and in June 1942 George Marshall placed Eisenhower in command of U.S. troops in Europe.

He headed the Allied invasion of French North Africa and then directed operations in Sicily and Italy. On Christmas Eve 1943, he was named supreme commander of the Allied Expeditionary Forces. D-Day, June 6, 1944 — the launching of the largest amphibious attack in history — was Eisenhower's decision after it had already been delayed one day. Eisenhower gambled on a break in the weather, but was also ready to take responsibility if it failed. Germany surrendered on May 7, 1945.

Eisenhower became president of Columbia University in 1948, but by 1950 became the supreme commander of the North Atlantic Treaty Organization.

He was twice elected president of the United States, running as a Republican. Although the 1950s are often today presented as idyllic, they were not. McCarthyism, the end of the Korean War, the creation of the Southeast Asia Treaty Organization, communist crackdowns in East Germany and Hungary, the partitioning of Vietnam, desegregation in the South, the launch of Sputnik, the creation of the National Aeronautics and Space Administration, the downing of the U-2 spy plane over the Soviet Union and the severing of diplomatic relations with Cuba took place while Eisenhower was in the White House.

Fact: He settled for being a cheerleader when a knee injury prevented him from playing football at the academy. He filled out resignation forms several times, but his classmates always talked him out of it.

Quote: "I could never wear my hat straight, and I couldn't be bothered with dust in the corner of my room," Eisenhower said, reminiscing about his academy days.

IMPACT

'Class the Stars Fell On'

Leaders such as five-star generals Dwight Eisenhower and Omar Bradley, and 59 generals in all, who served in World War II, were part of the USMA Class of 1915, known as "The Class the Stars Fell On." George S. Patton and Douglas MacArthur were West Point graduates as well.

Commanding the fronts

Eisenhower presided over the Allied forces in Europe, and Bradley was commander of the ground troops. Carl Spaatz, USMA Class of 1914, was commander of the Strategic Air Force. Patton, Class of 1909, was commander of the 3rd Army in Europe. Mark Clark, Class of April 1917, was commander in Italy. MacArthur was supreme commander of the Pacific.

Millions died

More than 19 million military personnel died in action worldwide, and more than 17 million civilians died during World War II.

9,000 from West Point

About 9,000 West Point graduates served and 769 died during the war.

OMAR N. BRADLEY

Title: USMA Class of 1915; commanding general, 1st Army, European Theater in World War II; Army chief of staff, 1948-49; first chairman of the Joint Chiefs of Staff, 1949-53; board chairman, Bulova Watch Co., 1958.

Born: Feb. 12, 1893, Clark, Mo.

Died: April 8, 1981, New York City.

Contributions: At the beginning of World War II, Bradley was commandant of the Infantry School at Fort Benning, Ga. The troops he commanded in North Africa contributed to the fall of Tunisia in 1943.

After the successful invasion of Sicily, he became 1st Army commander and participated in the planning of the invasion of France and in June 1944 was with his men on the Normandy beaches. For his consistent genuine concern about the welfare of his troops, he is known as the soldier's general.

As commander of the 12th Army Group, he continued operations throughout Europe until the end of the war.

Fact: Bradley was administrator of veterans' affairs from 1945-47.

Quote: "If he keeps up the clip he started, some of us will someday be bragging, 'Sure, General Bradley was a classmate of mine,'" Dwight D. Eisenhower wrote in his biography of Bradley in the cadet yearbook.

USMA graduate commanded secret project

Lt. Gen. Leslie Groves, USMA Class of November 1918, was placed in command of the Manhattan Project in 1942. Under the cloak of the Corps of Engineers, a sector of the government that oversees the construction of public projects, Groves was at the helm of one of the United States' best-kept secret projects.

It wasn't until the two atomic bombs fell on Nagasaki and Hiroshima that America's technological potential in the field of physics and as a world power was apparent.

"As far as I was concerned, his decision was one of noninterference — basically, a decision not to upset the existing plans," Groves said, crediting President Harry Truman with the decision to use the atom bomb.

GEORGE S. PATTON

Title: USMA Class of 1909; commanding general of the 7th army, 1942-44; commander of the 3rd Army European Theater, 1944-45.

Born: Nov. 11, 1885, San Gabriel, Calif.

Died: Dec. 21, 1945, Heidelberg, Germany, after an automobile accident near Mannheim.

Contributions: One of the most flamboyant of the American World War II generals, Patton's name is synonymous with brilliance, boldness and controversy. Nicknamed "Old Blood and Guts," he served with the tank corps in World War I — becoming a proponent of tank warfare and practitioner of it, as well — took part in the North Africa campaign in 1942 and, as head of the 7th Army, captured Palermo in 1943. In 1944 his 3rd Army tanks swept across northern France, and by December his forces played a huge role in defending Bastogne in the Battle of the Bulge. By March 1945 his units were crossing the Moselle River at the German frontier. His spectacular nature spawned a barrage of controversy and headlines: He carried ivory-handled pistols and his Jeep sported a bullhorn; he issued a public apology after slapping a hospitalized, shell-shocked soldier, and when he publicly criticized the post-war denazification policy, he was removed from command of the 3rd Army.

Fact: Patton came to the military academy from the Virginia Military Institute; he wrote poetry and was an avid student of military history, particularly the Civil War.

Quote: In a letter to his future father-in-law, he wrote: "It is hard to answer intelligibly the question 'why I want to be a soldier.'... I only feel it inside. It is as natural for me to be a soldier as it is to breathe and would be as hard to give up all thought of it as it would be to stop breathing."

HENRY H. 'HAP' ARNOLD

Title: USMA Class of 1907; commander, Army Air Corps during World War II; general of the Army; first general of the Air Force.

Born: June 25, 1886, Gladwyne, Pa.

Died: Jan. 15, 1950, Sonoma, Calif.

Contributions: An early proponent of air power, Arnold's advocacy helped lay the foundations for the U.S. Air Force. He rose through the ranks of the U.S. Army Air Corps to become its commander in 1938, and he ultimately commanded the Army air forces worldwide during World War II, where he played an important role in the development of strategic bombing — strikes against the enemy's industrial production. He was named a five-star general of the Army in 1944, and after the National Defense Act of 1947 created an independent Air Force, a five-star general of the Air Force.

Fact: Received flying instruction from Orville Wright in 1911.

Quote: Arnold described air power as "a three-legged stool — pilots, planes and airfields."

MATTHEW B. RIDGWAY

Title: USMA Class of April 1917.

Born: March 3, 1895, Fort Monroe, Va.

Died: July 26, 1993, Fox Chapel, near Pittsburgh.

Contributions: His attack on Sicily in July 1943 was the first major airborne assault in U.S. history; in 1942 he had converted the 82nd Infantry into the now famed 82nd Airborne Division; with his troops he parachuted into Normandy in June 1944.

Fact: Late in 1950, Ridgway, commanding the 8th Army in Korea during the Chinese communist offensive, started a counteroffensive that drove the Chinese out of South Korea. He succeeded Gen. Douglas MacArthur as Allied commander in the Far East and was promoted to four-star general in 1951, presiding over the end of U.S. occupation of Japan in 1952.

Quote: West Point "does not pretend to turn out finished Army officers. Its function ... is to develop the character of the fledgling officer, to instill in him the ideals and sense of duty, honor and patriotism that will sustain him throughout his career."

1950–PRESENT

Graduates command in Korean War

Right, A U.S. Army helmet from the battle of Pork Chop Hill, one of the bloodiest battles of the Korean War.

Spencer Ainsley

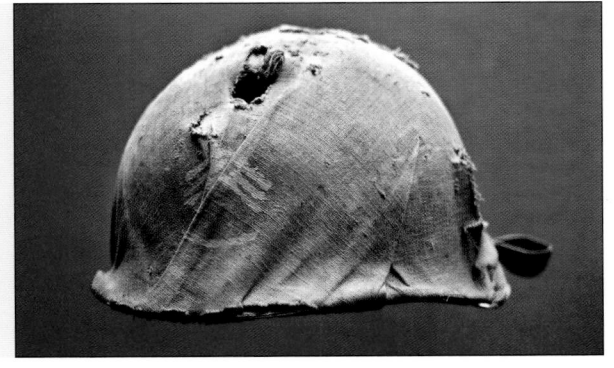

KOREAN WAR — 1950-53

On June 25, 1950, North Korea's People's Army crossed the 38th parallel and invaded South Korea. Two days later, President Harry Truman ordered the Air Force and Navy to help South Korea. North Korea drove the South Korean/United Nations forces back, but World War II hero and USMA graduate Gen. Douglas MacArthur led a turnaround, and advanced to near the North Korea/China border, before being driven back by a Chinese counter-offensive. After MacArthur repeatedly tried to direct foreign policy, he was removed by Truman and replaced by Gen. Matthew Ridgway, another USMA graduate, who offered to discuss a cease-fire in June 1951. An agreement was finally reached July 27, 1953.

1961
USMA registered as national historical landmark.

1965
Col. Edward H. White II, USMA 1952, becomes the first American to walk in space.

Richard Nixon

USA 32

1974
President Richard M. Nixon resigns.

1984
USMA acquires Ladycliff College in Highland Falls.

1986
Space Shuttle Challenger explodes after liftoff, killing the entire crew.

WAR WITH IRAQ
2003

WAR ON TERRORISM
2001-

| 1950 | 1960 | 1970 | 1980 | 1990 | 2000 |

KOREAN WAR
1950-53

1950
Gen. George S. Patton Jr. Monument, at right, is dedicated

VIETNAM WAR
1954-75

1964
President Lyndon Johnson signs legislation almost doubling the strength of the Corps to 4,400, by 1973.

Right, "Last Light Patrol" by William L. Prescott, 1967

1976
The first women (119) cadets arrive at West Point.

1980
Andrea Lee Hollen becomes first woman graduate.

1989
New Museum and Visitors Center opens to the public at South Post.

PERSIAN GULF WAR
1991

1991
General H. Norman Schwarzkopf, right, Class of 1956, leads Operation Desert Storm.

1991 The 1,000th African American and the 1,000th woman graduate from the USMA.

Images: **West Point Archives and Museum Collections, USMA; Gannett News Service**

U.S. joins battle against communism

Right, "The LZ" by William L. Prescott, depicts a helicopter landing zone during the Vietnam War.

West Point Museum Collections, U.S. Military Academy

Above, "Charlie Alpha" by John Dowd depicts a group of helicopters during the Vietnam War.

Below Right, "Defending the Base" by William L. Prescott, a watercolor depicting a battle in the Vietnam War, 1967.

West Point Museum Collections, U.S. Military Academy

ROLL CALL

Westmoreland leaves Vietnam

After the Tet Offensive, West Point graduate William C. Westmoreland, who had asked for more troops, was reassigned to Army chief of staff in Washington.

Millions served

More than 2 million Americans served in Vietnam, including 7,981 graduates of the U.S. Military Academy. And 273 of those West Point graduates were among the 58,000 who died.

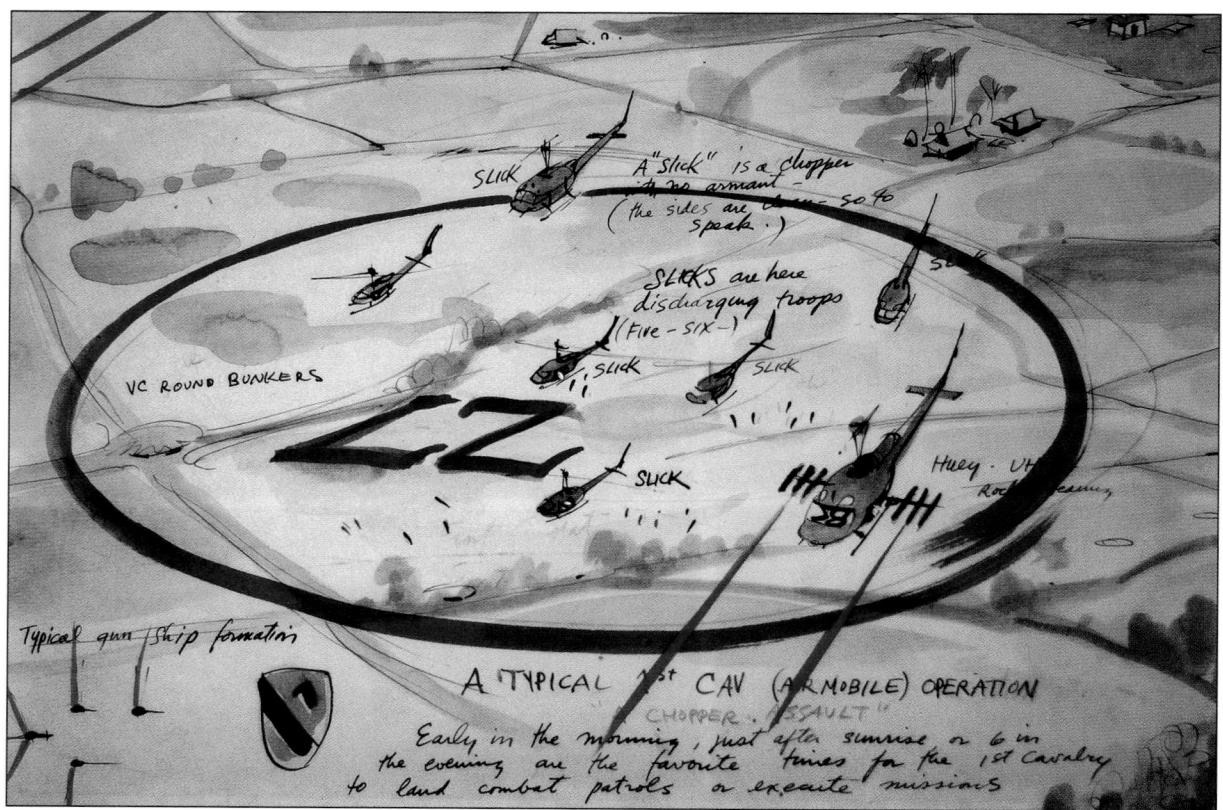

West Point Museum Collections, U.S. Military Academy

VIETNAM WAR — 1954-75

After the French lose a battle to re-establish colonial regime in Vietnam, the country is split in two. The United States backed the fledgling government of South Vietnam with military advisers and financial assistance beginning in 1959 and joined the war to stop South Vietnam from coming under communist control in 1964 with the Gulf of Tonkin Resolution. This allowed President Lyndon Johnson to order retaliatory strikes on North Vietnam.

USMA graduate Gen. William Westmoreland was commander of U.S. forces in Vietnam from 1964 to 1968, and Gen. Creighton Abrams, also from West Point, took over in 1968. On Jan. 31, 1968, 84,000 North Vietnamese guerrillas launched the Tet Offensive, regarded as the turning point of the war. The fall of South Vietnam in 1975 ended the war.

Hero brought 'hope of freedom'

The Vietnam War has been over for several decades, but the Congressional Medal of Honor was recently bestowed on a U.S. Military Academy graduate who was killed while he was a prisoner of war. The honor was given to Capt. Humbert Roque "Rocky" Versace in July 2002 by President Bush during a White House ceremony. It was the first time a Medal of Honor had been given to a Vietnam-era POW for actions that occurred in captivity.

Versace graduated West Point in 1959. He was captured by the Vietcong in 1963 in the Mekong Delta, tried several times to escape, and was executed two years later. During his first escape attempt three weeks after capture, Versace could only crawl due to back and knee wounds. He didn't make it far into the jungle before being recaptured.

"In his too-short life, he traveled to a distant land to bring the hope of freedom to people he never met," Bush said. "In his defiance and later death, he set an example of extraordinary dedication that changed the lives of his fellow soldiers who saw it first-hand. His story echoes across the years, reminding us of liberty's high price and of the noble passion that caused one good man to pay the price in full."

WILLIAM C. WESTMORELAND

Title: USMA Class of 1936, USMA superintendent 1960-63, chief of staff of the U.S. Army 1968-72.

Born: March 26, 1914, Spartanburg County, S.C.

Contributions: During World War II, Westmoreland commanded artillery battalions in Sicily and North Africa.

He commanded the 187th Airborne Infantry Regimental Combat Team in Korea.

During his stint as superintendent at West Point, Westmoreland expanded military training for cadets to include the preparation for the rigors of jungle warfare.

In 1968 he had nearly 500,000 Americans under his command during the Vietnam War. He was also promoted to chief of staff of the U.S. Army in 1968, and he retired from the Army in 1972.

Fact: Westmoreland was Time Magazine's "Man of the Year" in 1965.

Quote: "As a soldier prays for peace, he must be prepared to cope with the hardships of war and bear its scar." — the last sentence of Westmoreland's autobiography.

H. NORMAN SCHWARZKOPF

Title: USMA Class of 1956; commander in chief, Central Command, Operation Desert Storm.

Born: Aug. 22, 1934, Trenton, N.J.

Contributions: Schwarzkopf rose steadily through the ranks after returning a decorated combat veteran from two tours of duty in South Vietnam during the Vietnam War. Under his command, after six weeks of air bombardment of Iraq and its positions in Kuwait in 1991, allied ground forces retook Kuwait in 100 hours, destroying or incapacitating most of the Iraqi army, while sustaining minimal casualties. He retired from active service in 1991 after the Gulf War.

Fact: He commanded the ground forces in the U.S. invasion of Grenada in 1983 and by 1988 was a four-star general.

Quote: In a speech in May 1991 at the academy, Schwarzkopf told the Corps of Cadets: "The mothers and fathers of America will give you their sons and daughters ... with the confidence in you that you will not needlessly waste their lives. And you dare not. That's the burden the mantle of leadership places upon you. You could be the person who gives the orders that will bring about the deaths of thousands and thousands of young men and women. It is an awesome responsibility. You cannot fail. You dare not fail ..."

Spencer Ainsley

A collection of memorabilia about Gen. H. Norman Schwarzkopf at West Point.

'It was the first war we ever fought where the media had full rein, (where) they had no restraint. ... I mean that was a policy by the president and the enemy exploited it. It was something that plagued me from the very beginning.'

Gen. William Westmoreland
in a CNN interview about War in Vietnam

> 'We had a couple of cadets who wanted to leave West Point and join up as squad leaders and get in the fight. I had to talk to them from the 'poop' deck in the mess hall and say, 'Steady.'
>
> Their fight is 10, 20 years from now. There are plenty of things they're going to encounter ...
>
> They're young leaders. They wanted to get involved.'
>
> **Lt. Gen.**
> **William Lennox Jr.**
> superintendent of West Point, on the immediate reaction cadets had to the terrorist attacks on Sept. 11, 2001

Gannett News Service

Iraqi soldiers are captured during Desert Storm in 1991.

Answering Saddam's move

PERSIAN GULF WAR — 1991

West Point graduate H. Norman Schwarzkopf, Class of 1956, commanded Operation Desert Storm, the name given to the 1991 mission to expel Iraq President Saddam Hussein's forces from neighboring Kuwait. It took only months to succeed: Bombing began Jan. 16, the ground war began Feb. 23, and a cease-fire was accepted on March 3. About 3,000 USMA graduates served in the war, and three died.

U.S. leads strike against terrorism

WAR ON TERRORISM — 2001-

After the terrorist attacks on the World Trade Center and the Pentagon on Sept. 11, 2001, that killed an estimated 3,000 people, President Bush declared a global assault on terrorism.

The first strikes were launched Oct. 7 in Afghanistan against targets of the Taliban regime, the government harboring suspected mastermind Osama bin Laden.

Two West Point graduates died in a helicopter accident near the Philippines, related to the anti-terrorism mission.

Warren Zinn, Gannett News Service

Disarmament plea ends in war in Iraq

WAR WITH IRAQ — 2003

In March 2003, American forces went after Saddam Hussein again, this time in his own country. The United States — backed by mainly British troops — began attacks in Iraq in an effort to topple Saddam's regime after he refused to disarm. The United States began its military showdown with Saddam despite failure to get the United Nations Security Council's backing of the use of force against Iraq.

Left, Pfc. Joseph Dwyer, of Mt. Sinai, in Suffolk County, N.Y., runs while carrying an Iraqi boy injured during a battle between the U.S. Army's 7th Cavalry Regiment and Iraqi forces near the village of Al Faysaliyah, Iraq.

LEGACIES

THROUGHOUT THE WORLD AND BEYOND

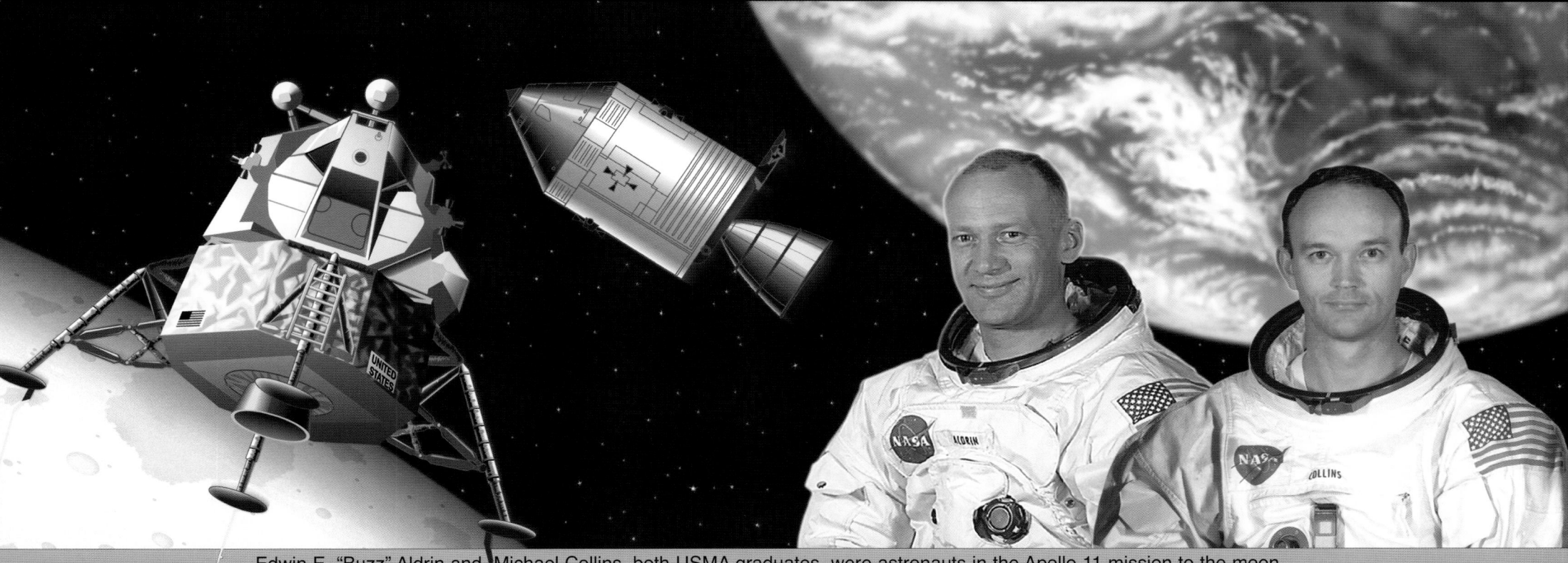

Edwin E. "Buzz" Aldrin and Michael Collins, both USMA graduates, were astronauts in the Apollo 11 mission to the moon.

Astronauts: NASA; Drawings: Dean DiMarzo

‘It turns out that if you are able to lead American troops, you can lead American business, you can lead American endeavors in space and you can be a politician.’

Rod Paschall, USMA Class of 1959, editor of MHQ, the Quarterly Journal of Military History

Below, The spacesuit worn by Frank Borman, USMA Class of 1950, commander of the first mission to orbit the moon.

West Point Museum Collections, U.S. Military Academy

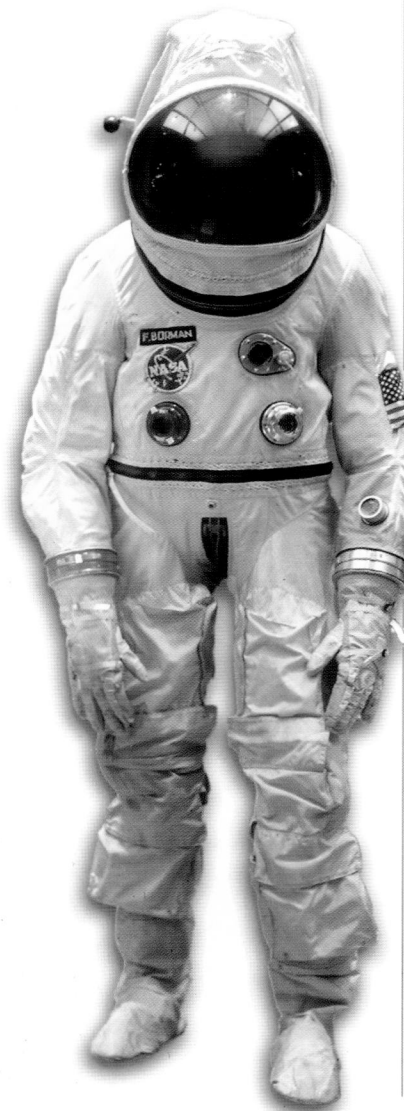

IN TIMES OF PEACE

A bastion of leaders

They're leaders in business, science and the arts — as well as on the battlefield.

Graduates of the U.S. Military Academy at West Point are expected to lead academically and to become Army officers. But they excel at much more.

"It is an institution that has a peculiar direction for creating leaders," said Rod Paschall, a 1959 graduate of West Point and editor of MHQ, the Quarterly Journal of Military History. "Few other institutions in the United States are created to create leaders, but West Point has been that way since 1802. It's a blood right."

The nation's first military academy, whose mission was to train students to become U.S. Army officers, was founded in March 1802. Some 58,000 men and women have graduated from West Point. Many of those graduates have gone on to fill leadership roles in the military, politics, commerce and society.

"It turns out that if you are able to lead American troops, you can lead American business, you can lead American endeavors in space and you can be a politician," Paschall said.

West Point graduates, while still Army officers, helped build the nation's infrastructure — canals, bridges, roads, lighthouses, railroads, harbors and more.

Academy graduates were responsible for building the Panama Canal under George Washington Goethals, the architect of the project and a member of the Class of 1880.

Leslie Groves, Class of November 1918, was a member of the Manhattan Project, which created the atomic bomb that was dropped on Hiroshima and Nagasaki, Japan, to end World War II.

Graduates take varied roles

West Point graduates fill roles as diverse as judge and neurosurgeon.

Judge Eugene R. Sullivan, a 1964 graduate, went to Georgetown University Law Center after serving his five years in the Army. He served as an attorney on President Richard Nixon's White House defense team during the Watergate crisis and has served as a member of the United States Court of Appeals Armed Forces since 1986.

They are statesmen:

■ John M. Shimkus, a 1980 graduate, represents Illinois in the U.S. House of Representatives.

■ John F. Reed, a 1971 graduate, represented Rhode Island in both houses of Congress.

■ Jim Nicholson, a 1961 graduate, served as chairman of the Republican National Committee.

West Point graduates have served as leaders of foreign countries. Jose Figueres, a 1979 graduate, is the president of Costa Rica, the longest-standing democracy in Latin America, and Fidel Ramos, a 1950 West Point graduate, was president of the Philippines from 1992 to 1998.

They are entrepreneurs:

■ Mark Hoffman is president and chief executive officer of Commerce One, which computerized business-to-business information exchanges, and founder of Sybase, a company that produces database software.

■ James Kimsey is a 1962 graduate and founding chairman of America Online.

They are athletes:

■ Mike Krzyzewski, a 1969 graduate, coaches the Duke University men's basketball team and used to coach at West Point.

■ Felix A. "Doc" Blanchard, Class of 1947, was a Heisman Trophy winner. The Heisman Trophy is awarded to the most outstanding college football player each year since 1935 and was named for John W. Heisman, the first athletic director of the New York City- based Downtown Athletic Club, which bestows the award.

West Point graduates are astronauts, bankers, scholars, lawyers, artists, poets and much more.

In 1965, Edward White II, a 1952 graduate, was the first American to walk in space. He was an astronaut from 1962 to 1967. He died in the 1967 Apollo I spacecraft fire.

And while most of these leaders are men, women will soon join their ranks.

"We just haven't had women long enough to really reach the high pedestals the guys have," academy historian Stephen Grove said. Women first entered the academy in July 1976, and the first woman, Andrea Lee Hollen, graduated in 1980.

Alison Jones was the first female West Point graduate to receive a Soldiers Medal, which is given to an individual who demonstrates heroism. She received the medal in May 1999 for her rescue and recovery efforts following the bombing of the American embassy in Kenya in August 1998.

Ed Ruggero, a 1980 graduate, followed a cross-section of cadets in June 1998 to document how the academy built leaders. He pub-

The building of the Panama Canal is captured in "Culebra Cut from South End," a 1913 watercolor by William Pretyman.

> **'It's a really big plus to have a West Point graduation if you're going into business.'**
>
> **Thomas Fleming**
> author "West Point: The Men and Times of the U.S. Military Academy"

Shoulder knots

These USMA professor's shoulder knots — a form of an officer's insignia of rank — were worn by Master of the Sword Antoine Lorentz from 1858 to 1885. This pattern was adopted in 1872 and worn in the U.S. Army through 1902.

West Point Museum Collections,
U.S. Military Academy

West Point Archives

Cadets in 1903 test the strength of a bridge made during an overland bridge-building exercise at the academy.

lished his findings in January 2001 in a book, "Duty First."

At West Point, he concluded, leadership is taught by example. It is inspirational, and cadets follow their leaders because they want to, not out of fear or for some carrot.

"There's no stopping someone like that," Ruggero said.

Novelist Thomas Fleming became interested in West Point after he was asked in 1969 to write a history of the academy by the Association of Graduates. His book is called "West Point: The Men and Times of the U.S. Military Academy."

A big plus in business

West Point, Fleming said, differs from other nations' military schools.

West Point "gives you a college degree along with a military education," he said. "It's really a big plus to have a West Point graduation if you're going into business."

The academy was created under President Thomas Jefferson, who previously had opposed the creation of a military academy on the grounds it would enhance the power of the military, which might someday threaten the republic.

Training in artillery and engineering for Army officers had been ongoing since 1794 at West Point. But on March 16, 1802, the "Act Fixing the Military Peace Establishment of the United States" created the academy and the Army Corps of Engineers out of the existing Corps of Artillerists and Engineers. Jefferson believed in the pursuit of science for practical applications, not for theory.

The academy was part of the Army Corps of Engineers until they were separated in 1866.

"Nation building was a part of the mission of the U.S. Army at that time, and it's a natural spin-off from protection to advancing society," Paschall said. "So you're going to see Army officers in all sorts of positions that would advance American society and industry."

GEORGE WASHINGTON GOETHALS

Title: USMA Class of 1880; appointed chairman and chief engineer of the Isthmian Canal Commission in 1907; governor of Panama Canal Zone, 1914-16.

Born: June 29, 1858, Brooklyn.

Died: Jan. 21, 1928, New York City.

Contributions: The dream of connecting the Atlantic Ocean with the Pacific Ocean without having to travel around the continent of South America came to existence under the leadership of George Washington Goethals.

This 1880 West Point graduate was known as a hard worker. Already appointed by Secretary of State William Howard Taft in 1907 to the Isthmian Canal Commission, Goethals was commissioned by President Theodore Roosevelt to head the construction of the canal as chairman and chief engineer after two previous chief engineers resigned.

The construction process of the canal underwent a number of catastrophes — mechanical breakdowns and explosions, including the mud slide at Cucarocha in 1913. Controversy over the canal project was strong in the United States, leaving many to question whether the project was still worth pursuing.

The ongoing political bickering in Washington and the horrendous living conditions, including rampant spread of infectious diseases like yellow fever and malaria, did not deter Goethals from completing his mission. Instead, it forced him to adopt a more meticulous style of leadership, determined more than ever to see the canal completed under his command.

His efforts paid off on Aug. 15, 1914, with the first ship to pass through the many locks and dams along the Panama Canal.

Fact: Under his leadership, the project was completed ahead of schedule and $23 million below budget.

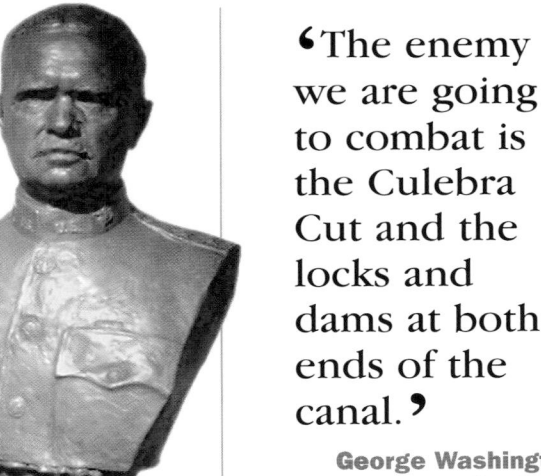

'The enemy we are going to combat is the Culebra Cut and the locks and dams at both ends of the canal.'

George Washington Goethals
speaking about the construction of the Panama Canal

Top, Gatun Locks at the Atlantic Ocean end of the canal. **Middle**, A bust of George Washington Goethals. **Below**, Panoramic view of the Culebra Cut.

Above, Capt. Benjamin Louis Eulalie de Bonneville.

'The result of his labors was a mass of manuscript, which he subsequently put at my disposal ... I found it full of interesting details of life among the mountains, and of the singular castes and races, both white men and red men, among whom he had sojourned. It bore, too, throughout, the impress of his character ... his kindliness of spirit, and his susceptibility to the grand and the beautiful.'

Washington Irving

Preface to "The Adventures of Captain Bonneville," an account of Capt. Benjamin Bonneville's travels

Benjamin L.E. BONNEVILLE

Title: USMA Class of 1815.
Born: April 14, 1796, near Paris, France.
Died: June 12, 1878, Fort Smith, Ark.
Contributions: The age of exploration of land west of the Mississippi River flourished during the turn of the 19th century, and Capt. Benjamin Louis Eulalie de Bonneville was determined to play a strategic role in its discovery.

Fur trade companies were exploding, settling in the West and Bonneville, being an avid trader, yearned for the opportunity to explore the frontier like fellow Army men Meriwether Lewis and William Clark.

In 1832, after many requests, Bonneville received permission from the War Department for a two-year leave of absence to explore the western frontier.

He began his three-year campaign, creating two of the first accurate geographical maps of the Northwest region. His adventures led him to discover the Great Salt Lake, the Green, Snake, Salmon and Yellowstone rivers; transverse the Sierras to California, and then connect his travel with the Santa Fe Trail. He documented the many Indian tribes and the varying number of plants and animals that inhabited the region.

Upon returning from his travels, Bonneville was dismissed by the Army for overstaying his leave. The Army dropped him from its payroll. President Andrew Jackson admired his contributions to the nation and had Congress reinstate him in 1836.

Although the salt flats and prehistoric lake in Utah are named after him, there is doubt he traveled and explored this particular region. Through his travels, the U.S. government recognized and seized the opportunity to take advantage of the West's rich depositories of natural resources.

Fact: In addition to Lake Bonneville and the Bonneville Salt Flats in Utah, the Bonneville Power Administration and the Bonneville Dam are named in his honor.

Left, A view of the Great Salt Lake from its southernmost point near Salt Lake City, Utah. The Great Salt Lake is what remains of the huge prehistoric Lake Bonneville which began shrinking 14,500 years ago after a natural dam in Idaho burst.

AP/Wide World Photos

Courtesy of Duke University

LEONIDAS POLK

Library of Congress

Title: USMA Class of 1827.
Born: April 10, 1806, Raleigh, N.C.
Died: June 14, 1864, Pine Ridge, Ga.
Contributions: Against his father's wishes, Leonidas Polk, upon graduating from West Point in 1827, left the military to become a minister of the Protestant Episcopal Church.

Polk was born into a respected military family. His grandfather, Thomas Polk, was the drafter of North Carolina's Mecklenburg Declaration of 1775, a precursor of the Declaration of Independence.

Polk turned his back on the military and followed the path of the church. He was appointed bishop of Louisiana in 1841.

As a fervent believer in higher education, Polk continued to preach its importance, eventually leading to his founding of the University of the South in 1857.

But with the onset of the Civil War, Polk changed his pacifist lifestyle and again established himself alongside other great military figures. Commissioned as major general in 1861, he became a dedicated preacher of the Confederate cause. In 1864, a Union cannon ball struck and killed him.

Fact: For his service, Polk earned the nickname "The Fighting Bishop."

Left, Sheet music from 1866, "Requiem: For the Confederate Dead," includes images of "Stonewall" Jackson (center) and Leonidas Polk (top right portrait).

> **'It is almost worth dying to be buried in such a beautiful place.'**
>
> **Gen. Patrick Cleburne** speaking about the land Leonidas Polk donated for St. John's Church in Maury County, Tennessee, a burial site for many Confederate soldiers

Courtesy of Duke University, Emergence of Advertising in America web site

Above, An image of a Baltimore & Ohio Railroad advertising poster from 1882. George Washington Whistler oversaw the B&O railroad in its early days.

GEORGE WASHINGTON WHISTLER

Title: USMA Class of 1819.
Born: 1800.
Died: April 1849, Russia.
Contributions: When the steam locomotive retired the horse and wagon, the demand for railroad construction exploded across the United States. Under President John Quincy Adams, George Washington Whistler was commissioned to begin building the first railroad line in the nation.

The Baltimore & Ohio Railroad was the first in a series of railroads Whistler would oversee. Displeased with early locomotive design, he resigned from the Army to become the chief engineer to the Proprietor of Locks and Canals in Lowell, Mass.

While working in Lowell, he built a locomotive and invented a new high-pitch whistle. The tune of his new invention screamed at a piercing decibel level, forever brandishing its tone as a symbol of America's thrust forward during the age of expansion.

In the 1840s, he designed a difficult section of the track through the Berkshires and attracted the attention of the czar of Russia, who asked Whistler to construct a railway connecting St. Petersburg with Moscow. Unfortunately, Whistler died in 1849, one year short of seeing his project completed.

Fact: While Whistler enjoyed a stellar career in the military, his son, James A. McNeill Whistler, was discharged for being deficient in chemistry.

The younger Whistler eventually became one of America's most famous painters.

ALEXANDER M. HAIG

Title: USMA Class of 1947; White House chief of staff, 1973-74; supreme allied commander in Europe of NATO forces, 1974-79; secretary of state 1981-82.

Born: Dec. 2, 1924, Philadelphia.

Contributions: As an American general and public official, Haig heavily focused on foreign policy. Haig served in both Korea and Vietnam, later returning to the United States as military adviser to Henry Kissinger from 1969-73.

During the Watergate scandal, Haig sat as President Nixon's civilian White House chief of staff between 1973-74.

He then returned to active military service, becoming the supreme commander of U.S. and NATO forces in Europe from 1974-79.

He served as secretary of state in 1981 under President Ronald Reagan. Failing to reach an accord on his authority in foreign policy issues, Haig resigned within a year of obtaining his seat on the president's Cabinet.

In 1988, Haig attempted to run for president on the Republican ticket but lost.

Fact: Haig was Reagan's first secretary of state, and is famous for claiming constitutional authority when he said, "I am in control here," after Reagan was shot in 1981.

Gannett News Service

Alexander Haig Jr., who served as Richard Nixon's civilian White House chief of staff, attended the former president's funeral in Yorba Linda, Calif., on April 27, 1994.

FIDEL V. RAMOS

Title: USMA Class of 1950; in the Philippines: army chief of staff, 1986-88; secretary of defense, 1988-92; president, 1992-98.

Born: March 18, 1928, Lingayen, Pangasinan, Philippines.

Contributions: Ramos is best known for the economic revival enjoyed in the Philippines during his presidency.

He became deputy chief of staff of the Philippine armed forces in 1981.

In 1986, Ramos supported Corazon Aquino after Ferdinand Marcos claimed victory in elections alleged to have been corrupt. A bloodless revolt called "People Power" installed Aquino as president.

She promoted Ramos to chief of staff and later named him defense secretary.

He served until 1992, when he took over the presidency with support from Aquino.

Ramos' efforts helped restructure the nation's government, which many had deemed too large. He is generally regarded as one of the most effective presidents in the nation's history.

Fact: Ramos served in the Philippine Armed Forces for 40 years, from 1951-91.

BRENT SCOWCROFT

Title: USMA Class of 1947, national security adviser to Presidents Gerald Ford and George H.W. Bush.

Born: 1925, Ogden, Utah.

Contributions: Having served as the national security adviser for two presidents, Scowcroft's expertise on international policy is highly regarded.

After graduating from West Point in 1947, Scowcroft earned his aeronautical rating as a pilot and later served in operational and administrative positions. His career led him to faculty positions at two prestigious U.S. service academies: U.S. Military Academy at West Point and U.S. Air Force Academy in Colorado.

In 1964, he was assigned to Headquarters U.S. Air Force in the Office of the Deputy Chief of Staff, Plans and Operations. Four years later, he was transferred to the Office of the Assistant Secretary of Defense for International Security Affairs. In 1970, he accepted a position with the Organization of the Joint Chiefs of Staff as special assistant to the director.

Scowcroft is retired from military service and now dedicates his time to advising U.S. and foreign corporate leaders on a number of international relations policies as president and founder of the Scowcroft Group.

Fact: Scowcroft earned his master's and doctorate in International Relations from Columbia University.

THORALF SUNDT JR.

Title: USMA Class of 1952; neurosurgeon.

Born: 1930.

Died: 1992.

Contributions: Sundt served as an engineer platoon leader and company commander with the 32nd Regimental Combat Team of the 7th Infantry Division during the Korean War.

When the Army denied his request for a leave of absence to attend medical school, he resigned and studied medicine at the University of Tennessee-Memphis.

In 1978, he co-authored a celebrated article in the New England Journal of Medicine in the field of open intracranial surgery on aneurysms. The next year, he was named chairman of the Department of Neurosurgery at the Mayo Clinic.

Sundt earned numerous honors and awards in his career, including Teacher of the Year in 1986 by the Mayo Fellows Association, out-

Gannett News Service

'So at a period where we should have been focusing on structures to improve the possibility that we could actually make some changes in the way the world operated ... we have frittered away the time.'

Brent Scowcroft
referring to 1991, in a 1999 keynote speech describing what has happened since the end of the Cold War

standing alumnus of the University of Tennessee-Memphis College of Medicine in 1988 and honorary president of the International Workshop on Intracranial Aneurysms in Atami, Japan, in 1989.

He was the vice chairman of the American Board of Neurological Surgery in 1989-90.

He also became editor of the Journal of Neurosurgery in 1989.

He was known as one of the pioneers of using surgical microscopes in neurosurgery, and he invented and designed devices that have reduced the dangers associated with surgical techniques.

Fact: Sundt performed more than 3,000 neurological procedures and authored more than 260 journal articles in the field of neurosurgery.

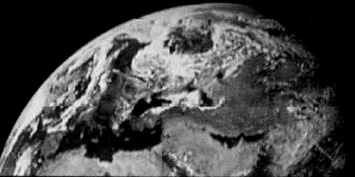

1957 –
First
manmade
satellite
in orbit –
Soviets
launch
unmanned
Sputnik. A few
weeks later,
Sputnik 2 carries
a dog into orbit.

1961 – First man
in space – Soviet
cosmonaut Yuri
Gagarin, 27,
circles the earth
once before safely
returning.

First American in
space – Alan
Shepherd.

1963 – First
woman in
space – Soviet
Valentina
Tereshkova.

1965 – First
American to walk
in space –
Edward White II
spends 21
minutes in
space outside his
vehicle.

1955
1956
1957
1958
1959
1960
1961
1962
1963
1964
1965

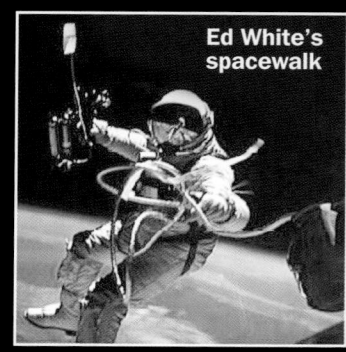

Ed White's
spacewalk

THE SPACE PIONEERS:

Four West Point grads played key roles in the space program during the 1960s when the Soviet Union and the United States were locked in a race to put men on the moon.

EDWARD
WHITE II
USMA CLASS OF 1952

THE FIRST AMERICAN TO WALK IN SPACE

Born in San Antonio, Texas, Nov. 14, 1930, Edward White II died in the Jan. 27, 1967, Apollo spacecraft fire at NASA Kennedy Space Center, Fla. An Air Force lieutenant colonel, White received flight training in Florida and Texas, following his graduation from West Point. He then spent three and a half years in Germany with a fighter squadron, flying F-86s and F-100s.

He attended the Air Force Test Pilot School at Edwards Air Force Base, Calif., in 1959 and was later assigned to Wright-Patterson Air Force Base, Ohio, as an experimental test pilot. He was named a member of the astronaut team selected by NASA in September 1962.

He was the pilot for Gemini 4 in June 1965. On that mission, he became the first American to walk in space.

FRANK
BORMAN
USMA CLASS OF 1950

COMMANDER OF THE FIRST MISSION TO ORBIT THE MOON

Frank Borman was born March 14, 1928, in Gary, Indiana. After receiving a bachelor of science degree from West Point and a master of science degree from the California Institute of Technology in 1957, Borman went on to command Gemini 7 and Apollo 8, two historic space missions.

An Air Force officer through 1970, Borman and James Lovell spent 14 days in orbit aboard Gemini 7 — the longest space mission at the time. Borman and his crew became the first space travelers to orbit the moon in 1968, reading from the Bible on Christmas Eve while transmitting images to a captivated audience on Earth.

BLAZING A NEW TRAIL

Edward White II, Frank Borman, "Buzz" Aldrin and Michael Collins took part in pivotal missions leading up to — and including — the first lunar landing.

MICHAEL
COLLINS
USMA CLASS OF 1952

COMMAND MODULE PILOT ON FIRST MOON LANDING MISSION

Michael Collins was born on October 31, 1930, in Rome, Italy. After receiving a bachelor of science degree from West Point, Collins enlisted in the Air Force, serving as an experimental flight test officer before being selected by NASA in 1963 to undergo astronaut training.

He served on pioneering space missions Gemini 10 and Apollo 11, taking over pilot duties at points in both runs. On the Apollo 11 mission, he orbited the moon as a safeguard while fellow astronauts Neil Armstrong and Buzz Aldrin became the first men to walk on the moon. After NASA, Collins became the first director of the Smithsonian Institute's National Air and Space Museum, and has also penned several books on space and space travel.

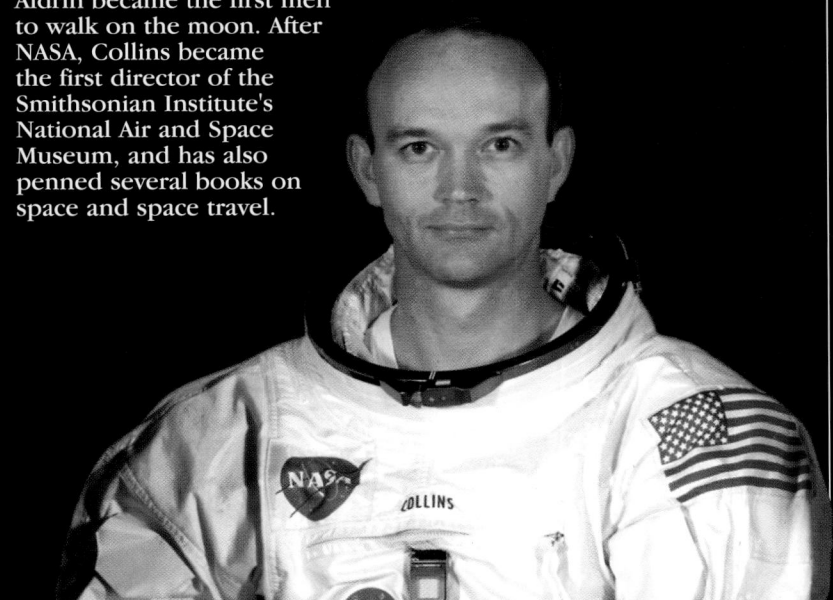

EDWIN E. 'BUZZ'
ALDRIN
USMA CLASS OF 1951

THE SECOND MAN TO SET FOOT ON THE MOON

Born in Montclair, N.J., in 1930, "Buzz" Aldrin joined the U.S. Air Force and flew his first missions during the Korean War, compiling 66 total missions. In 1966, Aldrin was selected by NASA to become an astronaut after his doctoral thesis at the Massachusetts Institute of Technology helped advance space technology. His flight on the Gemini 12 in November 1966 included a then record-breaking 5½-hour space walk.

Aldrin's most famous accomplishment was participating in the first lunar landing with fellow astronaut Neil Armstrong in June 1969. As the lunar module pilot of Apollo 11, Aldrin became the second person to walk on the moon. Aldrin retired from the Air Force in 1972, and has consulted with private businesses in addition to lecturing on space travel and design.

FIRST TO THE MOON

1967 – First space rendezvous – Frank Borman commands Gemini 7 for the first rendezvous of two spacecraft and an extended (nearly 14-day) orbit, proving men could survive in space long enough for a trip to the moon.

1967 – Apollo 1 crew killed – A spark ignites pure oxygen in the command module during routine testing, causing a fire that claims the lives of the three-man crew, including Edward White II.

1968 – First circumlunar flight – Frank Borman, William A. Anders and James A. Lovell become the first men to orbit the moon.

1965
1966
1967
1968
1969
1970
1971
1972

1969 - First men on the moon – Apollo 11 carries three astronauts to the moon. Michael Collins pilots the command module in orbit while Neil Armstrong and "Buzz" Aldrin land on the moon's surface below.

1972 – Last manned mission to the moon – Apollo 17.

THREE STEPS TO THE MOON

West Point graduates played vital roles in these three landmark missions

Apollo 8 | **FIRST MANNED FLIGHT AROUND THE MOON**

Gemini 4 | **FIRST AMERICAN TO WALK IN SPACE**

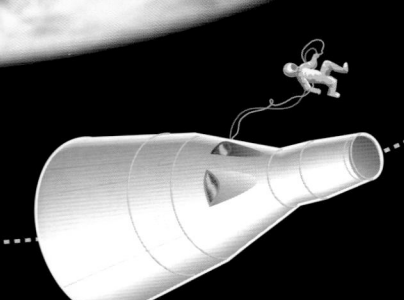

Four days, 62 orbits
Gemini 4 circled the earth 62 times, orbiting between 100 and 175 miles above the surface.

'It's the saddest moment of my life.'

Edward White, on ending his spacewalk and returning to his spacecraft.

To the moon and back
On Dec. 21, 1968, Apollo 8 was launched into orbit atop a towering Saturn V rocket. In 12 minutes, the three-man crew – Commander Frank Borman, William Anders and James Lovell – reached orbit around the earth and headed on toward the moon, shedding the rocket's bulky first few stages.

The ship reached a speed of 23,266 mph as it headed for the moon. The men rested and the next morning, 100,000 miles from home, they sent back live TV pictures.

Seven hundred miles above the moon's surface, Apollo 8 orbited for 20 hours, circling 10 times while taking photos of proposed landing sites.

On Dec. 27, the crew returned to earth successfully, having set the stage for the first lunar landing.

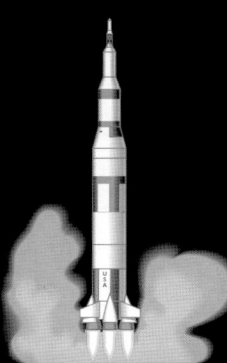

THREE PROGRAMS

 **Mercury**
Initiated in 1958, it was the United States' first man-in-space program. The project made six manned flights from 1961 to 1963.

Gemini
Named for its two-man crew, this was the second manned space program. It tested how well men and equipment stood up to two weeks of space flight and also perfected docking and landing methods.

Apollo
Milestones included the first humans to leave Earth's orbit and six manned moon landings.

Making the first step in space
On June 3, 1965, the Gemini IV carried two astronauts, Edward White II and James A. McDivitt, into orbit around the earth.

White made history when he left the capsule and spent 21 minutes floating in space connected to his ship by a tether, using a hand-held maneuvering unit that shot out compressed gas, allowing White to control his movements somewhat.

Going the distance
Different rocket designs were used for the different NASA programs. The towering Titan II rockets used in the Gemini missions would later be dwarfed by the Saturn V used to propel astronauts to the moon in the Apollo missions.

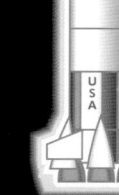

Mercury-Atlas
Mercury missions

Titan II
Gemini missions

Saturn V
Apollo Missions

Planning ahead
Moving around the earth at more than 2,000 mph, the moon presented a moving target for the Apollo spacecraft.

Scientists had to determine precisely where the moon would be three days after lift-off, when the spacecraft reached the moon's orbit.

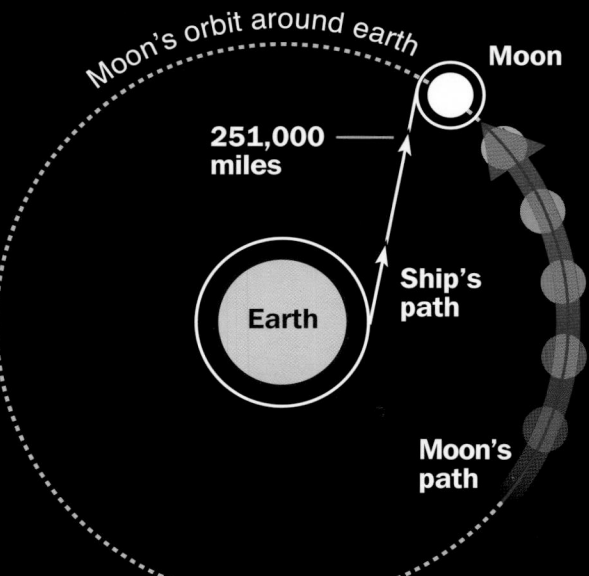

Moon's orbit around earth

Moon

251,000 miles

Earth

Ship's path

Moon's path

FIRST MEN TO LAND ON THE MOON

 The journey
Edwin "Buzz" Aldrin, Michael Collins and Neil Armstrong lift off aboard Apollo 11 on July 16, 1969, on a historic mission to land the first men on the moon. The first two stages of the 363-foot-tall Saturn V rocket propel the astronauts into Earth's orbit at speeds reaching 15,400 mph.

 Shooting for the moon
With the first two stages already shed, the third stage fires, sending the craft toward the moon at about 24,300 mph. The third stage is jettisoned, and the astronauts turn around the command and service modules to dock with the lunar lander.

 Separation, July 20
Upon reaching the moon, Collins pilots the command module in orbit while Aldrin and Armstrong climb into the Lunar Module "Eagle" and descend to the surface.

 Making history
Millions of people tune in to watch on television as Armstrong climbs down to the moon's dusty surface. Aldrin follows about 19 minutes later – shown at right.

 Exploration
The astronauts take samples, raise the American flag and learn to get around by taking long leaps. After 22 hours on the moon, the Eagle lifts off, heading toward a rendezvous with Collins and the command module.

 **Reunited**
Once Aldrin and Armstrong are back in the command module, shown at right, the Eagle is jettisoned and the three astronauts begin the long journey home.

 **Coming home**
The service module is jettisoned before the command module enters the earth's atmosphere at about 25,000 mph. The module endures searing heat as it slows to 325 mph before the parachutes open at 20,000 feet. The capsule splashes down safely in the Pacific Ocean, and the crew is picked up – shown at right.

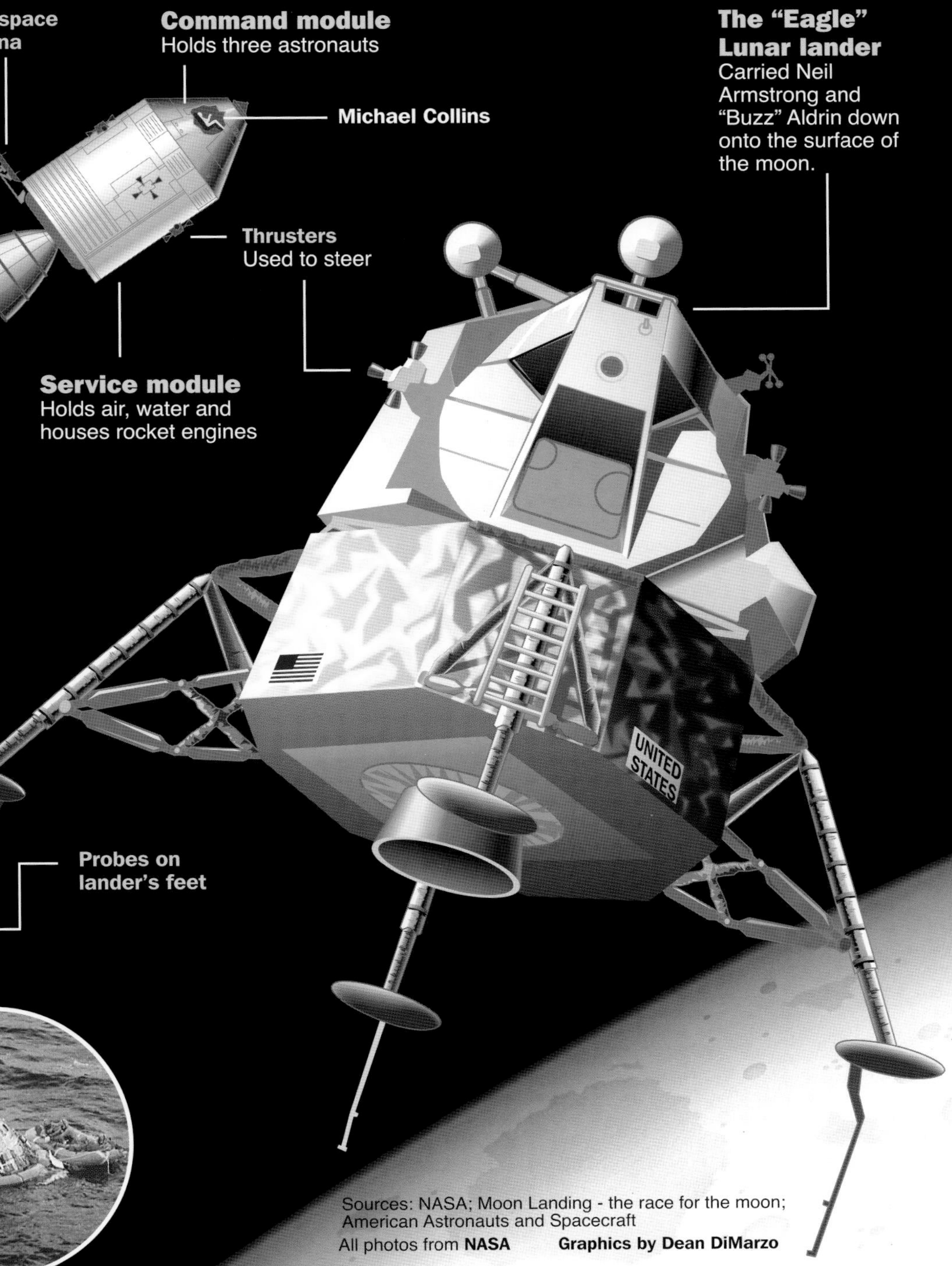

Deep space antenna

Command module
Holds three astronauts

Michael Collins

Thrusters
Used to steer

Service module
Holds air, water and houses rocket engines

The "Eagle" Lunar lander
Carried Neil Armstrong and "Buzz" Aldrin down onto the surface of the moon.

Probes on lander's feet

UNITED STATES

Sources: NASA; Moon Landing - the race for the moon; American Astronauts and Spacecraft
All photos from **NASA**   **Graphics by Dean DiMarzo**

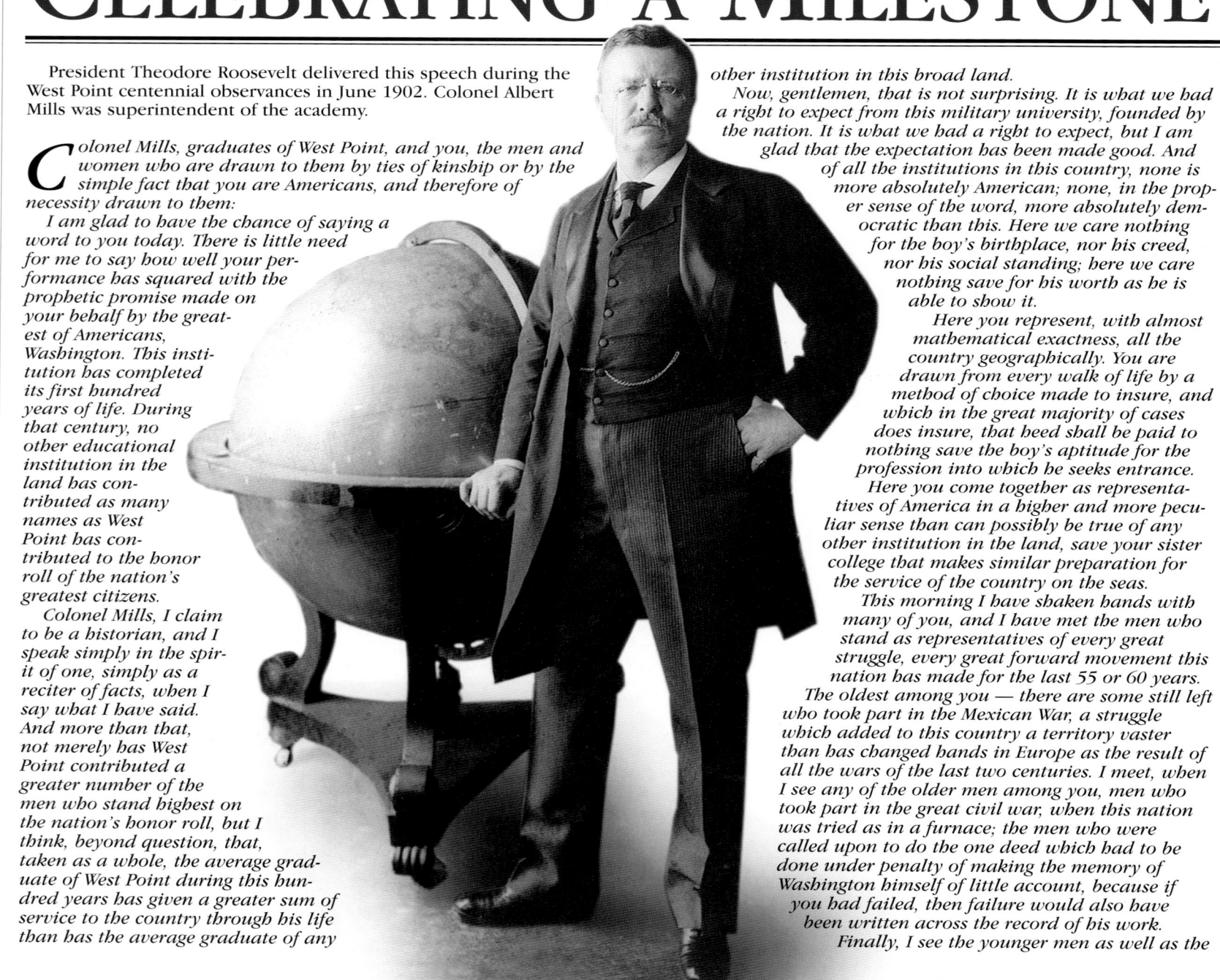

CELEBRATING A MILESTONE

President Theodore Roosevelt delivered this speech during the West Point centennial observances in June 1902. Colonel Albert Mills was superintendent of the academy.

Colonel Mills, graduates of West Point, and you, the men and women who are drawn to them by ties of kinship or by the simple fact that you are Americans, and therefore of necessity drawn to them:

I am glad to have the chance of saying a word to you today. There is little need for me to say how well your performance has squared with the prophetic promise made on your behalf by the greatest of Americans, Washington. This institution has completed its first hundred years of life. During that century, no other educational institution in the land has contributed as many names as West Point has contributed to the honor roll of the nation's greatest citizens.

Colonel Mills, I claim to be a historian, and I speak simply in the spirit of one, simply as a reciter of facts, when I say what I have said. And more than that, not merely has West Point contributed a greater number of the men who stand highest on the nation's honor roll, but I think, beyond question, that, taken as a whole, the average graduate of West Point during this hundred years has given a greater sum of service to the country through his life than has the average graduate of any other institution in this broad land.

Now, gentlemen, that is not surprising. It is what we had a right to expect from this military university, founded by the nation. It is what we had a right to expect, but I am glad that the expectation has been made good. And of all the institutions in this country, none is more absolutely American; none, in the proper sense of the word, more absolutely democratic than this. Here we care nothing for the boy's birthplace, nor his creed, nor his social standing; here we care nothing save for his worth as he is able to show it.

Here you represent, with almost mathematical exactness, all the country geographically. You are drawn from every walk of life by a method of choice made to insure, and which in the great majority of cases does insure, that heed shall be paid to nothing save the boy's aptitude for the profession into which he seeks entrance. Here you come together as representatives of America in a higher and more peculiar sense than can possibly be true of any other institution in the land, save your sister college that makes similar preparation for the service of the country on the seas.

This morning I have shaken hands with many of you, and I have met the men who stand as representatives of every great struggle, every great forward movement this nation has made for the last 55 or 60 years. The oldest among you — there are some still left who took part in the Mexican War, a struggle which added to this country a territory vaster than has changed hands in Europe as the result of all the wars of the last two centuries. I meet, when I see any of the older men among you, men who took part in the great civil war, when this nation was tried as in a furnace; the men who were called upon to do the one deed which had to be done under penalty of making the memory of Washington himself of little account, because if you had failed, then failure would also have been written across the record of his work. Finally, I see the younger men as well as the

Above, Celebrating the centennial of the U.S. Military Academy at West Point, 1902.

older ones; the men whom I have seen myself taking part in a little war — a war that was the merest skirmish compared with the struggle in which you fought from '61 to '65, and yet a war that has had most far-reaching effects; not merely upon the destiny of this nation, but therefore upon the destiny of the world — the war with Spain.

It was my good fortune to see in the campaign in Cuba how the graduates of West Point handled themselves; to see and to endeavor to profit by their example. It is a peculiar pleasure to come here today, because I was at that time intimately associated with many of these, your graduates, who are here.

On the day before the San Juan fight, when we were marched up into position, the officers with whom I was lost connection with the baggage and food, and I for supper that night had what Colonel Mills gave me. And the next morning Colonel Mills was with another West Pointer, gallant Shipp, of North Carolina. The next morning we breakfasted together. I remember well congratulating myself that my regiment, a raw volunteer regiment, could have to set it an example, men like Mills and Shipp, whose very presence made the men cool; made them feel collected and at ease. Mills and Shipp went with our regiment into action.

Shortly after it begun Shipp was killed and Colonel Mills received a wound from which no one of us at the time dreamed that he would recover. I had at that time in my regiment as acting second lieutenant a cadet from West Point. He was having his holiday. He took his holiday coming down with us, and just before the assault he was shot, the bullet going in, I think into the stomach,

going out the other side. He fell over, and as we came up I leaned over to him, he said "All right, Colonel, I am going to get well." I didn't think he was; but I said, "All right, I am sure you will," and he did; he is all right now.

There was never a moment during that time, by day or by night, that I was not an eyewitness to some performance of duty, some bit of duty well done, by a West Pointer, and I never saw a West Pointer failing in his duty. I want to be perfectly frank, gentlemen. I heard of two or three instances — you cannot get in any body of men absolute uniformity of good conduct; but I am happy to say that I never was an eyewitness to such misconduct. It was my good fortune to see what is the rule — what is the rule with only rarest exception — the rule of duty done in a way that makes a man proud to be an American, the fellow-citizen of such Americans.

Your duty here at West Point has been to fit men to do well in war. But it is a noteworthy fact that you also have fitted them to do singularly well in peace. The highest positions in the land have been held, not exceptionally, but again and again by West Pointers. West Pointers have risen to the first rank in all the occupations of civil life.

Colonel Mills, I make the answer that a man who answers the question must make when I say that while we had a right to expect that West Point would do well, we could not have expected that she would have done so well as she has done.

And now, in closing, I want to say one word to those who are graduating here, and to the undergraduates as well. I was greatly struck the other day by an article by one of your instructors, him-

> **'Your duty here at West Point has been to fit men to do well in War ... you also have fitted them to do singularly well in peace.'**
>
> **Theodore Roosevelt**

Right, Spectators watch a baseball game during centennial celebrations at the U.S. Military Academy at West Point, 1902.

'I do not have to ask you to remember what you can not forget — the lessons of loyalty, of courage, of steadfast adherence to the highest standards of honor and uprightness...'

Theodore Roosevelt

self a West Pointer, in which he dwelt upon the changed conditions of warfare, and the absolute need that the man who was to be a good officer should meet those changed conditions. I think it is going to be a great deal harder to be a first-class officer in the future than it has been in the past.

In addition to the courage and steadfastness that have always been the prime requirements in a soldier, you have to show far greater fertility of resource and far greater power of individual initiative than has ever been necessary before if you are to come up to the highest level of officer-like performance of duty. As has been well said, the developments of war during the last few years have shown that in the future the unit will not be the regiment nor the company nor troop; the unit will be the individual man.

The Army is to a very great extent going to do well or ill according to the average of that individual man. If he does not know how to shoot, how to shift for himself, how both to obey orders and to accept responsibility when the emergency comes where he won't have any orders to obey, if he is not able to do all of that, and if in addition he has not got the fighting edge, you had better have him out of the Army; he will be a damage in it.

In a battle hereafter each man is going to be to a considerable extent alone. The formation will be so open that the youngest officer will have to take much of the responsibility that in former wars fell on his seniors, and many of the enlisted men will have to do most of their work without any supervision from any officer whatsoever.

The man will have to act largely alone, and if he shows a tendency to huddle up to somebody else his usefulness is pretty near at an end. He must draw on his own courage and resourcefulness to meet the emergencies as they come up. It will be more difficult in the future than ever before to know your profession, and more essential also; and you officers, and you who are about to become officers, if you are going to do well, have got to learn how to perform the duty which, while becoming more essential, has become harder to perform.

You want to face the fact and realize more than ever before that the honor or the shame of the country may depend upon the high average of character and capacity of the officers and enlisted men and that a high average of character and capacity in the enlisted men can to a large degree only be obtained through you, the officers; that you have got to devote your time in peace to bringing up the standard of fighting efficiency of the men under you, not merely in doing your duty so that you can't be called to account for failure to perform it, but doing it in a way that will make any man under you abler to perform his.

I noticed throughout the time that we were in Cuba that the orders given and executed were of the simplest kind and that there was very little maneuvering, practically none of the maneuvering of the parade ground. Now I want you to weigh what I say, for if you take only half of it, you will invert it. I found out very soon in my regiment that the best man was the man who had been in the Regular Army in actual service, out in the West, campaigning on the Plains. If he had been a good man in the Regular Army in actual service on the Plains, he was the best man that I could get hold of. On the other hand, if he had merely served in time of peace a couple of years in an Eastern garrison, where he did practically nothing outside of parade grounds and barracks, or if he had been in an ordinary national guard regiment, then one of two things was true; if he understood that he had only learned 5 percent of war, he was 5 percent better than anyone else, and that was a big advance; but if he thought he had also learned the other 95 percent, he was worse than anything else.

I recollect perfectly one man who had been a corporal in the regular Army; this young fellow joined us sure he knew everything, confident that war consisted in nice parade-ground maneuvers. It was almost impossible to turn his attention from trying the very difficult task of making my cowpunchers keep in a straight line to the easier task of training them so that they could do the most efficient fighting when the occasion arose. He confused the essentials and the non-essentials. The non-essentials are so pretty and so easy that it is a great temptation to think that your duty lies in perfecting yourself and the men under you in them. You have got to do that too, but if you only do that you won't be worth your salt when the day of trial comes.

Now gentlemen, I do not intend to try to preach upon the performance of your duties here to you. It has been your special business to learn to do that. I do ask you to remember the difference there is in the military profession now from what it has been in past time; to remember that the final test of soldiership is not excellence in parade-ground formation, but efficiency in actual service in the field, and that the usefulness, the real and great usefulness, in the parade ground and barracks works comes in its being used not as an end, but as one of the means to an end. I ask you to remember that. I do not have to ask you to remember what you can not forget — the lessons of loyalty, of courage, of steadfast adherence to the highest standards of honor and uprightness which all men draw in when they breathe the atmosphere of this great institution.

— U.S. Military Academy Archives

SIGHTS • SOUNDS • SPORTS
GLORY OF PLACE, GLORY OF COMPETITION

The grandeur of the U.S. Military Academy at West Point is perhaps no place more evident than at Trophy Point, with its spectacular views of the Hudson River.

Spencer Ainsley

'Much of the history we teach was made by the people we taught.'

a West Point slogan that reflects academy graduates' place in American history

‘The architecture of the United States Military Academy at West Point reflects the history, traditions, and strengths of the United States of America as well as the character of its armed forces.’

THE ARCHITECTURE

Gothic stonework frames academy

"Masculine, muscular, military."

That's how West Point historian Stephen Grove views a campus made up largely of what the academy refers to as "military Gothic" architecture.

"It looks to me what a military academy should look like — rock-like, strong," Grove said.

Indeed, although the academy includes wooden structures and brick structures — among the latter the 1926 Hotel Thayer and the mammoth, modern and much criticized Eisenhower Hall (1974) — what stands out is the gray of the school's massive granite buildings.

Cohesiveness was an outgrowth of a 1903 contest begun by then-President Theodore Roosevelt, who had architectural firms vie to win approval to construct $6.5 million of new buildings.

Six entered and the winning firm was Cram, Goodhue & Ferguson of Boston.

Prior to the firm's efforts, the campus was "pretty grungy, with all types of things," Grove said, noting the goal was to create uniformity, while providing additional space for a growing cadet corps.

Museum specialist and conservator Paul Ackermann pointed to the architecture of the 1840 Ordnance Compound as being a precursor to other buildings. The granite Gothic Ordnance Compound, once used to house trophy weapons from war and now a club for senior cadets, was designed by then-school superintendent Richard Delafield.

"It's one of the buildings that survives today that determined the overall appearance of West Point," Ackermann explained. "A lot was built in response to it."

Buildings do deviate from the Gothic.

■ The Old (or Cemetery) Chapel of 1837 has Doric columns as part of its classic Greek revival style.

■ The superintendent's house, which was built in 1820 and is among the oldest buildings on campus — save for the Revolutionary War-era Forts Putnam and Clinton — is of Federal style, and has multiple chimneys and a lattice-trimmed porch.

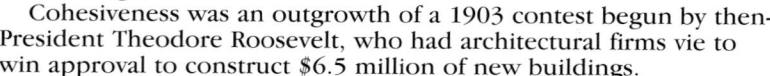

■ Other variations are found with the commandant's quarters (1820) and dean's house (1857), as well as with Cullum Hall (1895), a Greek classic building.

■ Large brick buildings, located on the south end of campus, served as stables for hundreds of horses used in cavalry training until the mid-1940s. They now house various things, including a bowling alley, offices and a post office.

The campus is full of towers, parapets and exterior dry moats, evoking a solid military theme found virtually everywhere. Stained glass in the famed 1910 granite Gothic Cadet Chapel contains the words "Duty, Honor, Country." Below is a limestone sculpture donated by Ulysses S. Grant's family. It depicts St. Michael, the patron saint of soldiers. The mural "War and Peace" sits above the altar in its predecessor, the Old Chapel, which was moved to the cemetery in 1910.

Taylor Hall (1910), the academy's administration building, features a fireplace mantel with sculptures of nine people from military history. But while Charlemagne is among the honored, so is King Arthur and other characters of legend.

And, indeed, as incongruous as it might seem, humor is present in West Point's architecture.

The outside of the Cadet Chapel features serious sculpture, such as Joan of Arc and soldiers, but also whimsical musicians and a man with a broom.

Poking fun at Patton

Funny-faced musicians also adorn the Hotel Thayer Crest Room. Gargoyle-like sculptures at the 1911 Thayer Hall, once the campus riding hall and now a classroom building, depict various horse scenes, with a knight and Indian prominent, along with a horse wearing a hat.

Folly is even found in the statue of George S. Patton, according to Karon Ray, the campus' senior tour guide and an unofficial campus historian. Patton once explained it had taken him five years to gradu-

Spencer Ainsley

The imposing military Gothic architecture that dominates the U.S. Military Academy is evident in this view looking south along the Hudson RIver.

Dean DiMarzo

Above, The view from the roof of the Cadet Chapel, looking north up the Hudson River.

LANDMARKS

A vast theater

Eisenhower Hall, with 192,000 square feet of floor space, is the second-largest auditorium in the Northeast, second only to Radio City Music Hall in New York City.

Centuries old

Revolutionary fortifications are the oldest structures at the academy, dating to about 1778.

Homes built in 1800s

The superintendent and commandant's house are the oldest residences. Both were built in 1820.

Kathy McLaughlin

Above, Family members of new cadets try to catch a glimpse of their cadet during R-Day (Reception Day) in 1999. **Top right,** A portrait of former President Ronald Reagan, who received the Thayer Award in 1989, is displayed in Taylor Hall.

Spencer Ainsley

ate because he couldn't find the library. His wife's response was to have the statue in his honor face the library — binoculars in hand.

The statue, like all monuments on campus, was privately funded, Ray noted, explaining "what's essential comes from public funds. All niceties and extras come from private funds."

Because the older buildings require maintenance, she joked that it sometimes appeared there were two seasons at West Point: "winter and construction."

Construction has sometimes meant the destruction of buildings whose passing is now much lamented. While the superintendent's house and Old Chapel were originally slated to be razed but were saved by outcry, only a small part of the cadet barracks, dating to the mid-1850s and housing some of the country's most famous soldiers, remains today.

Totally gone is the old ivy-covered library, designed by Delafield, which sat where the current 1964 library is.

Likewise, buildings from the 1870s were lost with the construction of Eisenhower Hall, the huge, brick performance area that is functional but blocks a good view of the Hudson River.

In his book on West Point's architecture, "The Campus Guide: West Point: U.S. Military Academy," author Rod Miller equates the construction to a betrayal similar to that of Benedict Arnold.

By and large, though, efforts have been made to maintain the campus' architectural integrity.

An upcoming project will have the main portion of the Hotel Thayer kept intact and an annex from the 1940s leveled as another hotel is built along with a large conference center.

The construction is, of course, in response to public demand to visit this famed institution, listed by Sports Illustrated as one of the best places in the country to watch football, with the backdrop of a 16,000-acre campus and its historic structures.

Hotel holds unique place in history

Xiva Pitman knows about the celebrities and dignitaries who graced the halls of the Hotel Thayer at the U.S. Military Academy at West Point.

Her memories sound like a Who's Who of American politics, sports and entertainment: Bob Hope. Red Skelton. Brooke Shields. President Dwight D. Eisenhower. Olympic gold medal swimmer Mark Spitz.

Pitman, a waitress at the hotel from 1956-1988, was there 20 years ago when the American hostages held by Iranian militants for 444 days were released. The 52 hostages landed at Stewart Airport and were whisked to West Point to be shielded from the prying press.

Pitman waited on the hostages, who all signed a menu for her. She later donated the menu to a local historian, who had it framed. Remarkably, of all the luminaries she served, she never got any of their autographs.

"We had to get busy and wait on them," the 81-year-old Highland Falls resident said.

Food, ambiance draw millions

The hotel continues to be a draw for celebrities and plain folk alike. The majestic building is host to about 300 weddings a year.

The hotel's dining room has become known for its elaborate Sunday brunches, which are attended by more than 1,400 people a week. And with an estimated 3 million visitors to West Point each year, the hotel is an attraction unto itself.

Built in 1926, the hotel is listed on the National Register of Historic Places. The Gothic-style building sits at the entrance to West Point.

A pair of stone lions greet visitors after they've climbed the 48 stairs to the hotel's front entrance. The lobby is marble-floored and adorned with circular candle chandeliers and flags of the nations.

Constructed to accommodate academy personnel and guests, the Hotel Thayer takes its name from Col. Sylvanus Thayer, superintendent of West Point from 1817-1833.

The granite structure was built to resemble a medieval fortress, with Gothic windows and turrets overlooking a rocky cliff and the Hudson River.

The hotel replaced the original West Point Hotel that opened in 1829 at Trophy Point. That structure was torn down in 1932, although an original gas lamp from the old hotel hangs in the Hotel Thayer lobby.

The hotel became one of the earliest real estate privatizations initiated by the Department of Defense.

A group of former West Point graduates formed Hudson River Partners, which has a 50-year lease on the hotel, with an option to renew for 25 more. The hotel technically is still owned by the federal government.

In 1998, the partnership led a $28 million effort to restore and refurbish the hotel. The modernization focused on expanding and reconfiguring existing rooms, which now number 150.

The rooms were redesigned to have spacious desks with dataport telephones and Internet access and voice mail messaging. New bathrooms are equipped with heat lamps, hair dryers and coffee makers.

Douglas Bennett, a founding and general partner of Hudson River Partners, said the renovations had to be in keeping with the historic character of the hotel.

"All of us have memories of the Hotel Thayer. We knew it needed to be brought up to the modern world," said Bennett, a 1964 graduate of West Point.

Hudson River Partners' next plan is a $30 million project to double the hotel's size. That plan calls for the creation of a conference center, meeting facilities with amenities, a new restaurant facing the Hudson River and health facilities. Bennett said the group hopes to have construction completed in 2004.

Left, Candle chandeliers and marble floors help showcase the stately main lobby of the Hotel Thayer.

Spencer Ainsley photos

Above, The front entrance of the Hotel Thayer.

VISITING THAYER

Hotel Thayer
Lodging, dining, conference facilities.
Call (800) 247-5047;
(845) 446-4731
www.thethayerhotel.com

'All of us have memories of the Hotel Thayer. We knew it needed to be brought up to the modern world.'

Douglas Bennett
USMA Class of 1964 and founding and general partner of Hudson River Partners, which leases Hotel Thayer

INSIDE THE CADET CHAPEL

A riveting blend of stained glass and stone

The architecture of the U.S. Military Academy's Cadet Chapel combines Gothic grandeur and scale with traditional religious symbolism, layering in distinctly military elements like this sword above the entrance (left). The chapel replaced a much smaller structure in 1910, now referred to as the Old Chapel. The Old Chapel was moved stone by stone from the central area of the academy and rebuilt in the cemetery where it now stands.

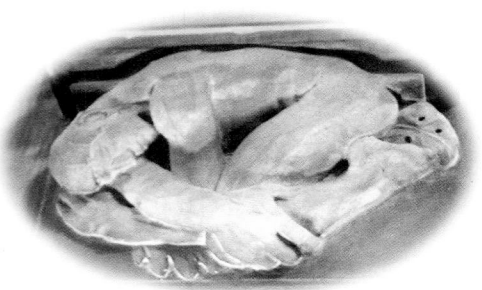

1837
Old Cadet Chapel built
The academy's first chapel has cannons from Revolutionary War embedded in the walls.

1902
USMA centennial spurs changes
Congress approves renovations at USMA, including a new chapel.

1903
Architects vie to design chapel
A competition is established for the design of the new chapel. The firm of Cram, Goodhue and Ferguson's winning proposal moves the location from the planned site at Trophy Point to a hill overlooking the barracks.

1909
Ground broken, cornerstone set
Construction begins on the massive Gothic structure. Much of the stone used for construction of the chapel is quarried on site, adding to the illusion that the building is part of the hillside upon which it is built.

1910
New Cadet Chapel opens
The last Mass is held at the Old Cadet Chapel. "The Corps," now the hymn of the Corps of Cadets, is played for the first time and the congregation moves up the hill for the dedication of the new chapel.

Visiting the chapel
Some evening Masses are open only to cadets, but Sunday Masses are open to the public. Visitors, above, also stop in during guided tours of the academy.

Heavenly glass
The chapel's ornate windows, above, were created by the Willet Stained Glass Studio. The final window was donated by the Class of 1976.

21,000 pipes and counting
The chapel has the world's largest church organ, with over 21,000 pipes ranging in size from 32 feet to about 3 inches tall. Additional pipes are added to the organ periodically.

Spiral staircases on either side of the lobby lead to the attic above the vaulted arch ceiling.

1911

Making music

A pipe organ with 2,406 individual pipes is installed in the Cadet Chapel. The organ will be added on to for many years.

For the missing soldiers

A pew to the left of the aisle, near the front of the chapel, is roped off and a candle is kept burning in memory of those who are missing in action.

The vaulted ceiling is 55 feet above the floor.

The chapel seats 1,500 people, including the choir.

Entrance porch on north side

Dean DiMarzo

Gothic atmosphere

From the vaulted ceiling and arched halls (above) to the ornate stone carvings and woodwork throughout the building, the Gothic style dominates. There is even a small dungeon below the entrance porch on the north side.

1916
The first of many
The first stained glass window is installed in the Cadet Chapel at a cost of $300. The exquisite designs that follow are numerous.

1950
Organ upgrade
For the second time, a larger organ console is installed to accommodate controls for the growing number of pipes.

1976
Finishing touches
The final two windows, given by the Class of 1976, are installed. They cost $300 each – the same price as the first ones.

St. Michael in marble

The massive altar, carved from a single block of marble, depicts the archangel St. Michael slaying a dragon. On each side of the altar there are large seven-branched candelabras with six angels holding various symbols of virtue.

‘As it has since it was first built, the Cadet Chapel serves as a daily visual reminder to the cadets of God's presence on this campus and his purpose for all who walk these hallowed grounds.’

Lt. Col. John J. Cook, chaplain of Cadet Chapel

The Cadet Chapel, which seats 1,500, is imposing in size, symbolism and beauty at the U.S. Military Academy.

14,000 pounds of musical metal

The chapel's bell tower, left, is equipped with a carillon and 12 bells. The largest is a "D" tenor bell weighing 3,500 pounds. Each evening, a cadet climbs the spiral stairs and crosses a catwalk above the chapel's domed ceiling to reach the bell controls (photo at far right). Religious songs and hymns are played and the hour is tolled.

Playing the big bells

The chapel's 12 enormous bells are controlled by levers and pedals on a console at the base of the bell tower.

A class tradition

From the 1920s on, it became a tradition for USMA classes to donate a stained glass window for their year and another window below that one for the class of 100 years earlier. Sixty years passed from the installation of the first stained glass window in 1916 to the last one in 1976.

Powering the pipes

Large blowers beneath the chapel provide the air needed to make thousands of organ pipes sound.

Reserved seating

The front right pew has a series of silver plates inscribed with the signatures of each of the past superintendents.

Faded glory revitalized

Civil War flags that adorned the walls have deteriorated over the years and are being replaced with modern replicas, left.

Dungeon

Entrance

Sources: Journal research; "The Cadet Chapel"; Lt. Col. John J. Cook, chaplain

Sanctuary

Choir

Organ

A chapel beneath the chapel

Located below the main chapel sanctuary is St. Martin's Chapel, right, used to celebrate Eastern Orthodox Mass.

Illustrations and photos: **Dean DiMarzo**

WEST POINT MUSEUM

Holding on to history's treasures

Circa-1865 inkstand of George W. Cullum, superintendent from 1864 until 1866.

THE MUSEUM

Museum hours

The museum at Pershing Center is open 10:30 a.m. to 4:15 p.m. daily. Call (845) 938-2203 or (845) 938-3590 or go to *www.usma.edu/ museum.*

Interesting facts

The museum has more than 45,000 artifacts in its collections, including uniforms, swords and weapons, a British military kettle drum captured from troops at the Battle of Saratoga, a Civil War bugle and a jeep from World War II.

Historic scientific instruments used in cadet classes.

The West Point Museum at the U.S. Military Academy offers a glimpse into the struggle our country has endured to maintain freedom, from the casing of an atomic bomb to the baton given to the Allies from the Nazis as a sign of surrender.

Now, more than ever, many feel the museum is a necessary and important attraction.

Located at Pershing Center, the museum holds four floors of military artifacts, including various uniforms of friends and foes, cadet artwork by Jefferson Davis, Ulysses Grant and James A.M. Whistler and weaponry, including cannons, swords and handguns. Many pieces embody West Point's role in training military leaders through the years.

Michael Moss, director of the museum, described the mission.

"The museum's goals are to support the education of the cadets, operate a public museum and protect and preserve the historical collections," he said.

Moss said that in the wake of the Sept. 11, 2001, attacks and the subsequent strikes in Afghanistan, the West Point Museum played a vital role in examining patriotism in America.

"It's a time to look at and to value tradition," Moss said.

To educate the cadets, the museum offers hands-on instruction with an up-close look at the historical artifacts. Here is where one can inspect an M-16 rifle or a homemade land mine as well as a diagram of Roman military strategy.

"(The cadets) know about material culture as well as conceptual history," Moss said.

Left, A portrait of Gen. Leonard Wood painted by Frederic Remington in 1909.

West Point Museum Collections,
U.S. Military Academy

The museum brought in more than 250,000 visitors in 2002, Moss said. Offering a public facility is a crucial role of the museum. Visitors may get a chance to see the items that identify the personalities and leadership qualities that established West Point's role in the shaping of the United States, from Dwight Eisenhower's popular dance card to a West Point doll from 1842, Gen. George S. Patton's submachine gun, Union general and president Grant's diploma and uniform as well as the sash worn by Confederate Gen. Robert E. Lee at the surrender at Appomattox, effectively ending the Civil War.

A unique look at military

In the Large Weapons Gallery one can find the housing to an atomic bomb of the type dropped on Nagasaki, effectively ending the Second World War. The cannon that fired the first American shot during World War I and a tank from that war are also there. Overlooking that exhibit are two murals depicting the invasion of Europe on D-Day, June 6, 1944, painted by a veteran.

The basement level, which acts as a balcony to the sub-basement, is home to the Small Weapons Gallery. The exhibit is a timeline that begins with primitive hand-held weapons (ancient clubs and tools made of wood and stone) and works its way through swords, spears,

'The museum's goals are to support the education of the cadets, operate a public museum and protect and preserve the historical collections.'

Michael Moss, director of the West Point Museum

West Point Museum Collections, U.S. Military Academy

"View of West Point Looking North" was painted in the mid-1860s by Robert W. Weir, who taught drawing at West Point for 42 years.

Spencer Ainsley

Cannons are among the military artifacts on display at the West Point Museum.

Theodolite
Instrument used in land navigation, map making and surveying, from the 19th century.

West Point Museum Collections, U.S. Military Academy

rifles, revolvers, pistols and machine guns. This detailed display, including some rarer, lesser-used firearms, is a must-see gallery for a Colt enthusiast.

The main floor holds the West Point Gallery and the History of Warfare Gallery. The West Point Gallery chronicles the USMA since its days as a fort during the Revolutionary War. Here, visitors can see how cadet uniforms have changed over the years, plus some displays of prestigious graduates, including Sylvanus Thayer, Lee and Grant, World War I general John J. Pershing and World War II generals Dwight D. Eisenhower and Omar Bradley.

The History of Warfare Gallery ties in closely with West Point's curriculum, as it examines warfare dating to Roman times and before. Displays of notable battles and legendary artifacts can be found here, including Napoleon's sword. Other pieces include artifacts found after the surrender of Nazi Germany and the plug that was pulled from the atomic bomb that fell on Nagasaki.

Tracing the Army's role
The second floor houses the History of the U.S. Army Gallery, showcasing the Army's role in supporting the nation. Spanning all aspects of the Army, exhibits focus on the westward expansion of the United States, the African-American regiments known as the Buffalo Soldiers, the top-secret plans behind the development of the atomic bomb and various architectural and aeronautical endeavors undertaken by the Army, including its role in satellite and space exploration.

Also on the second floor is the American Wars Gallery, offering a descriptive tribute to soldiers in wars throughout America's history, from militiamen of the Colonial period to soldiers who traversed the jungles of Vietnam. This is where George Washington's pistols, the British drum surrendered at the Battle of Saratoga and Geronimo's Winchester rifle are. The gallery is also where the Medal of Honor Wall stands, showcasing the West Point graduates who have been given the nation's highest military award.

Containing an extremely large, diverse and old collection, the West Point Museum tells a detailed story of how America maintained its freedom, and in 2001, after terrorist attacks, many felt the museum was a perfect place to seek inspiration.

"The role of West Point is to provide career officers to the U.S. Army," Brig. Gen. Eric T. Olson said. "I think the importance of that role is renewed for all of us in times like these. West Point officers have always been there for the nation in times of crisis."

Lt. Col. James Whaley, director of public affairs, agreed that the museum showcases America's determination.

"I think it's so important right now for people to see this museum and see the history that has been West Point, because it shows that, through adversity, those hills and valleys that we go through as a nation, the one constant through that has been the leadership of this academy," he said. "Now, as a nation, we face a valley. People can rest assured that the leadership that we're teaching at the academy will endure all the challenges that we face."

Above, An African-American Civil War soldier. **Right**, Weapons on display include machine guns from around the world. **Below**, Uniforms, maps and flags are among the thousands of artifacts. **Below right**, This oil on canvas shows a Zouave regiment during the Civil War.

West Point Museum Collections, U.S. Military Academy

General Pershing's campaign hat

This officer's hat was worn by Gen. John J. Pershing in the Punitive Expedition in Mexico, 1916-1917.

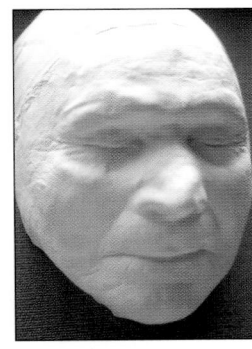

Sitting Bull mask

This plaster mask of the great Sioux chief Sitting Bull was created in 1880 by an unidentified artist.

Machine gun part

Ammunition magazine for Lewis machine gun.

> **'Through the Gothic portals of the U.S. Military Academy our nation's finest have passed.'**
>
> **Alexander Haig**, USMA graduate and former secretary of state, in "The Campus Guide: West Point. An Architectural Tour"

Frances Lehman Loeb Art Center, Vassar College

"Down the Hudson to West Point" was painted by Hudson River School painter Charles Herbert Moore in 1861.

VISITING WEST POINT

Tourists come for the forts, football

Army football games draw thousands of people to West Point each year.

The U.S. Military Academy's attraction as a tourist site is obvious, given the 3 million visitors a year from around the world who make their way to this citadel on the Hudson River.

There is much to see at West Point, the nation's oldest continuously occupied military post, which was declared a National Historic Landmark in 1960. Many come to capture the flavor and architecture of the country's first military service academy. Visitors can watch a cadet parade on The Plain, learn about the history of the U.S. Army, visit the graves of military heroes interred at the West Point Cemetery, or admire more than a dozen military monuments.

Visitors can also take in an Army football game at Michie Stadium, see a traveling musical, concert or dance performance at the 4,400-seat Eisenhower Hall Theater or attend a concert by the United States Military Academy Band.

Still others choose to visit Constitution Island, dine at Hotel Thayer or enjoy the spectacular scenery of the Hudson Highlands from Trophy Point.

Tours of West Point start at the Visitors Center. Located on the site of the former Ladycliff College Library outside the main Thayer Gate, the center offers historical and informational videos and maps, a full-scale cadet barracks room, a movie theater and a gift shop. In the wake of the 2001 terrorist attacks, visitors can expect extra security checks, and there is no longer access to the campus other than through guided bus tours beginning at the Visitors Center.

The graduates of West Point's Long Gray Line who emerged as the nation's leaders — from Robert E. Lee and Ulysses S. Grant to Dwight D. Eisenhower and Douglas MacArthur — are so intertwined with 225 years of American history that academy officials have adopted the slogan: "Much of the history we teach was made by the people we taught."

That history is contained at the West Point Museum, behind the Visitors Center, which by itself welcomes 250,000 visitors and thousands of school groups each year. The museum contains 45,000 artifacts, from military arms to military art, and is considered the oldest

IF YOU GO

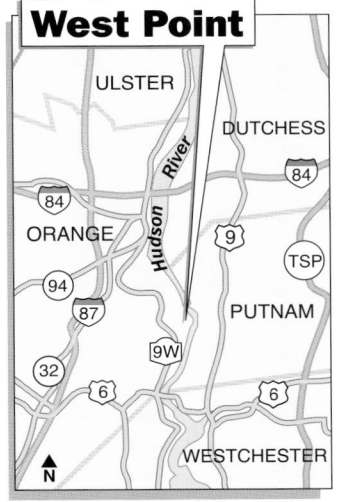

West Point

Visitors Center

9 a.m. to 4:45 p.m. daily. Call (845) 938-2638; (845) 446-3085 for gift shop. Guided tours April-October. Fees $6-$8. West Point Tours Inc. (845) 446-4724. *www.usma.army.mil/ publicaffairs/vic.htm*

Map labels

To Washington Gate
Cemetery
Old Cadet Chapel
Shea Stadium
Eisenhower Hall
Fort Putnam
Trophy Point
Michie Stadium
Washington Hall
to Stony Lonesome Gate
Cadet Chapel
Lusk Reservoir
Buffalo Soldier Field
Thayer Gate
Hotel Thayer
Visitors Center
Museum
HUDSON RIVER

A lamp-post banner heralds the 200th anniversary of West Point's founding.

IF YOU GO

The Chapels

■ The Cadet Chapel open daily 8:15 a.m. to 4:15 p.m; Protestant services, 10:30 a.m. Sundays.

■ Masses at Catholic Chapel of the Most Holy Trinity: 5:15 p.m. Saturdays, 9 a.m. and 11 a.m. Sundays.

■ Services at Jewish Chapel: 7 p.m. Fridays. Chapel open 9 a.m. to 4 p.m. weekdays, noon to 4 p.m. weekends.

All chapels: *www.usma. army.mil/chaplain/chapels. htm*

Eisenhower Hall

4,400-seat theater hosts musicals, concerts, comedians. Call (845) 938-4159; *www.eisenhowerhall.com*

Above, As a startling contrast between the old and the new, historic Fort Putnam, in foreground, rises above Michie Stadium.

Above, Jefferson Burges, a third-year cadet from Texas, practices the trumpet on the balcony of Cullum Hall, overlooking the Hudson River, in 2002.

and largest repository of military history in the Western Hemisphere.

Director Michael E. Moss said the museum serves as an academic facility for the Corps of Cadets, faculty and staff, with collections dating to the 1777 Battle of Saratoga during the American Revolution.

From Washington's pistols to Napoleon's sword

The museum's collections encompass the history of West Point and the U.S. Military Academy, the evolution of warfare and the development of the U.S. armed forces. Rare artifacts include George Washington's pistols, Napoleon's sword and a drawing by Grant.

Get a sweeping view of the Hudson River Valley from Fort Putnam, which was restored in the 1970s. It is open May through September. The fort, built in 1778 by Col. Rufus Putnam's 5th Massachusetts Regiment, is one of many forts constructed during the American Revolution to defend West Point.

Several chapels at West Point offer tourists a glimpse of the past and present. The Cadet Chapel, a Gothic cathedral of native granite on a hillside overlooking the Plain, was dedicated in 1910. It contains the largest church organ in the world.

The Catholic Chapel of the Most Holy Trinity, built in 1899 in the Norman Gothic style, contains 22 modern stained glass windows depicting soldier-saints from Christian history. And the Jewish Chapel, completed in 1984, contains an extensive Judaica collection and library.

'West Point officers have always been there for the nation in times of crisis.'

Brig. Gen. Eric T. Olson, about the role of the U.S. Military Academy

Karl Rabe

U.S. Military Academy cadets line up to be formally inspected by Gen. Colin Powell during a ceremony in 1998.

> **'**People can rest assured that the leadership that we're teaching at the academy will endure all the challenges that we face.**'**
>
> **Lt. Col. James Whaley**, director of public affairs at West Point

Spencer Ainsley

An aged tree located near the entrance to the Cadet Chapel frames a view north toward the Hudson River.

A band and a theater, for all to enjoy

Spencer Ainsley

The United States Military Academy Band plays as the Corps of Cadets prepare for a review in 2001.

Performing arts at the U.S. Military Academy at West Point have been around as long as the institution itself.

From the military band music of the early 1800s to the theatrical musicals of today, famous faces and recognizable performances have been part of the academy since it was established in 1802.

The first performance began with the creation of a band, and as West Point grew, so did the need for cadets to provide an audible order to their duty day. Today, the United States Military Academy Band is the oldest active band in the Army.

"Any time they march, they march to our drum beat," Sgt. Christopher Jones, a clarinetist in the USMA concert band and the band's spokesman, said of the cadets.

Band members are not cadets. Rather, they are full-time Army officers and professional musicians, most with advanced music degrees, stationed at West Point to support the cadets. Today, they are a staple at nearly every event, performing at military and patriotic ceremonies, public concerts, sporting events, television and radio broadcasts and various social activities for the Corps of Cadets and West Point community.

Several new works were commissioned for the band for West Point's bicentennial in 2002, and a composition contest drew 83 entries from all over the world.

Center hosts famous artists

An idea to create a building large enough to seat the entire Corps of Cadets in the mid-1970s led to another genre of performing arts at the academy. Eisenhower Hall, a 193,000-square-foot building with a 4,400-seat theater, was built with little expectation to draw in members of the community. But almost immediately it flourished to become a first-grade performing arts center and commonplace for cadets and the public.

"It has really gone beyond the idea of entertainment," said Bill Yost, director of performing arts at Eisenhower Hall. "We've introduced the cadets to the arts and at the same time have really been able to bridge the community."

Entertainers like Bob Dylan, Bill Cosby, Ray Charles, Fleetwood Mac, George Burns and the theatrical casts from "Cats," "West Side Story," "Evita" and "Les Miserables" have all been center stage.

The theater financially relies on ticket buyers, Yost said. "We do dance, and we do serious music, and we do rock and roll and country and comedy," he said. "We've accomplished what we set out to do."

Weekly performances are held at Eisenhower Hall, on the west bank of the Hudson Highlands on the grounds of the academy. The USMA band holds public performances all year. From mid-June to Labor Day, the summer outdoor concert series is held every Sunday at 7:30 p.m. at scenic Trophy Point overlooking the Hudson River. The rest of the year chamber and band music concerts are held.

Spencer Ainsley

A group of cadets march in their traditional parade uniforms on the Plain during a review in 2001.

'Any time they march, they march to our drum beat.'

Sgt. Christopher Jones
USMA band spokesman and clarinetist, about the cadets

U.S. Military Academy Archives

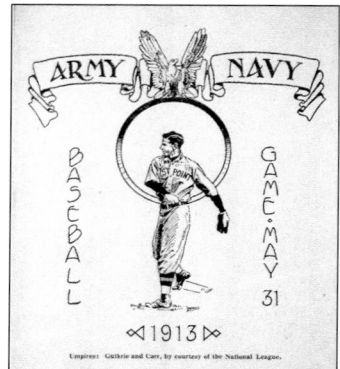

A program from an Army-Navy baseball game in 1913.

COACHES OF NOTE

Hockey

Jack Riley

Riley coached the Cadets' hockey team for 36 years (1950-1986), becoming the winningest coach in Army history with a record of 542-343-20. Riley also coached the 1960 U.S. Olympic hockey team to the country's first gold medal in hockey at the games in Squaw Valley, Calif.

Right, This 1935 painting by Albert W. Hampson reflects the intense rivalry between the Army and Naval academies — depicting Navy midshipmen on their way to remove Army's message from their mascot goat.

West Point Museum Collections, U.S. Military Academy

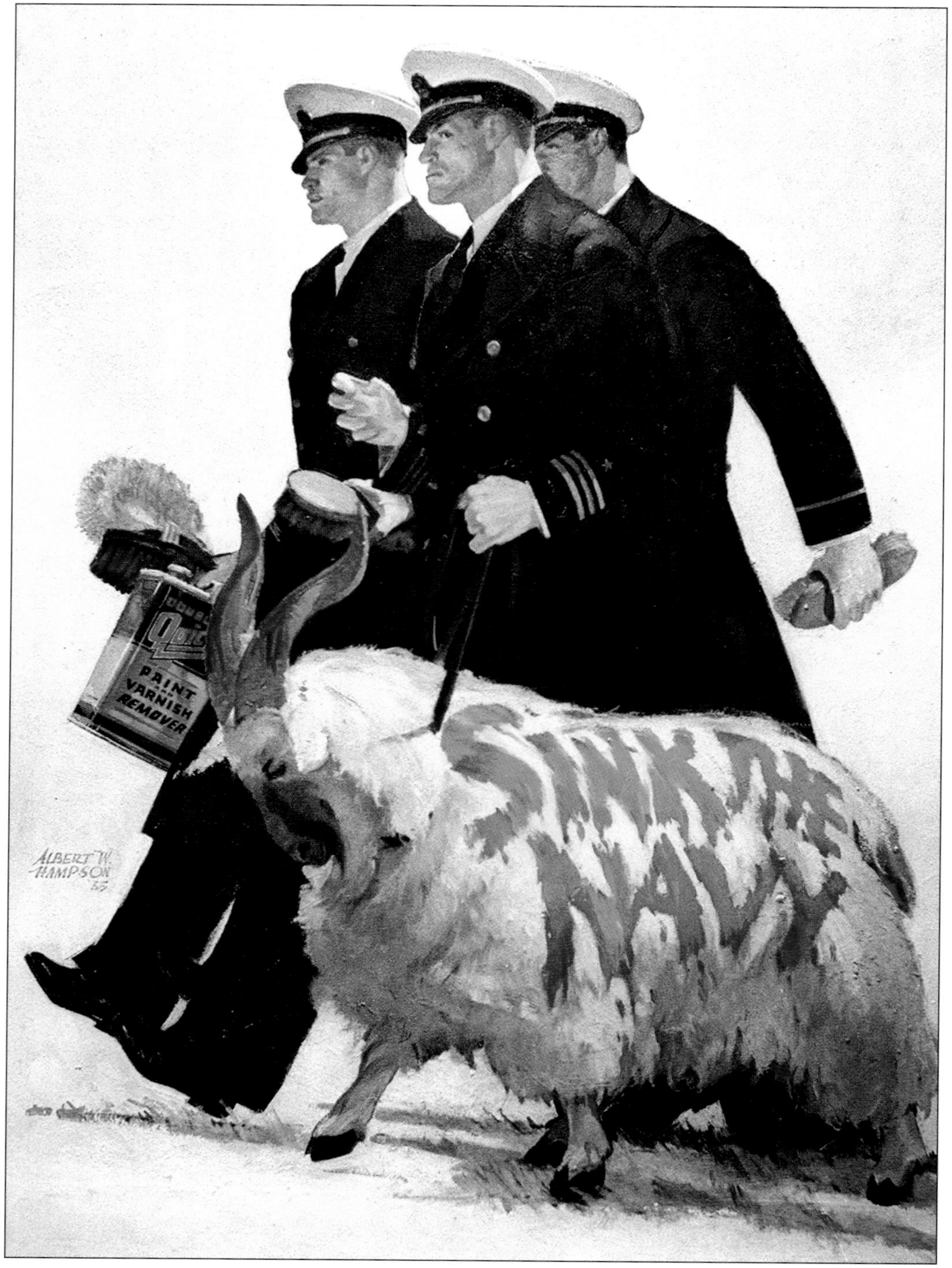

Cadet Sports

Much more than football

You go to West Point and you can expect to run.

And jump.

And shoot, sprint, tackle, tumble and yes, even swing a golf club.

Athletics is as much a part of the fabric of West Point as the salute.

"Every cadet is an athlete," Gen. Douglas MacArthur once said during his time as superintendent (1919-1922) at the U.S. Military Academy.

Michie Stadium, home to the Army football team, is the epicenter of sports at West Point. However, while Army football and the never-ending battle to defeat Navy stands alone in terms of prestige and tradition at West Point, the range of sports goes far beyond that.

Every cadet is required to participate in some form of athletics each semester, whether it's varsity, club or intramurals.

Dr. Woody Woodworth, director of competitive sports at West Point, oversees the club and intramurals programs. As far as participation, he said about 60 percent of the Corps of Cadets chooses intramurals. About 25 percent compete at the varsity level and are under the umbrella of the National Collegiate Athletic Association. And the rest are at the club level.

In all, Army has 25 intercollegiate (NCAA) sports, which include golf, gymnastics, riflery and wrestling.

The intramural program is cadet-led and cadet-run, as the cadets serve as players, coach-

Legendary coaches patrolled West Point sidelines

Lombardi. Knight. Krzyzewski. Riley. Riley?

When it comes to legendary coaches who have called plays from the sidelines at the U.S. Military Academy, three of the most famous coaches with ties to West Point are football's Vince Lombardi and basketball's Bob Knight and Mike Krzyzewski.

Earl "Red" Blaik is revered as the coach who led the football team during its World War II-era championships. But hockey coaches Jack and Rob Riley are legends, too.

Rob Riley completed his 16th season as head coach of Army hockey in 2002, making it 52 years that a Riley has been behind the bench. Rob succeeded his father, Jack, as coach in 1986. Jack Riley won 542 games behind the Army bench.

"It's been a great honor not only to follow my dad after his 36-year career," Riley said. "But to work with these outstanding men at West Point."

The Rileys are part of a glorious coaching tradition at West Point, which has been the final stop for some and a springboard for others.

Strong starts at academy

Another longtime coach at West Point is Jack Emmer, the most winning active coach among NCAA lacrosse coaches.

Two of the most prominent coaches who got their start at West Point are Krzyzewski, the head coach at Duke University, and Bob Knight, the head coach at Texas Tech and former coach at Indiana University. He led the Hoosiers to three NCAA titles. Both are members of the Naismith Basketball Hall of Fame in Springfield, Mass.

Krzyzewski was the head coach from 1975-80. Krzyzewski, Pat Harris and Tom Miller are the only head coaches in Army basketball history who have graduated from the academy. Between 1975-80, Krzyzewski's teams compiled a 73-59 record and made a National Invitational Tournament appearance in 1978.

After the 1979-80 season, Krzyzewski took over the men's pro-

Left, Coach Earl Blaik, center, with Felix "Doc" Blanchard, left, and Glenn Davis, stars of the 1940s Army team.

U.S. Army photos

gram at Duke. In 23 seasons, Krzyzewski has led the Blue Devils to a 590-175 record, been named Coach of the Year 11 times and won three NCAA titles.

Krzyzewski was recruited by and played for Knight from 1966-69. Knight was an assistant under "Tates" Locke from 1963-65 when the Cadets posted a mark of 40-15, and took over the program upon Locke's departure. Knight led Army to a 102-50 record in six seasons, making him the second-winningest coach in academy history. Only Leo Novak coached the Cadets to more victories, compiling a 126-61 record between 1927 and 1939.

Despite the success Army coaches have enjoyed on the hardcourt, the academy may be best known for the gridiron talent of the 1940s and '50s. From 1941-1958, Blaik led the Army football team to a 121-33-10 record and national titles in 1944 and 1945.

Playing against the backdrop of World War II, Army went undefeated in 1944, 1945 and 1946, with one tie, a 0-0 legendary battle against Notre Dame at Yankee Stadium on Nov. 10, 1946.

So dominant was Army in 1944 that the Cadets averaged 56 points a game and beat their opponents by an average of 52.1 points. Both are still Division I national records.

Players frequently got letters and telegrams from front-line soldiers and top generals. After the team beat Navy, 23-7, to cap the 1944 unbeaten season, the team received a telegram from a former Army football team manager: Douglas MacArthur. It read, in part, "We have stopped the war to celebrate your magnificent success."

Among the most notable assistants to serve under Blaik was Vince Lombardi. The coach, who led the Green Bay Packers to five championships, served under Blaik from 1949 to 1953.

COACHES OF NOTE

Basketball

Tates Locke

Locke coached Army for two seasons, compiling a 40-15 record. Locke left the post in 1965, and was replaced by his assistant, Bob Knight.

Bob Knight

Knight, above, coached at Army for six seasons, between 1965-71. He finished with an overall record of 102-50, making him the second-winningest coach in Army history.

Mike Krzyzewski

After playing under Bob Knight for four seasons and serving as a team captain, Krzyzewski went on to coach the Cadets from 1975-80. In five seasons, Krzyzewski was 73-59.

---

es, officials and administrators. A member of the faculty known as a sport educator oversees the activities. Teams are organized by company, so there are 32 teams with a championship at the end of the season.

The 22 club sports compete at the intercollegiate level, but none overlap with sports the academy competes in at the NCAA level. They include boxing, judo and team handball. At the club level, the coach-

es are volunteer officers and civilians on post. They are not paid.

"They are willing to devote their time to these cadets," Woodworth said, "and compete at a high level."

And at the U.S. Military Academy, competing at a high level is a daily expectation and one where the only requirement is a little blood, sweat and tears.

Above, This football trophy was awarded to the Class of 1898 for winning the 1896 intramurals.

Below right, Army's Ben Woodruff tries to block a Tulane University kick during the 2000 homecoming game at Michie Stadium.

COACHES OF NOTE
Football

Earl 'Red' Blaik

The winningest coach in Army history, with a record of 121-33-10 in 18 seasons (1941-58), Blaik led the Cadets to Associated Press national titles in 1944 and 1945.

Vince Lombardi

The legendary coach of the Green Bay Packers was an offensive and defensive backs coach at Army from 1949-53, under Blaik.

Tom Cahill

Cahill coached Army from 1966-73, compiling a 40-39-2 record. Cahill was named the National Coach of the Year in 1966 after leading the Cadets to an 8-2 record.

Bill Parcells

Before winning two Super Bowl titles with the New York Giants, Parcells was a defensive assistant coach for Army 1967-69.

Army beat Navy 6-4 on Nov. 28, 1908, at Franklin Field at the University of Pennsylvania in Philadelphia.

Tenacity propels Army on gridiron

On New Year's Day 1997, a charter flight bound from Shreveport, La., for Stewart International Airport in New Windsor settled at its cruising altitude.

Seated by one of the emergency exit doors was the 31st coach of the Army football team, a soft-spoken native of Ypsilanti, Mich., named Bob Sutton who never played college football and never served in the military.

Sutton stared out his small porthole window, his mind recalling the moments that had just ended Army's most successful season in recent school history.

Earlier, on New Year's Eve, the Black Knights of the Hudson had lost to Auburn in the Independence Bowl. Auburn led 32-7 going into the fourth quarter. Army rallied for 22 points and had a chance to tie the game when its kicker, J. Parker, missed a short field goal from 27 yards with 33 seconds remaining. It was Parker's first miss of the season after 17 successful attempts from within 40 yards.

Something struck Sutton as he reflected on the previous night's events. It wasn't that Army had won 10 games, a school record. Or that the Cadets had captured the coveted Commander in Chief's Trophy, the laurel of the round-robin series

between the three service academies. Nor was he thinking about how his team had played in its first bowl game in eight years, and just the fourth in school history.

Sutton was thinking about the comeback. Faced with a team that had completely dominated for three quarters, Army somehow had managed to come within one play of sending the game into overtime. Against players who were bigger and faster, and a deficit that would have brow-beaten most teams into resignation, his players had only become more resolute.

An Army comeback

Sutton saw something in that effort that wasn't drawn on a chalkboard but was from something much more profound — 100 years of football history and 200 years of military scholarship.

It wasn't just a comeback.

It was an Army comeback.

"I don't think there are many teams in the country that could have stayed at it as long as we did and get into a position to put the game into overtime," Sutton said. "That took an incredible amount of effort and a belief system that is so deeply rooted, it's hard to describe."

If one thing has remained constant in Army's more than 110 years of football, it is this unflagging resolve. It is a story of lifelong commitments to the team, the corps and the country.

And it all started with a bet.

A cadet named Dennis Michie founded the Army football team in 1890 in response to a friendly challenge from some Naval Academy midshipmen Michie met during a summer furlough. Michie, the son of a West Point philosophy professor, fought for administration approval and funding. The result was the first Army-Navy game, played on Nov. 29, 1890 at West Point. Navy, the more experienced team, won 24-0.

Michie played on Army's 1891 team that beat Navy at Annapolis and helped coach two more teams. On July 1, 1898, while leading a group of men near the San Juan River during the Battle of Santiago in Cuba, he became the first former Army football player to die in the line of duty. He was 28.

The Army team continued to grow during the 1890s but came into prominence for the first time after the turn of the century under Charles Daly. He earned All-America honors as Army's quarterback in 1901. Daly returned to coach Army twice, from 1913-16 and from 1919-22. In that time, his Army teams went 58-13 with three ties.

Army's success continued in the 1930s under coaches Ralph Sasse and Garrison Davidson. Neither coach lost more than three games in a season.

Legendary seasons

Army reached its highest level of success under legendary coach Earl "Red" Blaik.

Blaik attended West Point during Douglas MacArthur's tenure as superintendent. Blaik had resigned his commission and was enjoying a successful run as the head coach at Dartmouth. Although happy at Dartmouth, he felt the call of duty when West Point officials offered him the job before the 1941 season.

During his 18 seasons at West Point, Blaik won 121 games, lost just 33 and tied 10. He coached three national champion teams and three winners of the Heisman Trophy, college football's

highest individual award.

Newburgh resident Joe Steffy played on three of those teams, including the 1945 national champion, and coached under Blaik as an assistant from 1952-55.

"I think he taught a brand of leadership that they needed at West Point," Steffy said. "He had a way about him. He never raised his voice. He used first names. He called me Joe. He was very good at getting you prepared for the game. He was a good leader."

Army's success didn't stop with the war. From 1948-50, Army won 25 games and lost just one. The one loss: a 14-2 upset against Navy on Dec. 2, 1950.

Blaik's final season was in 1958. It was a remarkable season in many ways. Team captain Pete Dawkins captured the Heisman award. Flanker Bill Carpenter became known as the "Lonely End" and would go on to become a Vietnam War hero when he called a napalm strike on his own position minutes before he was about to be overrun by North Vietnamese soldiers.

The Cadets went 8-0-1 and finished third in the national polls. Only a 14-14 tie against Pittsburgh kept Army from another national championship.

And then it stopped. Blaik said his final farewell to Army football, and the Cadets vanished from the final national rankings until 1984. That's when second-year coach Jim Young installed the wishbone offense and led the Cadets to their first bowl appearance in school history, a 10-6 victory over Michigan State in the Cherry Bowl.

Army went on to make two more bowl appearances in the next four years, beating Illinois, 31-29, in the 1985 Peach Bowl and losing to Alabama, 29-28, in the 1988 John Hancock Sun Bowl.

Left, President Bill Clinton, center right, presents the Commander in Chief's trophy to the Cadets after their 28-24 victory over Navy at Veterans Stadium in Philadelphia in 1996. It was the first time since 1974 that a sitting president attended an Army-Navy game.

U.S. Army

'I never have regretted my sports obsession for a moment. It is almost trite to observe that in organized team sports, one learns the important art of group cooperation in goal achievement.'

Omar Bradley

'Upon the fields of friendly strife, are sown the seeds that, upon other fields, on other days, will bear the fruits of victory.'

Douglas MacArthur

FELIX 'DOC' BLANCHARD

Title: Football player (fullback).
Born: Dec. 11, 1924, Bishopville, S.C.
Contributions: Three-time All-America selection; led Army to national titles in 1944 and 1945; won the Heisman Trophy and Sullivan Award in 1945; was a placekicker and punter for the team as well; scored 38 touchdowns and ran for 1,908 yards in his career at Army; teammate of talented halfback Glenn Davis. The Heisman Trophy is awarded annually to the nation's top collegiate football player. The Sullivan Award is given annually to the most outstanding amateur athlete.

Facts: Son of a doctor who played football at Wake Forest and Tulane; was nicknamed "Little Doc" as a boy; led Army to three undefeated seasons; ran the 100-yard dash in 10 seconds in a dual meet against Cornell in 1945; won the IC4A shotput title that same year; after graduating from West Point, Blanchard entered the U.S. Air Force and became a jet pilot; elected to the National Football Foundation and College Hall of Fame in 1959; retired from the Air Force with the rank of colonel.
Quote: "Have just seen Superman in the flesh. He wears No. 35 on his Army jersey. His name is Felix 'Doc' Blanchard." — The words of Notre Dame coach Ed McKeever, sent on a telegram, following his team's 59-0 blowout loss against Army in 1944.

MIKE KRZYZEWSKI

Title: Played for USMA, 1966-1969; Army head men's basketball coach, 1975-1980; Duke University basketball coach, 1980-present.
Born: Feb. 13, 1947, Chicago.
Contributions: Working under former head coach Bob Knight as a player, Krzyzewski helped the team to a 51-23 record between 1966-1969. Krzyzewski captained the 1968-69 team that went 3-1 in the National Invitational Tournament. After West Point, his military service obligation included serving for two seasons as the head coach at the USMA prep school in Belvior, Va. In 1974-75 Krzyzewski worked with Knight, serving as a graduate assistant for the Indiana University Hoosiers. In his five seasons as West Point basketball coach, Krzyzewski guided the Black Knights to a 73-59 record, including a 20-win season in 1976-77. Army defeated archrival Navy in four of the five contests played during his tenure. At Duke, Krzyzewski won national championships in 1991, 1992 and 2001.
Fact: In 2001, Krzyzewski was a first-ballot inductee into the Naismith Memorial Basketball Hall of Fame.
Quote: Former Duke Player Shane Battier, the consensus 2001 National Player of the Year, on Krzyzewski: "Coach K instills not only the game of basketball in each of his players but teaches them a lot about life."

PETE DAWKINS

Title: CEO, Primerica Financial Services, based in Atlanta. Halfback, Army 1957-1959.
Born: March 8, 1938, Royal Oak, Mich.
Contributions: As a halfback, Dawkins won the 1958 Heisman Trophy, given to the top college football player. In his three seasons at Army, Dawkins was an offensive threat in the air and on the ground. He threw 16 passes, seven of which went for touchdowns; and he caught 27 passes, totaling 716 yards. Running, Dawkins rushed for 1,123 yards. He was his team's captain and class president at West Point before attending Oxford University on a Rhodes Scholarship, turning down a chance to play in the NFL for the Baltimore Colts. Following a 24-year career in the Army in which he was promoted to brigadier general, Dawkins became a partner with business giant Lehman Brothers. He became chief executive officer and chairman of Primerica Financial Services Inc. in 1991.
Fact: Dawkins had polio as a child.
Quote: In the 1959 "Howitzer," USMA's yearbook: "Pete firmly gripped our hands in deep and understanding friendship."

Chapter 6

CHARTING THE COURSE
LEADERS WHO SHAPED THE ACADEMY AND BROKE BARRIERS

Col. Sylvanus Thayer, one of West Point's most influential superintendents, is portrayed during an 1818 dedication of a monument in a painting by Jes W. Schlaikjer.

West Point Museum Collections, U.S. Military Academy

'Duty, Honor, Country. Those three hallowed words reverently dictate what you ought to be, what you can be, what you will be. They are your rallying points.'

Gen. Douglas MacArthur, in his speech on receiving the Thayer Award, May 12, 1962

Continued on page 103

THE SUPERINTENDENTS

Leaders change, the academy evolves

Being named superintendent of West Point has come to be the capstone to great military careers.

Whether the military men who have assumed the role got their luster from, or gave it to, the U.S. Military Academy, the 53 who have served as superintendents have been the driving force behind the institution's evolution.

When the academy was founded in 1802, the chief of the Army Corps of Engineers served as superintendent, dividing his duties and spending most of his time away from West Point, according to Stephen Grove, historian for the academy.

By 1817, when the "Father of the Military Academy," Sylvanus Thayer, was appointed, it was a full-time position. Established to train Americans in military engineering, West Point came into its own under Thayer's guidance, with an established curriculum and educational standards, codes of discipline and honor, and a library filled with European books on the art of war.

Dealing with issues such as curriculum, academic and military programs, honor and discipline, Thayer's tenure echoed through the next 170 years after he left in 1833, as notable succeeding superintendents tackled many of the same issues to help the institution change with the times.

Addressing the conduct of upper-class cadets toward the incoming

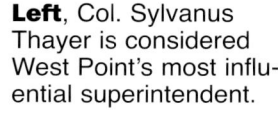

Left, Col. Sylvanus Thayer is considered West Point's most influential superintendent.
West Point Museum Collections, U.S. Military Academy

class — a relationship known to be harsh and unrelenting — has been an issue for years.

Lasting words

John M. Schofield, who served from 1876 to 1881, made a famous statement about this conduct in his 1879 speech, a statement cadets now have to memorize. The statement also addressed the relationship between instructing officers and their students.

"The discipline which makes soldiers of a free country reliable in battle is not to be gained by harsh or tyrannical treatment," he said, in part. "On the contrary, such treatment is far more likely to destroy than to make an army."

Visionary superintendents after each of the world wars saw the need to update the curriculum to instill more knowledge of world cultures and circumstances. But Douglas MacArthur after World War I and Maxwell D. Taylor after World War II had less success than Garrison H. Davidson in the late 1950s.

MacArthur did improve the military training and physical fitness programs, as well as create the Cadet Honor Committee to review

Sylvanus Thayer was the backbone of West Point

For Sylvanus Thayer, West Point was everything. And the academy owes everything to Thayer, its fifth superintendent.

Thayer headed the U.S. Military Academy for 16 years, longer than any other superintendent, and is known as the "Father of the Military Academy" for shaping a visionary course for the institution.

"He really gave his life to the academy," said Stephen Grove, historian at West Point. "He didn't marry, didn't have any kids. The academy was his life."

From 1817 to 1833, Thayer put to use his knowledge of European military thinking, an innate ability to lead and his background as an Army Corps of Engineers captain during the War of 1812.

After graduating from Dartmouth College in 1807, he entered West Point and completed studies in just a year. After graduating, he joined the Army Corps of Engineers and was commended for service during the War of 1812, Grove said.

But at the same time, he became convinced the U.S. Army was ill prepared, according to "Duty, Honor, Country: A History of West Point" by historian Stephen E. Ambrose. After peace returned in 1815, Thayer was sent to Europe to study the art of war and purchase European books that would become West Point's first library.

Appointed superintendent by President James Monroe, Thayer revolutionized the educational program, formalized discipline procedures and emphasized honor and integrity in a new way — three themes that remain central to the academy's mission to this day.

"In those days, an officer's word was his bond," Grove said. "That was the foundation of the present-day honor code."

Superintendents through the next century and a half would make significant changes to keep the academy up to date as concepts about curriculum, honor and discipline evolved. But no other had such a formative role in shaping the academy.

West Point Museum Collections, U.S. Military Academy

Top: A portrait of Sylvanus Thayer. **Above**, Thayer's presentation sword.

honor code breaches. Taylor established a place for classroom leadership training in an attempt to inspire motivation, rather than intimidation, in the Army ranks.

Under Davidson, though, multicultural studies — seen for years as a key to a thorough military training — took off, as did the study of electives.

Superintendents Andrew J. Goodpaster and Willard W. Scott are credited with redeeming reputation and morale at the institution after a tumultuous period in 1976, when an honor code scandal related to a test and the arrival of the first women candidates coincided with the nation's bicentennial, inspiring Congress to launch the West Point Study Group, an investigation into the academy.

Scott also fostered predecessor Davidson's sense of academic freedom when, in the first half of the 1980s, cadets were first allowed to choose to major in a variety of subjects rather than a prescribed curriculum.

Continued on page 104

DUTY, HONOR, COUNTRY

Gen. Douglas MacArthur, a West Point superintendent and World War II hero, received the Thayer Award from West Point more than 40 years ago. Here is the text of his famous "Duty, Honor, Country" speech, delivered on May 12, 1962.

General Westmoreland, General Groves, distinguished guests, and gentlemen of the Corps:

As I was leaving the hotel this morning, a doorman asked me, "Where are you bound for, General?" and when I replied, "West Point," he remarked, "Beautiful place, have you ever been there before?"

No human being could fail to be deeply moved by such a tribute as this (Thayer Award). Coming from a profession I have served so long, and a people I have loved so well, it fills me with an emotion I cannot express. But this award is not intended primarily to honor a personality, but to symbolize a great moral code — the code of conduct and chivalry of those who guard this beloved land of culture and ancient descent. That is the meaning of this medallion. For all eyes and for all time, it is an expression of the ethics of the American soldier. That I should be integrated in this way with so noble an ideal arouses a sense of pride and yet of humility which will be with me always.

Duty, Honor, Country. Those three hallowed words reverently dictate what you ought to be, what you can be, what you will be. They are your rallying points: to build courage when courage seems to fail; to regain faith when there seems to be little cause for faith; to create hope when hope becomes forlorn. Unhappily, I possess neither that eloquence of diction, that poetry of imagination, nor that brilliance of metaphor to tell you all that they mean.

The unbelievers will say they are but words, but a slogan, but a flamboyant phrase. Every pedant, every demagogue, every cynic, every hypocrite, every troublemaker, and, I am sorry to say, some others of an entirely different character, will try to downgrade them even to the extent of mockery and ridicule.

Words with lasting impact

But these are some of the things they do. They build your basic character, they mold you for your future roles as the custodians of the nation's defense, they make you strong enough to know when you are weak, and brave enough to face yourself when you are afraid.

They teach you to be proud and unbending in honest failure, but

humble and gentle in success; not to substitute words for actions, nor to seek the path of comfort, but to face the stress and spur of difficulty and challenge; to learn to stand up in the storm but to have compassion on those who fall; to master yourself before you seek to master others; to have a heart that is clean, a goal that is high; to learn to laugh yet never forget how to weep; to reach into the future yet never neglect the past; to be serious yet never to take yourself too seriously; to be modest so that you will remember the implicity of true greatness, the open mind of true wisdom, the meekness of true strength. They give you a temper of the will, a quality of the imagination, a vigor of the emotions, a freshness of the deep springs of life, a temperamental predominance of courage over timidity, an appetite for adventure over love of ease.

They create in your heart the sense of wonder, the unfailing hope of what next, and the joy and inspiration of life. They teach you in this way to be an officer and a gentleman.

And what sort of soldiers are those you are to lead? Are they reliable, are they brave, are they capable of victory? Their story is known to all of you; it is the story of the American man-at-arms. My estimate of him was formed on the battlefield many, many years ago and has never changed. I regarded him then as I regard him now — as one of the world's noblest figures; not only as one of the finest military characters but also as one of the most stainless. His name and fame are the birthright of every American citizen. In his youth and strength, his love and loyalty he gave — all that mortality can give.

He needs no eulogy from me or from any other man. He has written his own history and has written it in red on his enemy's breast. But when I think of his patience under adversity, of his courage under fire, and of his modesty in victory, I am filled with an emotion of admiration I cannot put into words. He belongs to history as furnishing one of the greatest examples of successful patriotism; he belongs to the present, to us, by his virtues and by his achievements.

In 20 campaigns, on a hundred battlefields, around a thousand campfires, I have witnessed that enduring fortitude, that patriotic self-abnegation, and that invincible determination which have carved the heart of his people. From one end of the world to the other he has drained deep the chalice of courage.

As I listened to those songs of the glee club, in memory's eye I could see those staggering columns of the First World War, bending under soggy packs, on many a weary march from dripping dusk to drizzling dawn, slogging ankle-deep through the mire of shell-

'(The Thayer) award is not intended primarily to honor a personality, but to symbolize a great moral code — the code of conduct and chivalry of those who guard this beloved land of culture and ancient descent. That is the meaning of this medallion.'

Gen. Douglas MacArthur
on receiving the Thayer Award

shocked roads, to form grimly for the attack, bluelipped, covered with sludge and mud, chilled by the wind and rain; driving home to their objective, and, for many, the judgment seat of God. I do not know the dignity of their birth but I do know the glory of their death. They died unquestioning, uncomplaining, with faith in their hearts, and on their lips the hope that we would go on to victory. Always for them Duty, Honor, Country; always their blood and sweat and tears as we sought the way and the light and the truth.

And 20 years after, on the other side of the globe, again the filth of murky foxholes, the stench of ghostly trenches, the slime of dripping dugouts; those boiling suns of relentless heat, those torrential rains of devastating storms; the loneliness and utter desolation of jungle trails, the bitterness of long separation from those they loved and cherished, the deadly pestilence of tropical disease, and the horror of stricken areas of war; their resolute and determined defense, their swift and sure attack, their indomitable purpose, their complete and decisive victory — always victory. Always through the bloody haze of their last reverberating shot, the vision of gaunt, ghastly men reverently following your password of Duty, Honor, Country.

The code which those words perpetuate embraces the highest moral laws and will stand the test of any ethics or philosophies ever promulgated for the uplift of mankind. Its requirements are for the things that are right, and its restraints are from the things

Left, Gen. Leslie R. Groves, USMA Class of 1918, presents Gen. Douglas MacArthur with the Thayer Award on May 12, 1962.

U.S. Military Academy Archives

Right, The words of Gen. Douglas MacArthur, shown in a portrait taken in Manila in 1945, are forever linked with West Point.

AP/Wide World Photos

---

that are wrong.

The soldier, above all other men, is required to practice the greatest act of religious training — sacrifice. In battle and in the face of danger and death, he discloses those divine attributes which his Maker gave when he created man in his own image. No physical courage and no brute instinct can take the place of the Divine help which alone can sustain him.

A 'boundless frontier'

However horrible the incidents of war may be, the soldier who is called upon to offer and to give his life for his country, is the noblest development of mankind. You now face a new world — a world of change. The thrust into outer space of the satellite, spheres and missiles marked the beginning of another epoch in the long story of mankind — the chapter of the space age.

In the five or more billions of years the scientists tell us it has taken to form the earth, in the three or more billion years of development of the human race, there has never been a greater, a more abrupt or staggering evolution. We deal now not with things of this world alone, but with the illimitable distances and as yet unfathomed mysteries of the universe. We are reaching out for a new and boundless frontier. We speak in strange terms: of harnessing the cosmic-energy; of making winds and tides work for us; of creating unheard of synthetic materials to supplement or even replace our old standard basics; to purify sea water for our drink; of mining ocean floors for new fields of wealth and food; of disease preventatives to expand life into the hundred of years; of controlling the weather for a more equitable distribution of heat and cold, of rain and shine; of space ships to the moon; of the primary target in war, no longer limited to the armed forces of an enemy, but instead to include his civil populations; of ultimate conflict between a united human race and the sinister forces of some other planetary galaxy; of such dreams and fantasies as to make life the most exciting of all time.

And through all this welter of change and development, your mission remains fixed, determined, inviolable — it is to win our wars. Everything else in your professional career is but corollary to this vital dedication. All other public purposes, all other public projects, all public needs, great or small, will find others for accomplishment; but you are the ones who are trained to fight: yours is the profession of arms — the will to win, the sure knowledge that in war there is no substitute for victory; that if you lose, the nation will be destroyed; that the very obsession of your public service must be Duty, Honor, Country.

Others will debate the controversial issues, national and inter-national, which divide men's minds; but serene, calm, aloof, you stand as the nation's war-guardian, as its lifeguard from the raging tides of international conflict, as its gladiator in the arena of battle.

For a century you have defended, guarded and protected traditions of liberty and freedom, of right and justice. Let civilian voices argue the merits or demerits of our processes of government; whether our strength is being sapped by deficit financing, indulged by federal paternalism grown too mighty, by power groups grown too arrogant, by politics grown too corrupt, by crime grown too rampant, by morals grown too low, by taxes grown too high, by extremists grown too violent; whether our personal liberties are as thorough and complete as they should be. These great national problems are not for your professional participation or military solution. Your guidepost stands out like a ten-fold beacon in the night, Duty, Honor, Country.

You are the leaven which binds together the entire fabric of our national system of defense. From your ranks come the great captains who hold the nation's destiny in their hands the moment the war tocsin sounds. The Long Gray Line has never failed us. Were you to do so, a million ghosts in olive drab, in brown khaki, in blue and gray, would rise from their white crosses thundering those magic words, Duty, Honor, Country.

This does not mean that you are warmongers. On the contrary, the soldier, above all other people, prays for peace, for he must suffer and bear the deepest wounds and scars of war. But always in our ears ring ominous words of Plato that wisest of all philosophers, "Only the dead have seen the end of war."

The shadows are lengthening for me. The twilight is here. My days of old have vanished tone and tint; they have gone glimmering through the dreams of things that were. Their memory is one of wondrous beauty, watered by tears, and coaxed and caressed by the smiles of yesterday.

I listen vainly for the witching melody of faint bugles blowing reveille, of far drums beating the long roll. In my dreams I hear again the crash of guns, the rattle of musketry, the strange, mournful mutter of the battlefield.

But in the evening of my memory, always I come back to West Point. Always there echoes and re-echoes Duty, Honor, Country.

Today marks my final roll call with you, but I want you to know that when I cross the river my last conscious thoughts will be of The Corps, and The Corps, and The Corps. I bid you farewell.

— **U.S. Military Academy Archives**

JOHN M. SCHOFIELD

Title: USMA Class of 1853; secretary of war, 1869; USMA superintendent, 1876-1881; commander of the Army 1888-95.
Born: Sept. 29, 1831, Chatauqua County.
Died: March 4, 1906, St. Augustine, Fla.
Contributions: Schofield became one of 43 fully commissioned brigadier generals from Illinois during the Civil War. His troops captured Wilmington, N.C., and defended Franklin, Tenn., in 1864. He earned prestige for his heroism in the Civil War, eventually receiving the Medal of Honor for heroism. After the Civil War, he served as secretary of war, superintendent of the USMA, and commanding general of the U.S. Army.
Fact: Schofield graduated seventh in his class at West Point. Schofield Barracks, a U.S. Army post about 30 miles north of Honolulu, is named after him. He was the first to recommend acquiring Pearl Harbor as a naval base.

OLIVER O. HOWARD

Title: USMA Class of 1854; USMA superintendent, 1881-1882; founder of Howard University in Washington, D.C.; president of Howard, 1869-74.
Born: Nov. 8, 1830, Leeds, Me.
Died: Oct. 26, 1909, Burlington, Vt.
Contributions: Howard became a mathematics professor at West Point in the 1850s and was about to become a minister when the Civil War broke out. An abolitionist, Howard was made a colonel in command of the 3rd Maine Regiment. After leading a brigade at the Battle of Bull Run, Howard was promoted to the brigadier general of volunteers in September 1861. At the Battle of Fair Oaks (Seven Pines) on June 1, 1862, Howard had two horses shot from under him and his right arm was shattered by two bullets. However, he continued to fight until the Confederates retreated. His arm was amputated. He received the Medal of Honor for his bravery. After the war, Howard headed the Freedmen's Bureau. He founded Howard University in 1867. He continued to serve the army as a commander, directing several campaigns against Native Americans. One of his most famous occurred in eastern Oregon, where he negotiated with Chief Joseph. Howard was also superintendent of West Point. He later wrote several books detailing his military and Indian affairs.

MAXWELL D. TAYLOR

Title: USMA Class of 1922, USMA superintendent, 1945-49; commanding general of U.S. forces in Korea, 1953; U.S. chief of staff 1955-59; chairman of the Joint Chiefs of Staff, 1962-64; ambassador to South Vietnam 1964-65; special consultant to President Lyndon Johnson 1965-69.
Born: 1901, Keytesville, Mo.
Died: April 19, 1987, Washington, D.C.
Contributions: During his stint as superintendent, Taylor helped modernize the institution's curriculum. He implemented a formalized program for leadership instruction and also helped to form the department of behavioral sciences.
During World War II, Taylor commanded the 101st Airborne Division. In 1944, Taylor was the first U.S. general to arrive in France during the Allied Invasion. He commanded a parachute assault in the Normandy Campaign and in the Battle of the Bulge. He served as the U.S Army's chief of staff from 1955 to 1959. In 1961 he served as President John F. Kennedy's military adviser. He advocated the maintenance of conventional infantry as a prudent alternative to nuclear weapons in war.
Fact: Taylor established the USMA Preparatory School in Newburgh on June 25, 1946. The Maxwell D. Taylor Leadership award is presented to the graduate cadet candidate selected by a special board for being tops in overall excellence.
Quote: "Unless you are prepared to use our planes to knock out Cuban planes, then you shouldn't have started the thing in the first place." — Taylor during the Kennedy administration, on the Bay of Pigs invasion.

> **'The discipline which makes the soldiers of a free country reliable in battle is not to be gained by harsh or tyrannical treatment. On the contrary, such treatment is far more likely to destroy than to make an army.'**
>
> **John M. Schofield**
> defining discipline during an address as USMA superintendent in 1879

BREAKING BARRIERS

‘With the corps, I don't think race and gender played a major role, if any.’

Sakima A.G. Brown
1998 West Point graduate

Right, In 1877, Henry O. Flipper became the first African American to graduate from the U.S. Military Academy at West Point.

Black grads take top posts in Army

Dazell Green remembers the day his daughter told him she wanted to go to the U.S. Military Academy.

Green had been at a community gathering in the City of Poughkeepsie, about a 45-minute drive from West Point. A community activist had told the group they should encourage sending their children to one of the military academies because they have so much to offer.

Green returned home, told his family about the speech he heard that day and asked his children who wanted to go.

"My daughter Sakima, age 7 at the time, stood up and said, 'I do,' " Green said.

Thanks to inspiration from her father and a lot of hard work, Capt. Sakima A.G. Brown, Class of 1998, brought about her dream. Today, she has the distinction of being the first African American from the City of Poughkeepsie to graduate from West Point. Brown went on to Officers' School in Virginia.

Over the two centuries the U.S. Military Academy has been in existence, the impact of African Americans has grown.

Black cadets make up approximately 8 percent of the 4,000 cadets who attend the USMA. The Class of 2004 included 103 African Americans out of its 1,179 cadets, or 8.7 percent.

More than 1,000 graduate

The number of black graduates of the USMA totals 1,654 through the Class of 2001. The 1,000th black graduated from West Point in 1991.

■ James W. Smith became the first African American admitted to the academy in 1870.

■ Henry O. Flipper became the first African American to graduate in 1877. The son of slave parents, Flipper was stationed with the 10th U.S. Cavalry after graduation.

When Col. William Rufus Shafter became Flipper's commanding officer in 1881, he replaced Flipper as quartermaster and planned to replace him as commissary when he could find a replacement. When Flipper discovered commissary funds missing from his trunk, he tried to conceal the loss until the money could be found. However, he was accused by his commanding officer of embezzlement and conduct unbecoming an officer. He was court-martialed and found

U.S. Military Academy Archives

HENRY O. FLIPPER

Title: USMA Class of 1877; officer in Tenth Cavalry 1878-81; special agent to Department of Justice 1893-1901; interpreter/translator for the U.S. Senate 1919-21; assistant to secretary of the Interior 1921-23; prominent surveyor and engineer in Latin America and American Southwest.

Born: March 31, 1856, in Thomasville, Ga.

Died: May 3, 1940, in Atlanta.

Contributions: Henry O. Flipper graduated from the U.S. Military Academy in 1877 as the institution's first black graduate. He was the fifth to enter West Point.

After graduation, he was stationed with the 10th U.S. Cavalry and assigned to frontier duty. He was discharged from the Army in 1882 for conduct unbecoming an officer. In 1976, the Army Board of Corrections cleared Henry Flipper's name and issued an honorable discharge certificate to his descendants. He was also awarded a posthumous pardon.

After his army career, Flipper enjoyed a career as surveyor and engineer in the Southwest and Latin America. He worked as a surveyor for several American land companies between 1883 and 1891 in Chihuahua and Sonora.

He opened a civil and mining engineering office in Nogales, Ariz., in 1887. Beginning in 1901, Flipper spent 11 years in northern Mexico as an engineer and legal assistant to mining companies.

After working for the U.S. Senate as a translator and interpreter and serving as assistant to the secretary of the interior, he worked in Venezuela from 1923 to 1930 for William F. Buckley Sr.'s Pantepec Petroleum Company.

He retired in 1931 and lived the rest of his life in Atlanta with his brother.

Fact: An annual West Point award in Flipper's memory is presented to the graduate who best exemplifies "the highest qualities of leadership, self-discipline, and perseverance in the face of unusual difficulties as a cadet."

Quote: "I was thoroughly humiliated, discouraged and heart-broken at the time. I preferred to go forth in the world and by my subsequent conduct as an honorable man and by my character disprove the charges." — Flipper, after being discharged from the military.

Benjamin O. Davis, Jr.

Born: 1912 in Washington, D.C.

Title: USMA Class of 1936.

Contribution: Benjamin O. Davis, Jr. assumed command of the first black air unit, the Tuskegee Airmen, in 1942. He led this unit in 200 escort missions, and they never lost a bomber to German aircraft fire. He later assumed command of the all-Black 332nd Fighter Group with which he flew 60 combat missions. He was awarded the Distinguished Flying Cross and the silver star. He was promoted to brigadier general in 1953, and like his father before him, became the highest-ranking black officer in the armed forces.

---

innocent of embezzlement but guilty of conduct unbecoming an officer. Flipper was dismissed from the Army in 1882.

In 1976, the Army Board of Corrections concluded Flipper's punishment and subsequent conviction were "unduly harsh and unjust." An honorable discharge certificate was presented, and President Bill Clinton awarded him a posthumous pardon in 1999.

Flipper did work as a surveyor, engineer, translator and interpreter after his Army career. He worked for the U.S. Senate as a translator and served as assistant to the Secretary of the Interior. He died May 3, 1940, in Atlanta at 84.

■ Ohio natives John H. Alexander and Charles Young became the second and third African-American graduates in 1887 and 1889, respectively. The fourth was Benjamin O. Davis Jr. of Ohio, who became the first African-American general officer in the Air Force.

■ Roscoe Robinson Jr. graduated from the academy in 1951. Thirty-one years later, he became the first African-American four-star general in the history of the U.S. Army.

■ In 1962, Fred A. Gordon was the 41st African-American graduate. Twenty-five years later, he became the academy's first African-American commandant.

■ David Ramsay became the 47th African American to graduate from the USMA in 1964, with honors and the rank of cadet captain. Ramsay was one of the first African Americans to fly with the U.S. Air Force ThunderBirds. Ramsay was killed in action in Vietnam on Aug. 17, 1970. He was a recipient of the Purple Heart, Distinguished Flying Cross, two Meritorious Service Awards, Bronze Star, Vietnam Campaign Medal, Air Force Good Conduct Medal, two Air Medals, National Defense Service Medal, Silver Star and Vietnam Service Medal. A memorial was unveiled in his honor in his hometown of Roxbury, Mass., on Nov. 20, 1999.

■ Brig. Gen. Vincent K. Brooks, deputy director of operations and the chief military spokesman for the 2003 U.S.-allied coalition war with Iraq, graduated from West Point in 1980. In his senior year he was the first African-American cadet to be elected first captain, the highest ranking cadet officer and leader of the corps of cadets. In 2002, he was the first member of his class to be nominated for flag rank (a general officer), and he is the third member of his family to reach the rank of general. In June 2002, his brother, Brig. Gen. Leo Brooks Jr., was named West Point's commandant of cadets, a position second only to superintendent at the academy.

While African-American women like Sakima Brown could have faced barriers, she said she did not.

"With the corps, I don't think race and gender played a major role, if any," she said. "We were overcoming obstacles on a daily basis. It was teamwork, teamwork. If one doesn't make it, then the whole group doesn't make it."

ROSCOE ROBINSON JR.

Title: USMA Class of 1951, commanding general of 82nd Airborne Division 1978-80, commanding general of U.S. Army, Japan, 1980-82, U.S. representative to NATO Military Committee 1982-85.
Born: Oct. 11, 1928, in St. Louis.
Died: July 22, 1993, in Washington.
Contributions: Robinson saw action in the Korean War shortly after graduation. He served as a battalion commander in Vietnam. His medals included the Distinguished Service Medal, the Silver Star with Oak Leaf Cluster, the Legion of Merit with two Oak Leaf Clusters, the Distinguished Flying Cross and the Bronze Star Medal.

In 1987, after his retirement, he was named to oversee the work of a panel that re-examined the Korean War performance of some black Army units that were criticized at the time.

Robinson received the Distinguished Graduate Award at a cadet review in May 1993. The award is given to those whose "character, distinguished service and stature draw wholesome comparison to the qualities for which West Point stands, as epitomized by its motto — 'Duty, Honor, Country.' "

Fact: In 1982, Robinson became the first African-American four-star general in the Army.

> **'**Throughout a military career that took him to the pinnacle of his profession, he overcame adversity with courage and an enduring dedication to duty.**'**

Statement on Distinguished Graduate Award for Roscoe Robinson Jr. first African-American four-star general in U.S. Army

Right, USMA Superintendent Lt. Gen. Daniel W. Christman speaks to two veterans of the Buffalo Soldier regiments, Sgt. Sanders Matthews, center, and Staff Sgt. George Washington Howe, during the 34th annual Buffalo Soldiers Ceremony at the USMA, 1996.

The Buffalo Soldiers

It had nothing to do with where they were from, and the nickname of the men of the 9th and 10th U.S. Cavalry Regiment was thought up by their Indian foes, but the "Buffalo Soldiers" adopted it with pride.

The black American troops who served on the western frontier after the Civil War were a horse cavalry first created by the Army Reorganization Act of 1866. Various regiments of Buffalo Soldiers served in the U.S. Army in one capacity or another for about 80 years.

Early on, the 9th and 10th Cavalry took part in 11 campaigns against hostile Indians, engaging in over 125 battles and skirmishes, most in Texas and New Mexico. Besides participating in these battles, they guarded borders, apprehended bandits and cattle thieves and maintained order in unruly territories.

In the Spanish-American War, both regiments were active. They both took part in the Battle of San Juan Hill, while the 10th extricated the "Rough Riders" from difficulty and then joined with them in the assault on the blockhouse.

After the turn of the century, there was duty in the Philippines, and later a detachment of the 9th Cavalry was assigned to West Point to help training cadets in riding and mounted drill. A

Lee Ferris

squadron of the 10th Cavalry eventually replaced it, and remained at West Point until its inactivation in 1946. Today, an athletic field that was once known as Cavalry Plain is dedicated to the Buffalo Soldiers.

Twenty-three men of the 9th and 10th Cavalry were awarded the Congressional Medal of Honor.

Women overcome chilly reception

Melissa Parrish and Alison Adas were barely a year old when Kathleen Snook graduated from West Point some 20 years ago.

But today they are benefiting from the trailblazing decision of Snook and others to be among the first women to enroll at West Point.

Snook graduated from West Point in 1980, the first class to include women, and now teaches math at the academy. Parrish and Adas are both seniors.

"Things have definitely changed, and women are much more accepted and integrated," Snook said.

However, women still cannot hold some combat positions in the military, and some people still object to their presence.

"It's so important for the military academy to be representative of society," Snook said. "Shouldn't we be educating all kinds of leaders for military and societal leadership?"

The class that entered West Point last July was the 26th to include women. Women have remained at about 16 percent of the incoming class each year.

In 1975, Congress ordered the integration of the military, and women entered West Point in 1976.

Andrea Lee Hollen was the first woman to receive a West Point diploma in 1980.

But in 1976, women were not well received, academy historian Stephen Grove said. An overwhelming number of cadets and officers were hostile to the idea of women there.

But now, more than 20 years later, "it's a different world," Grove said. Women have made the academy more "humane."

Even in 1989, change was dramatic as Cadet Kristin Baker became the first woman brigade commander — West Point's top cadet honor.

The harassment of the plebes, which the academy had been trying to eliminate for decades, also began to decline with the arrival of women.

Women in the academy today are much more comfortable with themselves, Snook said.

Neither Parrish nor Adas said they have had a problem or said they felt out of place in the male-dominated academy.

"I never saw any sexual discrimination. I have not encountered any form of sexual harassment," Parrish said. "I don't think it's an issue. But you need to be aware of it."

Parrish, who is barely five feet tall, said her physical size can be a drawback.

"Appearance is important," she said, "and a lot of times a big strong male in a leadership position — that will be an advantage."

Adas said she wasn't sure how she would be treated by her superiors when she arrived, whether they would ease up because she was a woman.

"I was pleasantly surprised," she said. "It didn't happen. I don't ever feel that there's a barrier based on gender."

A portrait of Andrea Lee Hollen, the first woman to graduate from the U.S. Military Academy at West Point.

West Point Museum Collections U.S. Military Academy

Andrea Lee Hollen

Born: February 17, 1959, in Pennsylvania.

Title: USMA Class of 1980.

Contributions: A Rhodes Scholar, Hollen was the first woman graduate of the U.S. Military Academy.

Hollen was the first female to receive her diploma because of her class rank. The first 50 to receive diplomas in a graduating class go by class rank, and she was the first female in the top 50 and thus, the first graduate.

Hollen went to Oxford for her master's degree and was a major when she left the Army in 1992.

Kristin Baker

Born: May 23, 1968, in North Dakota.

Title: USMA Class of 1990.

Contributions: Baker was the first woman brigade commander, the top ranking cadet in terms of leadership, of the U.S. Corps of Cadets. This is the same position held by John J. Pershing and Douglas MacArthur when they were cadets.

Baker is still in the Army and is stationed in Washington, D.C.

THE FIRST DAY

Right center, Sakima Green gets the traditional cadet haircut on R-Day. While men receive crew cuts, the women have their hair cut short.

Kathy McLaughlin photos

Above, Green takes a physical fitness test on Reception Day, the start of a six-week basic training session for plebes.

‘Sakima said she was going to West Point, and she's done it.’

Dazell Green,
speaking about his daughter,
Reception Day 1994

THE FIRST DAY

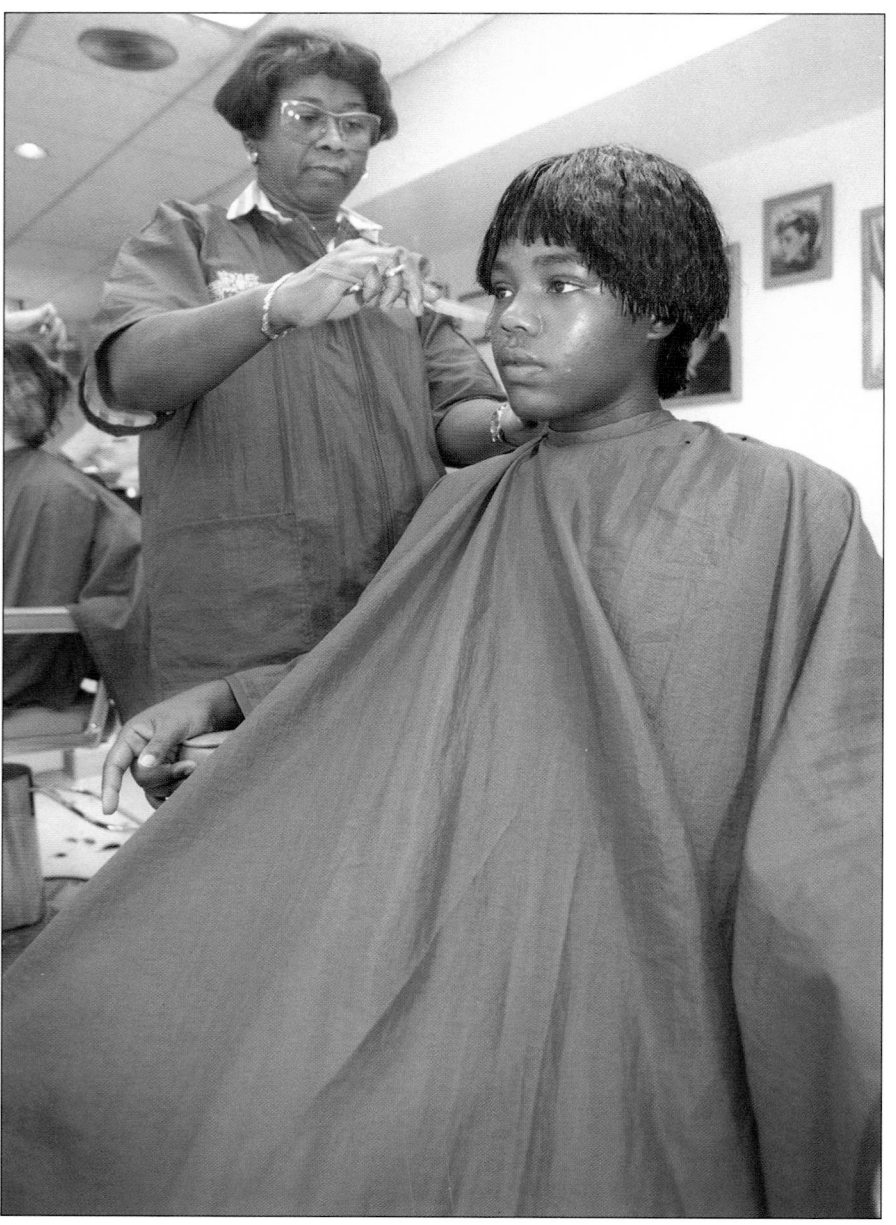

Below, Sakima Green signs in under the watchful eye of her company's 1st Sgt. T.J. McGrath, but she has to stretch as she carefully keeps behind the designated line on the floor.

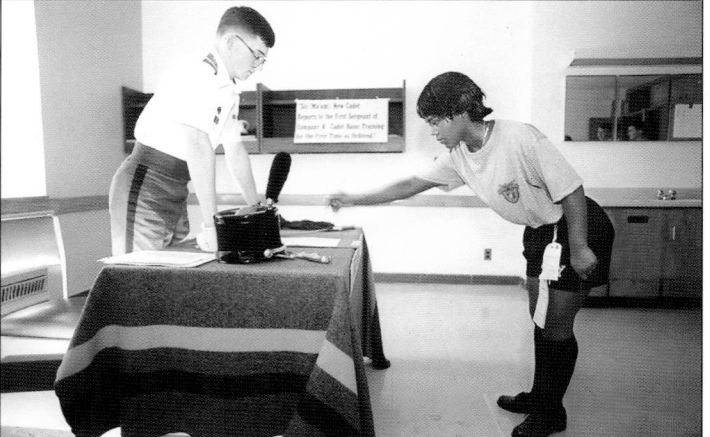

Girl lands dream spot at the Point

Sakima Brown, who is from Poughkeepsie, was profiled by the Poughkeepsie Journal on her first day as a cadet at the USMA in 1994. She was single then, and her last name was Green. After growing up in the City of Poughkeepsie, N.Y., she attended the private Oakwood School in a nearby community before entering the U.S. Military Academy. She graduated from West Point in 1998, and the following week, she married another academy graduate.

Since she was a little girl, Sakima Green dreamed about going to West Point. And Monday she realized that dream when she traded her civilian clothes for military issue – a pair of gray trousers and a white shirt – during Reception Day for the Class of 1998.

"I figure if I can make it through here, then there's no stopping me," said Sakima Green, of Poughkeepsie.

Her parents are confident she will. "Sakima said she was going to West Point, and she's done it," said Dazell Green about his daughter.

"The first thing that came to my mind as we walked

'I figure if I can make it through here, then there's no stopping me.'

Sakima Green, new cadet, R-Day 1994

While Sakima Green listens to drill instructions, some of her fellow cadets carry their assigned clothes and duffle bags.

'Yes, it's a stressful environment. But we're building leaders of the future.'

1st Sgt. T.J. McGrath, R-Day 1994

Kathy McLaughlin photos

Sakima Green waits with fellow members of Alpha Company on one of the many stops during her first day at the academy.

around the Point was that she's a pioneer. She'll be a great leader – that's what pioneers are," he said.

During R-Day 1994, about 1,160 new cadets reported to the U.S. Military Academy. They went through admissions processing, were fitted with their initial issue of military clothing, got haircuts, and took their first lessons in marching, military courtesy and discipline.

They ended the day marching before their families and taking the Oath of Allegiance. R-Day is an initiation of sorts to six weeks of Basic Training, known by all who have gone through it as "Beast Barracks."

Green, a 1993 graduate of Oakwood School in the Town of Poughkeepsie, spent 1994 at the U.S. Military Academy Prep School in Fort Monmouth, N.J. She is a "prepster" in military lingo, and she said the experience will give her an edge over the other new cadets. She was confident about the four years before her.

"I know how to march, how to shine shoes, how to salute. We're expected to know more and are automatically given leadership roles," the 18-year-old said.

All went smoothly for Green as she progressed through her training: She was fitted for her uniform, got her hair trimmed to Army regulation and was instructed on the proper way to salute.

Her problem came when she had to manage a long stretch to a table – with toes at "the line" – and sign in with her company. After several tries, each followed by a loud reprimand from 1st Sgt. T.J. McGrath, she was finally successful.

"Yes, it's a stressful environment," McGrath explained later. "But we're building leaders of the future. We have to make sure these people can deal with the stress. The Army is not an easy lifestyle."

Teamwork crucial

At the orientation center, Lt. Col. Dean Russell greeted cadets and parents. He warned the group of the rigors of the training – the emotional and physical demands – and he left them with a few words of advice: "You've got to have a sense of humor. ... You must remember that everything is based on teamwork. ... And most important, take one day at a time."

The cadets, from every state in the nation as well as eight foreign countries, had only a few minutes to say goodbye to loved ones.

Luke Herbert, 18 and from Rhode Island, appeared calm as he spent a few last minutes with his parents, Maureen and Peter.

"It hasn't quite hit me entirely yet, but I'm starting to get a little nervous," Herbert said. "My plan is to keep a sense of humor and try to have some fun."

Kathy McLaughlin photos

Above, An upper classman checks Sakima Green's tags on R-Day. The tags indicate the progress she has made moving into the academy.

‘You've got to have a sense of humor ... And most important, take one day at a time.’

Lt. Col. Dean Russell
R-Day 1994

Above, Sakima Green lines up with fellow members of Alpha Company.

'The first thing that came to my mind as we walked around the Point was that she's a pioneer. She'll be a great leader – that's what pioneers are.'

Dazell Green, Poughkeepsie, speaking about his daughter Sakima, who entered West Point in 1994

Kathy McLaughlin

Sakima Green salutes an upper classman prior to lining up for her next check-in station on R-Day (Reception Day) in 1994. Green graduated in 1998.

Chapter 7

STUDENTS & TRAINING
BUILDING AND TESTING LEADERS OF CHARACTER

Shaun Lenard Marzett, left, and Matthew David Magennis, center, embrace after graduation in 2002.

Karl Rabe

'It's a tough thing, getting through West Point, and I think the country expects it to be that way.'

George Seip, Class of 1942, veteran of World War II, Korean War and Vietnam War

'It's hard academically, physically and emotionally. ... They don't cut you any slack.'

George Seip, Class of 1942

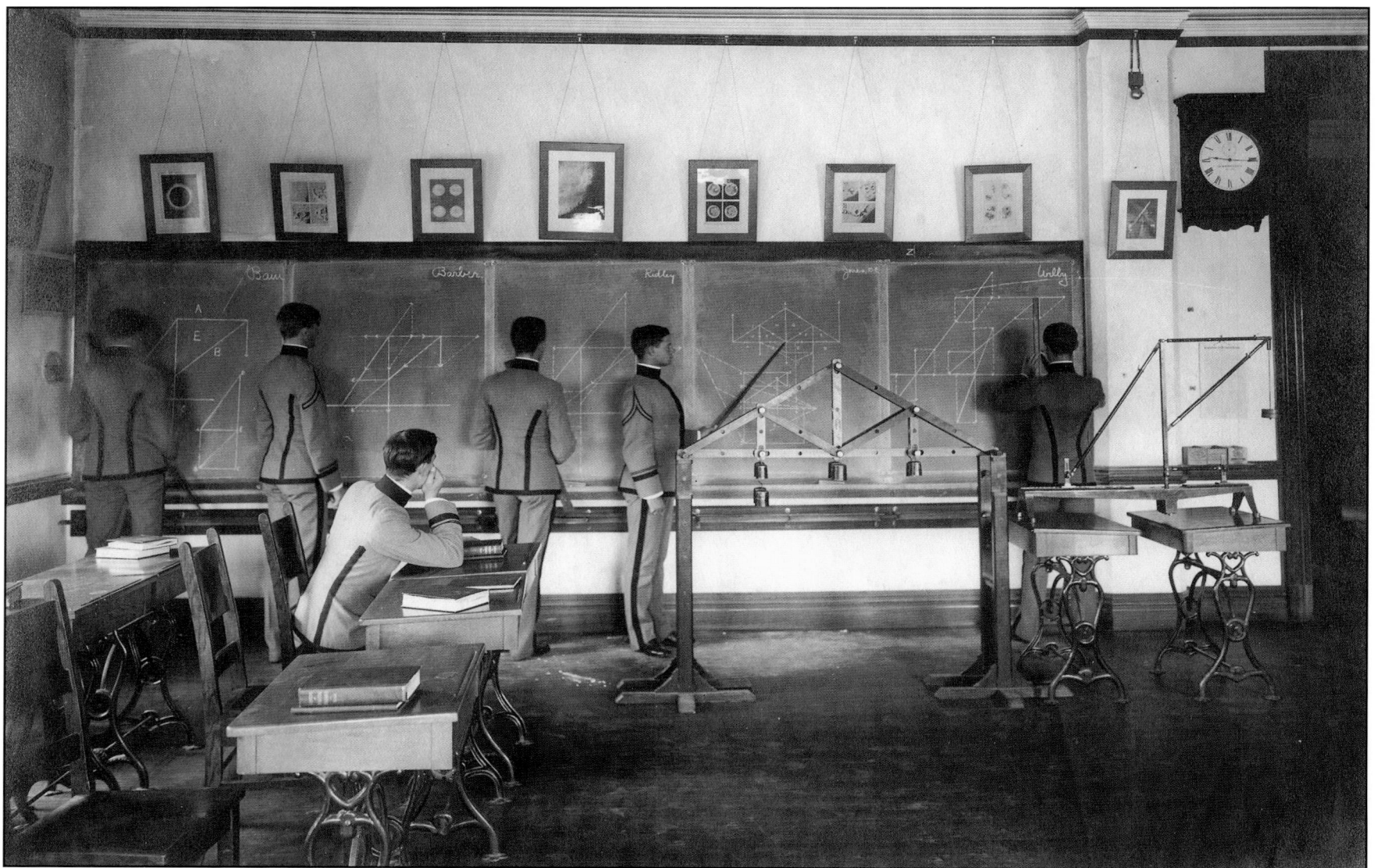

U.S. Military Academy cadets attend a class in mechanics on Oct. 1, 1903.

THE CORPS OF CADETS

Discipline molds leaders, forges bonds

For more than 200 years, the U.S. Military Academy at West Point has been in the business of producing leaders. The bottom line?

Ulysses S. Grant. Robert E. Lee. Dwight D. Eisenhower. Douglas MacArthur. George S. Patton. Omar Bradley. H. Norman Schwarzkopf.

All were members of the "Long Gray Line."

Two of West Point's 58,000 graduates — Ulysses S. Grant and Dwight D. Eisenhower — became president of the United States. Six served as chairmen of the Joint Chiefs of Staff. There are astronauts, members of Congress, governors, judges, authors and captains of industry who started their careers in the Corps of Cadets.

"It's a place for people who want to become leaders," said Col. Michael Jones, director of admissions at West Point and a member of the Class of 1970.

"Graduates are commissioned as second lieutenants in the U.S. Army and have a five-year service commitment. In exchange for that commitment, you get a great education and leadership training and share in an experience that will shape the rest of your life," he said.

Diversity is key at West Point

There is no such thing as a typical cadet, West Point historian Stephen Grove said. By design, the academy attracts and trains men and women from all socio-economic, racial and religious backgrounds, from every congressional district in the nation and from several

'It's a place for people who want to become leaders.'

Col. Michael Jones
West Point director of admissions and 1970 West Point graduate

Darryl Bautista

Above, West Point Cadet Mark Thompson of Simi Valley, Calif., sprints through a water crossing during the 2001 Sandhurst contest. Teams from West Point, Canada and the United Kingdom took part in the military competition.

Left, The Corps of Cadets stands in formation at 6:55 a.m. in front of Washington Hall before breakfast.

Spencer Ainsley

LONG GRAY LINE

West Point adopted gray as the color of the uniform in 1816 because of an embargo. It couldn't get indigo ink to make blue. Gray pants are worn with the uniform in fall and winter; white pants are worn in spring and summer.

Academy grows

■ West Point has about 4,000 cadets because that's the number Congress has mandated for the institution. Prior to 1964, the number was 2,500.

■ Even though cadets can major in such diverse subjects as English, history or political science, every graduating cadet receives a bachelor of science degree.

■ 25 intercollegiate varsity sports and more than 100 organized extracurricular activities.

■ Core curriculum ranges from 26 to 30 courses, depending on major.

foreign countries.

"From its earliest days, West Point has been very representative of the country," Grove said. "By requiring the academy to appoint a cadet from every congressional district, Congress ensured the nation will always feel involved and have a stake in the success of West Point."

With rigorous academic, physical and moral standards, only the best and brightest are accepted to the academy. A profile for the Class of 2004 noted that of 10,893 applicants, 1,188 were admitted. Of those, 91 percent ranked in the top two-fifths of their high school class.

There were 63 high school valedictorians in the class, 686 members of the National Honor Society, 222 high school class presidents, 155 Eagle Scouts and 1,045 varsity athletes.

Not all graduate

The academy is not for everyone. About 200 members of each incoming class of plebes quit or are dismissed by the time the class graduates.

Jones, whose son graduated from the academy in 1996 and

whose daughter graduated in 2001, said those who survived "gain tremendous maturity and organizational skills. You learn to persevere to achieve a goal and you develop a willingness to sacrifice what you want as an individual for the benefit of a group."

You also become part of a brotherhood, said Cornwall resident George Seip, 85. A member of the Class of 1942, Seip said he "graduated right into World War II. I'm a veteran of Korea and Vietnam, too."

Seip, who retired in 1970 as a lieutenant colonel, said the rigors of life as a West Point cadet fostered a kinship among all those who experienced them.

"It's a tough thing, getting through West Point, and I think the country expects it to be that way," he said.

"America wants cadets to live up to a higher standard. It's hard academically, physically and emotionally, and they don't cut you any slack. If you mess up, you're out. There are no second chances. If you get through it, you feel a bond with those who came before you and those who come after you. Most turn out to be pretty good people. I think history proves that."

Commencement traditions made of gold and silver

Not long after earning a class ring, graduates of West Point will often get a wedding ring.

The tradition of cadets getting married on graduation day dates to 1835, according to Stephen Grove, U.S. Military Academy historian.

It was that year cadets were first barred from getting married while at West Point, prompting a rush to the altar each graduation day since.

But it is the tradition of graduates getting a class ring, once unique to West Point, that has spread to most other academic institutions.

"The ring is really the most notable," Grove said. "But they didn't always have rings; some years they selected cuff links instead."

Why or how the tradition started is unknown.

The oldest military academy in the nation, West Point is rich with tradition from its Cadet Honor Code — which states "a cadet shall not lie, cheat,

A cadet ring

steal or tolerate those who do" — to its enduring commitment to "Duty, Honor, Country," to the "Long Gray Line" of West Point graduates who have gone on to be leaders on the battlefield, the halls of government and the corporate world.

When graduates are commissioned as Army second lieutenants, they are required to give a silver dollar to the first person who salutes them, according to another long-standing tradition. That practice goes back to at least the 19th century.

Some believe there is another practice that began at the academy and has become universal.

"There is some claim that one of the professors used chalk on a board during the 1820s," Grove said, "which is thought to be one of the first times chalk was used for education."

Then and now

In the beginning, there was no national testing and applying to West Point was much like getting into regular colleges. High school principals and family friends wrote endorsements and selection was informal, without consideration of class rank and tests. Some people were admitted even without the equivalent of a high school education while others already had college degrees.

Today, applicants have to meet stringent academic requirements as well as leadership and physical criteria. They also need a recommendation from a congressional representative.

Right, a cadet wears a full dress uniform, including a shako hat with black feathers. The jacket stripes indicate this is a cadet lieutenant in his senior year.

U.S. Military Academy Archives

West Point cadets pose for a photo, circa 1900.

It takes even more work to become a general

■ The cost of the four-year West Point experience, including tuition, room, board, medical and dental expenses, is paid by the U.S. government. Cadets, as members of the Army, receive an annual salary of $7,200, which helps to pay for uniforms, books, a personal computer, supplies and incidental living expenses. A deposit of $2,400 to $3,000 is required to cover costs during the first year.

■ The USMA ranks fourth among the nation's colleges and universities in number of Rhodes scholars; it has had 70. Since 1973, 32 cadets have won Hertz Foundation fellowships in Applied Physical Science disciplines, and 11 cadets since 1983 have been awarded Marshall Scholarships to attend a British university.

■ West Point does not teach the "art of war." Its main curriculum is in the sciences and humanities. If you want to become a general, you have to go to the Command and General Staff College, and then the U.S. Army War College.

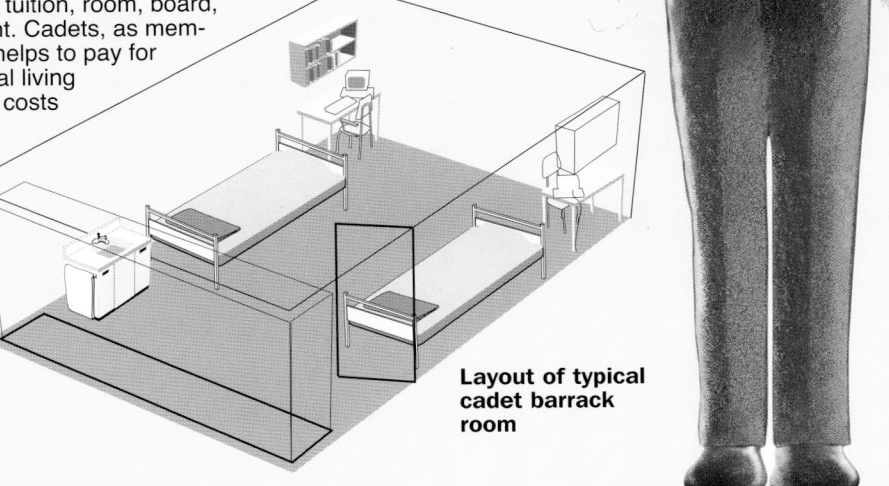

Layout of typical cadet barrack room

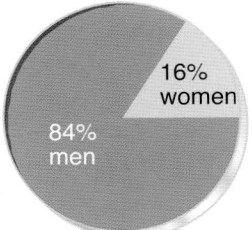

The school in 2003

Male cadets predominate, but student diversity has grown.

16% women

84% men

■ 4,004 full-time students, as of February 2003.

■ For 2003-2004 school year, about 12,600 applied, about 1,230 will be admitted.

■ Students come from 53 states and territories and 18 other countries.

Percentages

■ Out of state: 92%
■ Reside on campus: 100%
■ International: 0.9%
■ African Americans: 8%
■ Asian Americans: 5%
■ Hispanic Americans: 6%
■ Native Americans: 0.5%

More than an academy

■ West Point is not just a campus or military post, it's actually a military reservation.

■ The U.S. established a military college so it wouldn't have to depend on foreign engineers during times of conflict.

Larry Seil illustrations

'We're looking for a well-rounded student, academically and physically.'

Darby McNulty, executive officer of admissions

U.S. Military Academy Archives

As part of their physical regimen, hundreds of U.S. Military Academy cadets perform calisthenics in the central barracks area on March 17, 1904.

MAKING THE CUT

Tough scrutiny ensures quality

Adam Cerniglia of Wappingers Falls doesn't know what he would have done if he hadn't been accepted to West Point. "I really didn't want to go to any other school," the graduate of Roy C. Ketcham High School said.

Cerniglia was one of 10,890 applicants for the West Point Class of 2004. When basic training began in July 2000, 1,188 of them reported as the academy's newest cadets.

Representing less than 11 percent of the applicant pool, these were the survivors of one of the most demanding college selection processes in the country.

They were the ones who met not only the stringent academic requirements, but leadership and physical requirements as well, all accompanied by a recommendation from a congressional representative.

But there are other ways to gain admission to the U.S. Military Academy.

The Secretary of the Army is allocated cadetships for children of career military personnel, deceased or disabled Armed Forces veterans and recipients of the Medal of Honor.

Those enrolled in a Junior or Senior Army Reserve Officer Training Corps program are eligible, as are soldiers of the Regular Army, Army Reserve and Army National Guard.

Limiting number of cadets

The number of applicants admitted varies slightly each year in order to keep the total enrollment at 4,000. Narrowing the applicant pool to 1,100 or so is no simple matter.

"It's a daunting process," said Darby McNulty, executive officer of admissions. "The first thing we do is try to break it down so it's not so intimidating."

To do this, McNulty strongly suggests potential applicants start the process early. Because most congressmen won't accept a request for a nomination after the fall, he said applicants should get started in the spring of their junior year in high school.

Also, if a health problem is discovered during a physical, early treatment may be needed to help the applicant meet physical requirements before deadline.

Most applicants are varsity athletes when they apply, giving them a strong advantage in that category. Of those accepted for the Class of

Spencer Ainsley

Cadet Betty Simbert, Class of 2002, practices a routine with the USMA cheerleading squad inside Cullum Hall at West Point.

> **'I was a straight-A student in high school with very little effort. I came here, and it was a totally different world.'**
>
> **Adam Cerniglia**
> West Point cadet

Rigid rules teach cadets essential order and discipline

In their dormitory rooms, cadets have to stack their books on the shelves in descending order, beginning with the tallest one on down.

They have to fold the socks in their drawers so the crease of the roll resembles a smiley face. They have to hang their uniforms in the closet in a particular order and with a given amount of space in between each garment.

OK, it's the U.S. Military Academy. It has rules and regulations like the rest of the Army, maybe even more so.

But what's the deal with the books and smiley socks?

It's "to establish and maintain good order and discipline," according to the U.S. Corps of Cadet Standard Operating Procedure, a big, fat rules and regulations book that tells cadets how to dress, walk, talk and treat fellow cadets and superiors.

Some examples:

■ "When the door of a cadet's room is closed, persons desiring entry will knock and await acknowledgment before entering."

■ "A male cadet may offer his arm to a lady when walking conditions permit."

And so forth.

What's the point? The Reserve Officers' Training Corps, through which 75 percent of Army officers are commissioned by going to college and taking military science courses, doesn't impose these kinds of rigid demands on its people.

But ROTC isn't the world's premier military academy.

"If West Point's core values are Duty, Honor and Country, this targets duty," said Maj. Tony Burgess (Class of 1990), the regulations and discipline officer for the Corps of Cadets.

"Without these rules, it's chaos and you're not going to get the West Point experience. It prepares them to be successful in the Army" where the key to success is following orders, preferably to the letter, no matter how arcane or irrelevant they may seem, Burgess said.

2004, 1,045 (88 percent) had played varsity sports in high school, and nearly half of them had been team captains.

"We're looking for a well-rounded student, academically and physically," McNulty said.

Rather than looking at grade point averages, admissions counselors are more concerned with how a student ranks in comparison to his or her peers. Nearly three quarters of cadets were in the top 20 percent of their high school class.

Applicants need blessing of congressional representatives

After a prospective cadet passes the physical and academic requirements, there's still the obstacle of a congressional letter of recommendation.

Because each senator and representative can nominate only 10 candidates, the competition at this step can be intense.

"That was definitely the most rigorous and nerve-racking part of the process," Cerniglia said.

He appeared before a committee appointed by U.S. Rep. Sue

Kelly, R-Katonah. After the committee interviewed him about why he believed he was qualified, he earned the nomination from Kelly's office. In April of his senior year, three months before basic training, Cerniglia received his letter of acceptance.

After classes began, however, he found he hadn't anticipated how difficult it would be.

"I was a straight-A student in high school with very little effort," he said. "I came here, and it was a totally different world."

He said it was the support and mentoring of some upperclassmen in his company that helped him get through the first difficult year.

"There's a tremendous amount of support here," McNulty said. The guidance from upperclassmen is what keeps the cadet retention rate around 80 percent, he said.

McNulty also points to the lengthy and competitive admissions process as a way of keeping the retention rate high, by allowing only the strongest of the candidates in.

"It's a very demanding four years here; that's why we cover all our bases," McNulty said. "It's a tough, but fair, process."

Rigorous demands keep cadets in top competitive shape

A year after entering the U.S. Military Academy, New Paltz High School graduate Sebastian Salas continues his adjustment to a demanding military life.

This includes fine-tuning his backhand in tennis. Salas completed his freshman season on the men's tennis team with a 17-12 record in singles.

But being an athlete is only a small part of Salas' physical and mental challenges at West Point. Being a student at the academy combines three educational disciplines — military, academic and athletic. The days are long and require strong time management skills by cadets.

"It was more than I expected," Salas said. "With the rigid schedule, I don't have much free time. I regret it sometimes when times are hard. But I like it to the extent I know I'm getting a great education."

Juan Salas, a native of Chile, was also a stranger to West Point before his son expressed an interest in the academy.

"It's an amazing institution to be a part of," Juan Salas said. "I personally have a lot of respect for those kids. They work very hard and they have to be highly motivated to stay there and go through the rigorous military, academic and sports programs. I think

Americans should be pretty much at ease with the leaders they are making."

Physical fitness is only a part of being in the academy; yet, it's one of the many demands a cadet must endure. They must have the discipline to remain in shape.

"It forces you to prioritize," said Peter Quimby, a retired Army captain and former West Point baseball player from Rhinebeck. "You learn pretty quickly only the most fit will survive. Once there, if you can't prioritize, you can get eaten up in the system."

Twice a year, all cadets, including athletes, are required to take the Army Physical Fitness Test. The test has three parts, a 2-mile run and a check to see how many push-ups and sit-ups a cadet can do in a 2-minute span. The cadets are graded based on age and gender.

The Army also will keep tabs of a cadet's weight, and cadets must meet requirements based on age and gender.

Highland's Gene Ventriglia, the women's soccer coach at Army, started the program in 1985.

"From my perspective, we're getting much more dedicated and skilled athletes," he said. "I wouldn't have thought 15 or 20 years ago, we'd reach the level it has now. The cadets are so much more aware of what needs to be done."

‘You learn pretty quickly only the most fit will survive.’

Peter Quimby
retired Army captain and former West Point baseball player

GETTING MARCHING ORDERS

After saying goodbye to their parents at Eisenhower Hall on R-Day (Reception Day) in June 2001, new candidates take a tense and silent three-minute bus ride across campus to begin the registration process before they are assigned a room.

Spencer Ainsley photos

Above, A female candidate leads a long line of men moving toward a check-in station during Reception Day activities at Thayer Hall. Women have been attending the academy since 1976 and represent about 16 percent of the Corps of Cadets.

Right, Cadet John Nakat of Honolulu, who graduated in 2001, concentrates on his studies in West Point's Grant Hall. Cadets must fulfill a rigorous academic curriculum.

Above, The cadets' freshly-laundered uniforms are placed on racks outside the cadet barracks.

A new candidate sits motionless while getting the traditional haircut on R-Day (Reception Day) at West Point. While many new candidates arrived at West Point with short hair, this man's hair was longer and bleached blond. The haircut, always done with an electric razor, takes about three minutes.

Left, Ryan Mark Ciovacco, right, of the Town of Poughkeepsie, and a member of USMA Class of 2004, speaks with plebe Justin McFarlin of Monroe during the 6:55 a.m. formation in front of Washington Hall. Once cadets enter their second year, they have the responsibility of nurturing the development of one freshman for the year.

Above, A view from Trophy Point shows one of the giant links in the chain that stretched from West Point to Constitution Island during the Revolutionary War to keep British ships from sailing up the Hudson River.

Left, The insignia of rank worn by the first captain of the Corps of Cadets.

Spencer Ainsley photos

Right, This ornate handle is on the main entrance door to the Cadet Chapel. The chapel, built of granite in the form of a cross, is noted for its military Gothic architecture. It was dedicated in 1910 and is used for Protestant services.

Spencer Ainsley photos

TO THE AMERICAN SOLDIER

Above, The American Soldier Monument, dedicated in 1980, honors Americans killed in combat. The monument was designed by Felix de Weldon, who sculpted the classic scene of soldiers raising the flag at Iwo Jima.

Opposite page, A worker inside the cadet mess at Washington Hall clears tables in front of the 2,450-square-foot mural that depicts the 20 most decisive battles through the ages. The mural, by T. Loftin Johnson, was the largest mural in New York state when completed in 1936.

Spencer Ainsley photos

Above, Cadet Capt. Brent Lorenzo Dial, of Bowie, Md., commands the attention of a new candidate on R-Day (Reception Day) while teaching the proper form for saluting at the academy. Once new cadets receive the bulk of their clothing and other personal items, they learn how to salute and march in formation under the scrutiny of seasoned cadets.

Above, The bell tower of the Cadet Chapel rises above the academy's fall foliage.

Right, The Corps of Cadets marches in formation.

❝I hope I can share with these cadets some of why this education matters, how it helped me and how it might help them in the Army.**❞**

Michael Wright
USMA Class of 1989, former cadet who returned as a professor

HONING THE MIND

'Rotating faculty' assures expertise

After graduating from the U.S. Military Academy in 1989, Houston native Michael Wright served as an officer in Fort Hood, Texas, in Korea and at other Army posts.

Through a program in which the Army sends officers to earn master's degrees, he was able to return to West Point about four years ago, this time as a social sciences professor.

"I hope I can share with these cadets some of why this education matters, how it helped me and how it might help them in the Army," said Wright, a major who has also served as the dean's executive officer.

With 62 percent of the 500 academic professors serving as temporary "rotating faculty" from the field Army, the academy ensures its students are exposed to the latest ideas in graduate-level study and military service. The remainder are senior military faculty, said Col. George Forsythe, vice dean for education. Both types of professors have doctoral degrees, ensuring cadets get the depth they need, he said.

"We call it a blend of excellence because we get a variety of different perspectives, with everybody working on the same goals," Forsythe said.

West Point has 13 academic departments in the basic sciences, engineering, humanities and social sciences. Course titles range from "Colloquial Arabic," "Military Readings in Chinese" and "Contemporary Creativity," to "Land Use Planning and Management" and "Photonics Engineering."

Morten Ender, an associate professor of sociology, said he was drawn to West Point because he specializes in military history. He is one of the permanent, non-military faculty members.

"I think the curriculum overall is more demanding. All of my courses are more demanding than the courses I taught at civilian schools," he said.

Focus shifts away from engineering

Cadets at West Point used to fall in behind their section marcher and proceed in cadence to every class at the military academy.

Although the title section marcher is still used, the student's duties are limited to taking roll for professors and reporting that cadets are ready to begin class.

As for marching together, that wouldn't be practical. After the late 1950s, West Point started to veer from its one-size-fits-all math, science and engineering curriculum and allowed cadets to take electives.

"We had a heavy emphasis on engineering because of our historical legacy," said Col. George Forsythe, professor and vice dean for education, referring to West Point's transformation from a military garrison during the American Revolution to a corps of artillerymen and engineers, then into the first engineering school in the United States.

Members of the Class of 1962 took 48 classes, including two electives. The curriculum school officials approved for students who graduate in 2005 calls for 40 classes, 10 of which will be electives. There is less emphasis on engineering and more on information technology. The students will take a class their senior year in which they integrate the subject with others. Cadets can also take additional electives beyond the 40 courses.

Humanities subjects rise

School officials have gradually increased arts and humanities courses over the years, Forsythe said. The core curriculum now requires 16 classes in the humanities and social sciences and roughly 14 in math, science and technology.

The changes make sense, he said, since West Point is not simply an Army prep school. Its purpose is to train cadets who will be leaders in military and civilian life, and who will have a lifelong passion for learning.

"It's in the service of liberating the mind and using the sciences as well as the arts," Forsythe said.

"It doesn't make sense for us to say using the equipment is more important than leading the people," he said.

Humanities and social sciences are the most popular majors and fields of study, comprising 55 percent of students. Thirty-three percent pursue engineering, and 12 percent, math and science. All receive a bachelor of science degree.

Morten Ender, an associate professor of sociology in his fourth year teaching at the academy, said the number of sociology majors grew from five to 25 in his first three years. Although much has changed since the late 1950s, the curriculum is still considered traditional compared with other colleges.

Well-rounded education

Although some might think the large core curriculum anachronistic, school and Army officials decided it is the proper way to prepare well-rounded officers, academy historian Stephen Grove said.

Bulletin boards in Thayer Hall show a range of legal courses, from National Security Law and The Law of War for Commanders, to Legal Philosophy and Jurisprudence, and Contracts, Torts, Warranties.

Cadets can also hone in on modern history, military history, or military art and science. They can learn about the histories of joint operations or revolutionary warfare, the history of world religions and the Making of Modern America.

Outside of academics, cadets spend time absorbing the intricacies of soldier skills, military values, field experience and leadership skills. They have two semesters of academics a year, an intersession in which they learn military science, and a summer of training or military detail.

Above, West Point cadets parade in June 1995 prior to graduation day ceremonies.

'We had a heavy emphasis on engineering because of our historical legacy.'

Col. George Forsythe,
Professor and vice dean for education

Right, A team from the United States Military Academy at West Point prepares to land their launch during the annual Sandhurst competition.

Darryl Bautista

West Point Archives

Above, Cadets are trained in fencing techniques during Gym class, 1903.

Bottom right, Cadets perform tank maneuvers with state-of-the-art computer simulated programs. The two cadets here act as tank driver and weapons loader as they navigate across a desert landscape.

Spencer Ainsley

Learning the art and science of fighting

A lot more is required of cadets at the U.S. Military Academy than studying and going to class. As future Army officers, they must become acquainted with the art and science of war.

That means learning tactics and operations from the ground up. And most of all, learning how to take orders and, ultimately, how to give them.

The military part of a cadet's education "is a continual immersion in leader development" starting from private and progressing to corporal, then sergeant and finally lieutenant, said retired Col. Joe Adamczyk (Class of 1972), former brigade tactical officer. It's always conducted during the summer before classes begin.

Freshmen and sophomores do seven weeks of Cadet Summer Training in an area southwest of the main buildings. Junior and senior cadets and a task force of experienced soldiers from the 10th Mountain Division at Fort Drum supervise the training.

During their first summer, the cadets learn basic individual soldiering skills such as marksmanship, mountaineering and preparing for nuclear, biological and chemical attacks.

The next summer, they function within small command units such as squads and platoons. The units conduct tactical missions, such as a raid.

By the third and fourth summers, the older cadets are ready to lead the younger ones. And they go anywhere in the world where there's an Army presence to take over a real Army platoon for several weeks.

Cadets may also attend and graduate from one or more of the rough-and-tumble Army schools, anything from air assault training to combat diving training.

Poe the writer, Leary the rebel didn't last at the Point

Resigning from the U.S. Military Academy at West Point does not doom a former cadet to a lifetime of disgrace and anonymity.

Edgar Allan Poe became one of America's best-known writers after he was booted from the academy in 1831 for absences from roll calls and parades.

Timothy Leary, who preached his turn on, tune in, drop out mantra from an estate in Millbrook in the mid-1960s, entered West Point in 1940 and left in 1941. He then earned a doctorate in psychology from the University of California at Berkeley. He taught there and at Harvard University before becoming an icon of the 1960s counterculture.

He died in 1996.

"I believe it was a military bearing kind of problem," Alan Aimone, special collections librarian at the U. S. Military Academy at West Point, said of Leary's departure. "He was too much of a free spirit."

Reasons for leaving varied

Thumbing the through "Official Register of Officers and Cadets at the United States Military Academy," Aimone found Timothy Francis Leary had among the highest math scores in his class. He was also at the top in other ways.

"He had 152 demerits," Aimone said, as he scanned the record. "That was between July 1, 1940, and May 31, 1941. ... Only three cadets had more."

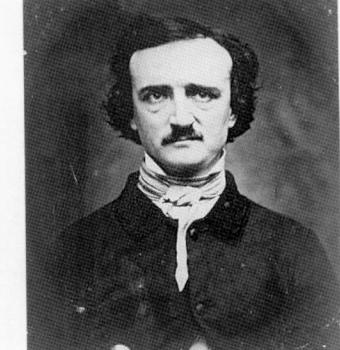

Library of Congress

Some leave the academy for less ignominious reasons.

"Sometimes the people who didn't make it had an offer to go to a Harvard or a Stanford," Aimone said. "These are high-ability people. ... Sometimes they dropped out because of a medical problem, or because they were needed at home to help their family."

Frail health forced Edward Maynard to resign. A member of the Class of 1835, Maynard became a dental surgeon and inventor, the first to fill teeth with gold foil in 1838.

Some still joined the military.

John Cleveland Robinson left in 1838. He later fought in the Mexican War. He retired as a major general from the Army and received the Medal of Honor for gallantry in the Civil War.

Andrew Hull Foote left West Point for the Naval Academy. He founded a temperance society, and his campaigning for sobriety led to the abolishment of the spirit ration in 1862.

Others had political careers.

Benjamin Grubb Humphreys, among a group of cadets dismissed after a student riot on Christmas Eve 1826, became Mississippi's first elected governor after the Civil War. William Gilpin became the first governor of the Territory of Colorado after leaving the academy in 1835.

Above, Edgar Allan Poe
Right, Timothy Leary

Impish artist, son of a graduate, gets kicked out of the academy

James A. McNeill Whistler, the American painter famous for the portrait he did of his mother, was not so popular with his professors at West Point. He was a little too impertinent for the Army.

In a drawing class, West Point historian Stephen Grove said, Whistler was supposed to draw a bridge over a river.

He did, but he had two boys fishing from the span. Get those boys off the bridge, the instructor said.

The next drawing showed them fishing from the river bank.

Get those boys out of the picture, the instructor ordered. The final attempt showed two little tombstones by the river.

Whistler's father, George Washington Whistler, had a stellar career as a cadet. He graduated in 1819. The junior Whistler did not. His aborted career at West Point lasted from 1851 to 1854 when he was discharged for being deficient in chemistry and conduct.

West Point Museum Collections, U. S. Military Academy

A humorous set of sketches by James A. McNeill Whistler while he was a student at the academy. They show a cadet on watch duty as his posture relaxes over time.

Right, A cadet walks past the Cadet Honor Code, which in 12 words states the doctrine all cadets must live by during their education at West Point.

Spencer Ainsley

Karl Rabe

Above, The USMA Cadet Glee Club prepares to record the hymn "The Mansions of the Lord" for the movie "We Were Soldiers," starring Mel Gibson.

Cadets bound by 12 simple words

THE CADET HONOR CODE

A CADET WILL NOT LIE, CHEAT, STEAL, OR TOLERATE THOSE WHO DO.

It's a simple code all West Pointers must live by: A cadet will not lie, cheat, steal or tolerate those who do.

As easy to understand as it is strict, the Cadet Honor Code is also only the minimum standard of ethical behavior taught — and expected — at the Point.

Though fundamental to the development of military officers, the honor code was not formalized in academy publications until 1947, academy historian Stephen Grove said.

"It came down through the English culture, where an officer's word was his bond. All cultures value essentially the same thing, going back to the Bible," he said.

Grove said the academy's code of conduct grew out of an officer's commitment to always tell the truth in both the spoken and written word.

"Really, it was about lying," he said. "(Superintendent Sylvanus Thayer) impressed that upon the cadets in the 1800s. In fact, cheating was frowned upon, but people weren't thrown out for it."

In 1905, someone wrote a letter to the academy asking if cheating was a violation of the honor code. Officials wrote a return letter stating it was not.

When Superintendent Albert Mills, who served from 1898 to 1906, saw that response, he immediately sent a correction indicating it was a matter of honor. He formally added cheating to the traditional prohibition against lying.

Stealing had always been an offense that could end a military career, according to the Army's criminal justice system.

"There is also the non-toleration clause," Grove said. "You are honor-bound to report (an infraction) if you see it. If you do not, you are as guilty as the person who committed it."

Today, a process is in place for cadets accused of lying, cheating or stealing.

First, the person charged must review the allegation with an honor code representative, then stand for a cadet-led investigation.

If there is sufficient evidence, a full hearing is held. Once cadets vote on the case, the academy superintendent has the final say.

West Point's commitment to a brand of ethics not often found in today's society begins seeping into a cadet's psyche almost immediately.

Maj. Shannon Cox, a 1990 West Point graduate and now the Special Assistant to the Commandant for Honor Matters, said she remembered hearing about the honor code and worked on memorizing it the very first day she hit campus.

She said she understood its gravity when she began removing her eyeglasses after she had finished her classroom work, so there was no way she could see someone else's paper if her head wasn't pointed straight ahead or at her desk.

And it wasn't only the idea of being accused of cheating; there was also the responsibility of reporting someone else who was.

"That's probably the hardest part of the code for people to internalize," Cox said. "But it's taught here as a professional responsibility."

Cox said officers who leave West Point and end up in combat must uphold the honor code because without it, a platoon's safety could be compromised.

The fact cadets are responsible for prosecuting honor code violations sets the military academies apart from most universities, where faculty and administrators watch over a school's ethics.

"The cadets police themselves," Cox said.

That's a tradition that won't likely change. In a special introduction to a "White Paper" about the code and honor system, former academy Superintendent Lt. Gen. Daniel W. Christman talked about their importance.

"The Honor Code, perhaps above all else, binds graduates of all eras; it allows us to 'grip hands' across the ages," Christman wrote. "What must never change is our focus on the values of honor and integrity. To this end, the Honor Code will forever remain the key element of West Point's cadet development program."

Leadership code promotes respect, not abusive hazing

The man who would lead the World War II Allied forces and who would become president of the United States demeaned a plebe at the U.S. Military Academy as part of hazing, the institutionalized pressure put on new cadets.

Dwight Eisenhower told the young man he "looked like a barber," before finding out that was exactly the plebe's occupation before he came to the Point, according to an account by historian Stephen Ambrose.

"I've just done something that was stupid and unforgivable," Eisenhower told his roommate, swearing never to participate in such ridicule again. "I managed to make a man ashamed of the work he did to earn a living."

Hazing was outlawed by an act of Congress in 1901, growing out

of a federal inquiry into physical abuse that had led to the death of Cadet Oscar Boz.

A few years after leaving the academy, Boz died of tuberculosis some said was brought on by the fights and other conditioning abuse he endured at the school.

Though older cadets were no longer allowed physically to hurt plebes, the mental and emotional abuse remained until about 1990, when a new code of cadet leadership moved away from the plebe-style system and more toward leadership based on respect.

"The Army has known for a long time that you will get more from people by inspiring them to do well," academy historian Stephen Grove said.

"You don't have to yell and scream at people to put them under pressure."

Spencer Ainsley

Above, After saying goodbye to their parents at Eisenhower Hall on R-Day (Reception Day) in June 2001, new candidates take a bus ride across campus to begin the registration process.

Stringent military justice system takes cue from civilians

West Point's criminal justice system mirrors the non-military one, but has specific laws geared toward the armed forces.

West Point, like the other three national military academies, operates under the Uniform Code of Military Justice, which Congress adopted in 1951. The code lays out crimes and the process of prosecution, defense and automatic appeals.

West Point commanders, who hold the ranks of lieutenant general and brigadier general, act as prosecutors, deciding whether to have cases prosecuted or handled administratively by staff judge advocates.

The code calls for federal military prison time for some crimes that would bring far lesser punishment in the civilian world. A person who misses work could be fired, but a military person convicted of being absent without leave could go to prison, said Col. Patrick Finnegan, director of West Point's Department of Law and a former staff judge advocate.

Some convictions can bring a dishonorable discharge or bad con-

duct discharge. The death penalty is possible for murder, as well as for disobeying or striking an officer during war time.

"The code exists to handle crimes," Finnegan said, "and secondly, for commanders to enforce discipline."

Criminal cases are called courts martial and are heard by a judge or a tribunal of at least five officers. If the defendant chooses trial by tribunal, the panel not only decides guilt or innocence but also the sentence.

All verdicts and sentences are automatically reviewed by the academy's commandant and by the military appellate court. Appeals also are heard by a court of five civilians appointed by the president. The U.S. Supreme Court would hear any final appeals.

Congress adopted the Uniformed Code of Military Justice to give defendants rights similar to civilian courts, Finnegan said. The code came in response to perceived abuses in convictions and sentencing of military personnel during World War II, he said.

IN THE BARRACKS

Spencer Ainsley photos

There are rules and regulations for all aspects of cadet life at the United States Military Academy. For example, the books Cadet Ryan Mark Ciovacco keeps on his desk must be neatly arranged by height, from left to right.

Right, Cadet Ryan Ciovacco has developed a technique for maintaining the shine on his shoes. Black polish, a cotton cloth and a little exhaled air are the perfect combination for daily shoe maintenance.

At 6 a.m., Ciovacco uses a time-honored technique to remove loose threads from the bottom of his pants before breakfast. He said the flame from a lighter seals the edge of the pants.

It's details, details, details

When Cadet Ryan Mark Ciovacco, USMA Class of 2004, wakes up at 5 a.m., he is not thinking of duty, honor or country. He is hunting down specks of dust, traces of lint, any smudge or wrinkle that has crept into his room or onto his shoes or uniform. The only constant is his bed, which was made the first day of the academic year, then not again until he becomes a junior. "Most cadets make their bed once, then sleep on top of it every night," Ciovacco said. "There is not enough time to make the bed every day."

From 5 to 6 a.m. nothing matters but the perfect shine, the perfect crease of his pants, perfect order in his closet and a perfect shave. Following the rules and regulations that have defined West Point for 200 years is often daunting. But Ciovacco, from the Town of Poughkeepsie, is all too aware of the academy's legacy, a training ground for some of the nation's greatest leaders.

Excerpts from 'Barracks Arrangements Guide'

Above, Ciovacco cleans the mirror and sink in his room every morning before his day begins. Every cadet's room is inspected on a daily basis for cleanliness and order.

Left, At 6:15 a.m., Ciovacco, Class of 2004, carefully irons his shirt in his room before attending morning formation at 6:55 a.m. and breakfast in Washington Hall. Ciovacco is a graduate of Arlington High School in Poughkeepsie.

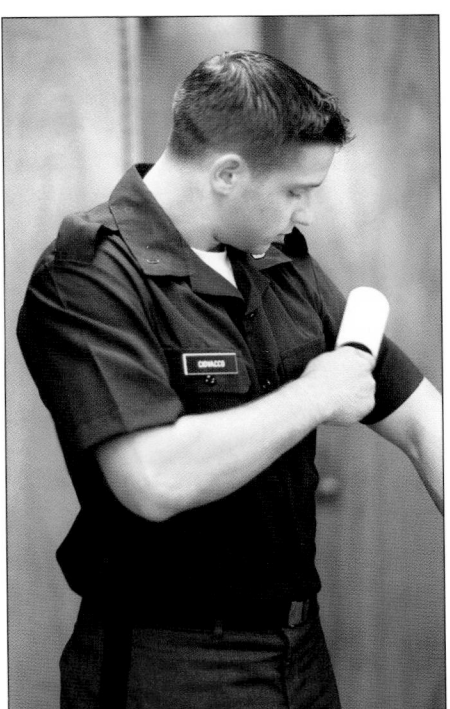

Left, Ciovacco uses a special brush to remove lint from his shirt before attending the 6:55 a.m. cadet formation in front of Washington Hall.

Spencer Ainsley photos

Footgear
Will be displayed at foot of the bed under the nametag. Starting from the bedpost: combat boots, low quarter, and pumps (women). In the wardrobe, shower shoes on the left, and slippers on the right. For first class cadets: maximum of four pair of civilian shoes (non-athletic) per cadet in coat closet.

Knickknacks
Displayed on desk or bookshelf (not on bureau). Knickknacks will be appropriate items, which do not detract from the military appearance of the room. Only three knickknacks per cadet are authorized for display (dolls, stuffed animals, teddy bears, and Class Souvenirs are considered knickknacks). First Class cadets are authorized a maximum of six knickknacks.

Underclothes
Stored in second bureau drawer folded into squares.

Towels
One on towel rack folded in half (thirds for 2nd and 3rd cadets in two-person room). All others in 2nd or 4th drawer of the bureau or on top shelf of the wall locker as appropriate.

‘There is order to everything at West Point. The books above my desk must be arranged according to height, from left to right, tallest to shortest.’

Ryan Mark Ciovacco, USMA cadet

Ciovacco averages four hours of sleep each night, considering his rigorous curriculum, athletics and intensive late-night study routine.

SPANNING GENERATIONS

Legacy of service found in bloodlines

Retired Col. Jeffrey Rogers, whose father and grandfather graduated from West Point, said he was never pressured to attend the academy.

He grew up around soldiers and was comfortable with Army life. When he was about 17, he applied to West Point, motivated by his "desire to serve the nation, to have the privilege and honor to lead soldiers."

He graduated in 1968, served in Vietnam and later became the chief of the Army's finance corps. He retired from active duty in 1994. Rogers now lives in Manchester, Conn., with his wife, Carlyle, the daughter of a West Point graduate.

Following father

Rogers' sons are all graduates of the academy: 2nd Lt. Spencer Rogers graduated in June 2001; Capt. Carter L. Rogers, in 1991; Bryant V.S. Rogers, in 1994. Their relationship with the academy has made their close family even closer, Jeffrey Rogers said.

"It gives our family a very special heritage and a very special bond, and it revolves around service to the nation."

The Rogers family is not unique. Many families have West Point as a legacy.

Katherine King Miller Corliss said she remembers watching the first women graduate from the academy in 1980 and thinking she would like to do the same. In 1998, Corliss became the seventh generation of her family to graduate from the West Point. Like Rogers, Corliss said she was not pressured to attend. She, too, had been

Generations join 'Long Gray Line'

Above, Retired Col. Jeffrey Rogers, center, poses with his sons, Cadets Carter Rogers, left, and Bryant Rogers, in 1990.
Right, Retired Lt. Col. Harry Rogers III poses with grandson Spencer Rogers in 2000.

introduced to Army life through her family. Her father, Jeremy King Miller, graduated in 1973, served five years and then left the Army. Her grandfather had achieved the rank of general, and as she was growing up, the view from his post made Army life look pretty good, she said.

For Corliss, there is a pride in the accomplishment of having survived the rigors of West Point and come out standing. It was the strength her family gave her that helped her most during her cadet days.

"On the days when it was hard and you were ready to pack it up, one of the things that motivated me was having my family to cheer me on," said Corliss, a first lieutenant, who has served as a signal officer handling communications and electronics at Fort Bragg, N.C. Christopher Corliss, her husband, is a 1999 academy graduate.

Pride in the service he has given to the nation, as well as the achievement of graduating from West Point, are also paramount to retired Col. Seth Hudgins Jr., who is president of West Point's alumni organization, the Association of Graduates.

His father graduated from the academy, and Hudgins "knew Army" growing up. Hudgins was in combat in Vietnam within a year of graduating in 1964. He served two tours in Vietnam and 26 years in the Army.

"I was very proud that I had done what my father had, that I had accomplished and achieved what he had back in 1939," Hudgins said.

His son also chose a military career, opting to attend the U.S. Naval Academy at Annapolis, Md. Seth Hudgins III is a lieutenant commander who flies jets off aircraft carriers and has been involved in the war against terrorism.

Hudgins said he feels a bond with his son that exists beyond their friendly rivalry at the annual Army-Navy game. Part of it is they are both graduates of a service academy.

"I'm very proud of him, of his decision to serve his country," Hudgins said.

> **'**On the days when it was hard and you were ready to pack it up, one of the things that motivated me was having my family to cheer me on.**'**
>
> **Katherine King Miller Corliss**
> 1998 West Point graduate

> **'**It gives our family a very special heritage.**'**
>
> **Retired Col. Jeffrey Rogers**
> 1968 West Point graduate

Karl Rabe

Above, President George W. Bush is saluted by West Point valedictorian Erica J. Watson before she receives her diploma in June 2002.

Right, After four demanding years at the U.S. Military Academy at West Point, cadets celebrate graduation with hugs and laughter.

Darryl Bautista

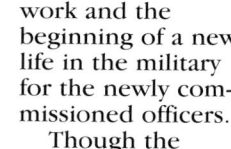

GRADUATION DAY

Traditions mark end, and beginning, for new officers

The children, varying in size and age, lined up across the 40-yard line at Michie Stadium at West Point, many leaning forward with a hand on a knee.

As the sun began to peek through a gray sky that morning — and the Class of 2001 joined the "Long Gray Line" of West Point graduates — the children readied for a mad dash that has become an annual graduation day tradition at West Point over the past half century.

Moments after taking the oath of office, and being commissioned as second lieutenants, the graduates tossed their hats into the air as the ceremony — and their careers as cadets — officially came to an end.

Then the children scrambled all over the field to retrieve a hat to keep as their own.

Another scramble soon followed as some of the newly commissioned officers headed to the chapel to get married — their first opportunity to do so since entering the academy four years earlier. Cadets are not allowed to marry while attending West Point.

No time for marriage

"The four-year experience is demanding enough," West Point historian Stephen Grove said. "You can't spend the time that you legitimately should on a marriage in this kind of environment."

Graduation day at West Point is the culmination of four years of

work and the beginning of a new life in the military for the newly commissioned officers.

Though the academy itself is marking its bicentennial, the Class of 2003 is actually the 205th graduating class. It's also the 24th class to graduate women. No classes graduated in 1810 or 1816 and there were two graduating classes in 1861, 1917, 1918 and 1943 because of the wars going on at the time.

The first documented hat toss took place in 1946, but Grove said it's not out of the realm of possibility that graduates had done that decades before. Grove said 19th-century cadets would sometimes take off their caps and throw them down on the ground and stomp on them.

Another graduation day ritual designed to honor the class "goat" — the graduate who finishes at the bottom of the class academically — only came about in 1968. Every member of the class gives a silver dollar to the goat, which he receives at graduation.

But the term goat itself had its roots much earlier in the academy's history.

Until the 1880s, the lower-ranking members of the class were known as "immortals," Grove said, but that soon changed.

"There was a Spanish-speaking professor who taught the lower cadets who wore a goatee," he said. "The lower-ranking cadets became known as goats."

'The four-year experience is demanding enough. You can't spend the time that you legitimately should on a marriage in this kind of environment.'

Stephen Grove, West Point historian, on the abundance of weddings following graduation at the academy

Darryl Bautista

Commencement day is also wedding day for some of the graduates of the U.S. Military Academy.

'Whenever duty called, the men and women of West Point have never failed us. I know you never will.'

President Bill Clinton
speaking at West Point commencement in 1997

'We are fighting a war with different methods but not different moralities ... You will find you are prepared because you are the men and women of West Point.'

President George W. Bush
speaking at West Point commencement in 2002

Kathy McLaughlin

Cadets receive their diplomas as President Bill Clinton reviews the commencement ceremonies in 1993.

Karl Rabe

President George W. Bush is given a sabre by the USMA Class of 2002, presented by class President Joseph Da Silva in June 2002.

Karl Rabe

The United States Military Academy graduating class of 2002 stands during the graduation ceremonies at Michie Stadium. There were 958 graduates.

Presidents and future presidents

The magnificence of the U.S. Military Academy's history and its surroundings draw millions of visitors every year. Among the visitors, a few notables stand out: the U.S. presidents who have addressed the cadets at commencement ceremonies.

1902: Theodore Roosevelt handed out diplomas, but did not speak at the graduation. He spoke instead at the academy's centennial observance the day before.

1908: William Howard Taft, who was Secretary of War at the time. He was elected president later that year.

1916: Woodrow Wilson

1935 and 1939: Franklin Roosevelt

1947: Dwight David Eisenhower, as chief of staff of the Army

1955: Eisenhower as president

1962: John F. Kennedy

1975: Gerald Ford

1981: Ronald Reagan

1991: George Bush

1993 and 1997: Bill Clinton

2002: George W. Bush

Presidents Eisenhower and Ulysses Grant were the two West Point graduates who became president, but only Eisenhower came back as a graduation speaker.

'We produce leaders of character. That's what we do. We produce them for the Army. We produce them for the nation ... The academics may change ... the science and math are going to advance. But the basic core of what we do – leaders of character – will not change.'

Lt. Gen. William J. Lennox., Jr., USMA superintendent, 2002

Darryl Bautista

Cadets toss their hats into the air as they celebrate graduation in 2001 from the U.S. Military Academy at West Point.

INDEX

Kosciuszko Monument, 8

Kosciuszko, Thaddeus, 8, 38

Kosloski, Nancy, 19

Koster, Samuel W., 104

Krzyzewski, Mike, 62, 97, 100

Kuwait, 59-60

L

Ladycliff College, 57, 91

Lafayette, Marquis de, 32

Lake Champlain, Battle of, 32

Lampert, James B., 104

Leary, Timothy, 135

Lee Barracks, 6

Lee, Robert, E., 22, 41, 43-49, 86, 88, 91, 102, 119

Lennox, William, Jr., 4, 60, 104, 145

Leo, Anthony, 3, 29

Leavenworth, Fort, 55

Levy, Simon, 11, 29

Lewis, Meriwether, 66

Lichtenberg Tennis Center, 13

Lincoln, Abraham, 43-45

Lindbergh, Charles, 53

Little Big Horn, 49-50

Locke, Tates, 97

Lombardi, Vince, 97-98

"Long Gray Line," 119, 142

Longstreet, James, 46

Lorentz, Antoine, 64

Lovell, James, 70-72

M

MacArthur, Arthur, 46

MacArthur Barracks, 6

MacArthur, Douglas, 4, 8, 12, 46, 53, 55-57, 91, 96, 97, 100, 101-106, 111, 119

MacArthur, Jean, 8

Mahan Hall, 7

Maher, Marty, 19, 24

Marchers, 123

Marchesani, Tony, 13

Marcos, Ferdinand, 68

Marshall, George, 12, 55, 99

Martalear's Rock, 28, 30

Mase, Roy W., 17

Maxwell D. Taylor Leadership Award, 107

Maynard, Edward, 135

McClellan, George B., 46

McFarlin, Justin, 129

McGrath, T.J., 112, 114-115

McKeever, Ed, 100

McKinley, William, 50

McNulty, Darby, 122-124

Meade, George, G. 49

Merritt, Wesley, 103

Mexican War, 16, 22, 46-49, 74

Michie Stadium, 9, 12, 13, 52, 91, 96, 98-99, 142, 144

Military Academy Prep School, 115

Miller, Jeremy King, 141

Miller, Rod, 80

Miller, Tom, 97

Mills, Albert, 74-75, 136, 103

Mission Statement, 3

Missionary Ridge, Battle of, 46

Monroe, James, 103

Montgomery, Fort, 29, 30

Moore, Bryant E., 104

Moore, Charles Herbert, 90

Moore, Griselda, 36

Moore, John, 36

Moore, Stephen, 36

Morse, Samuel, 42

Moss, Michael, 86, 87, 92

Motto, U.S. Military Academy, 4

Mount Defiance, 38

Mount Giulian, 37

N

Nakat, John, 127

Napoleon, 88, 92

National Aeronautics and Space Administration (NASA), 55, 70-71

National Defense Act of 1947, 56

Nazis, 86

NBC, 24

Nebel, C., 43

New Orleans, Battle of, 42

Nicholson, Jim, 62

Nicola, Lewis, 35

Nixon, Richard, M., 57, 62, 68

North Atlantic Treaty Organization, 55

Notre Dame, University of, 97

Novak, Leo, 97

O

Oakwood School, 112, 115

Old Cadet Chapel, 16, 17, 42, 82, 91

Olson, Eric T., 88, 93

Operation Desert Storm, 57, 60

Oriskany, Battle of, 31

Spencer Ainsley